THE POWER OF POINT·OF·PURCHASE ADVERTISING:

MARKETING AT RETAIL

RETAIL IS DETAIL!

READ & ENJOY.

Bill Smith

ONWARD & UPWARD!

John A. Schley

POPAI

**POINT·OF·PURCHASE
ADVERTISING INTERNATIONAL**
Now P-O-P Stands For Proof Of Performance™
WWW.POPAI.COM

THE OFFICIAL TEXTBOOK OF POINT·OF·PURCHASE ADVERTISING INTERNATIONAL

THE POWER OF POINT·OF·PURCHASE ADVERTISING:

MARKETING AT RETAIL

EDITED BY ROBERT LILJENWALL

POPAI

**POINT·OF·PURCHASE
ADVERTISING INTERNATIONAL**
Now P-O-P Stands For Proof Of Performance™
WWW.POPAI.COM

Point-Of-Purchase Advertising International
1660 L Street NW
10th Floor
Washington, DC 20036
p: 202.530.3000
f: 202.530.3030
www.popai.com

Graphic Design:
Mercury Publishing Services
Rockville, Maryland

Printed in USA
ISBN 0-9707099-1-9

CONTENTS

CONTENTS

FOREWORD

Dick Blatt, President & CEO
Point-Of-Purchase Advertising International (POPAI)

Education is one of the key goals of POPAI, the only nonprofit, global trade association of the marketing-at-retail industry. Education helps to keep the benchmarks high for our industry and advances not only companies that use knowledge best but also the careers of our most educated practitioners. This new edition of the industry's only existant textbook is intended to further inform and help educate.

POPAI holds regional seminars called POPAI UNIVERSITY ON THE ROAD and on the Internet called POPAI UNIVERSITY ON THE WEB. We also offer a Certified Point-of-Purchase Professional (CPP) designation. Members can receive credits toward a CPP designation with every POPAI UNIVERSITY seminar they attend.

Moreover, POPAI has undertaken national, comprehensive research to better understand which signage and placement of P-O-P work best to lift sales in supermarkets, in convenience stores, and in drug stores. In 2003, the prestigious Advertising Research Foundation endorsed our White Paper on how to measure the number of audience impressions created by P-O-P advertising. Taken together, these research studies make point-of-purchase advertising a measured medium for the first time in the industry's history. Now, marketers can forecast their return on investment in P-O-P advertising and better integrate P-O-P into their marketing mix.

In this book you will learn about consumer behavior and its implications for P-O-P advertising, as well as the design, engineering, and manufacturing expertise required to bring a successful campaign to a retail environment. You will understand not only the terminology used in the field but also the trends that are shaping P-O-P advertising and influencing decisions made by retailers, brand marketers, and P-O-P producers.

New in this edition is a phrase you see on our cover: *"marketing at retail."* We used to call P-O-P advertising "in-store" advertising. That definition has broadened to include the outside of the store too—the store's colors and logo recognizable at a glance as well as each store's way of branding itself as it markets a wide range of products, including private labels. "Marketing at retail" captures the new, wider horizon for P-O-P advertising.

Please look at what else POPAI can offer you on our Web site, www.popai.com. Visit our online POPAI Library of information culled from hundreds of sources. Our online POPAI Creative Gallery of award-winning P-O-P displays gives you the industry's best source of creative ideas. We offer affordable memberships in POPAI to professors and students interested in the field as well as to industry practitioners.

On behalf of POPAI, welcome to our industry, and thank you for investing your time in reading the work of our contributing writers and editors—all leaders in our field. I want to thank Brian McCormick of Rapid Displays and Ed White of E and E Display Group for their guidance as Co-Chairs of the Textbook Task Force, Robert Liljenwall for his skills as the editor, and Mark DellaPietra, POPAI's staff liaison to the project. We hope that you find this textbook to be your companion and guide as you learn the many ways that point-of-purchase advertising increases sales and builds brands.

PREFACE

Robert Liljenwall, Managing Director
ProCreative Services

This is the first revision of the highly successful first POPAI textbook, *Marketing's Powerful Weapon: Point-of-Purchase Advertising*, published in 2001. The response to the publication was outstanding, because it provided— for the first time—a complete overview of the point-of-purchase industry, written by top professionals in their fields.

As the global organization responsible for promoting and monitoring the point-of-purchase advertising industry, POPAI brought together industry leaders to create a definitive guide and textbook for P-O-P professionals—brand marketers, retailers, P-O-P vendors and suppliers, advertising and promotional agencies, and especially for newcomers to the industry. One of the most important functions of this publication is for it to serve as the teaching guide and benchmark for the CPP exam (Certified Point-of-Purchase Professional). This examination process greatly assists POPAI in creating long-term professional standards and executives who are thoroughly trained and educated about all facets of the point-of-purchase advertising industry.

Each of the contributors for this updated version again provide their insight, opinion, and industry knowledge to help the reader better understand the evolving and fast-changing world of point-of-purchase advertising.

We changed the title of the publication to reflect the broadening influence that the point-of-purchase advertising industry is having on retail. "Marketing at retail" is a term that is growing in awareness and acceptance among all three stakeholders—retailers, brand marketers, and P-O-P vendors and suppliers. Not only is the industry providing innovative and effective point-of-purchase displays through all retail segments, but the broadening influence of new technologies and methods of reaching the consumer both inside and outside the retail environment are helping retailers and brand marketers move product as never before.

Marketing at retail is where it is happening. Remember, point-of-purchase advertising is the last three feet of your marketing plan.

We have several new contributors this time around: Frank Mulhern, Ph.D., Professor of Integrated Marketing Communications for Northwestern University, has written Chapter 1, covering "marketing at retail" and how point-of-purchase advertising has broadened its influence in retail. Denise Ogden, Ph.D., from Penn State University, has joined with her husband, Doc Ogden, Ph.D., Kutztown University, to update Chapter 2. We have two new chapters—Jeff Sandgren discusses trends in technology in Chapter 8, and Doug Adams provides a thorough review of POPAI's measured medium research in a Special Report section.

We have four outstanding editorials on a vast array of subjects contributed by John Anderson, Jim Einstein, Merrill Howard, and John Sakaley.

The POPAI Editorial Board, headed by Ed White and Brian McCormick, supervised the project from its inception to insure that the entire book represented the "state of the art" of the P-O-P industry.

As the Editor, it was clear that the first publication was successful in addressing the core issues facing industry education: Creating a comprehensive document that would further the understanding of the P-O-P industry especially for mid-level managers and new entrants into the industry who needed a one-stop publication that contained "all they needed to know."

We placed POPAI's *Point-of-Purchase Advertising Desktop Reference Guide*, the complete P-O-P industry glossary, on a CD with each book so that readers could load this onto their computers for easy reference.

It is also important to note that this publication would not have succeeded without the diligent and positive contribution of POPAI Manager of Educational Services Mark DellaPietra, who devoted countless hours of coordination, proof reading, and working with our publisher, Mercury Publishing Services. We need to recognize John Laine for his tireless editing efforts to insure that all the "i"s were dotted and "t"s crossed.

In conclusion, all involved in this project believe that this effort continues to strengthen the professionalism of the point-of-purchase advertising industry. And we also continue to believe that P-O-P advertising is marketing's most powerful weapon.

ABOUT THE EDITOR

ROBERT LILJENWALL

Mr. Liljenwall is managing director of ProCreative, a marketing and branding consultancy in Newport Beach, CA. He teaches strategic marketing and brand identity management at University California—Los Angeles Extension University. He travels widely in his consulting business and lectures on global trends in marketing at retail. He served as co-Editor and co-author of the first POPAI publication, *Point-of-Purchase Advertising: Marketing's Powerful Weapon*. He is currently writing a book on "marketing up the food chain" and consulting in the United States and Mexico. He received a BA in journalism from San Jose State University and an MBA from Pepperdine University.

"The defining aspect of marketing at retail, and for that matter the moment of truth for all of marketing, is the point of transaction where the customer chooses to make a purchase, takes possession of a product or consumes a service, and pays in real dollars."

Marketing at Retail and Marketing Management Today

FRANCIS J. MULHERN, PH.D., ASSOCIATE DEAN
DEPARTMENT OF INTEGRATED MARKETING COMMUNICATIONS
MEDILL SCHOOL OF JOURNALISM, NORTHWESTERN UNIVERSITY

INTRODUCTION

In the span of a few decades, the field of marketing has evolved into a sophisticated combination of market research, product development, pricing, physical distribution, service delivery, and marketing communications. In this evolution, two prevailing elements have come to together to form a platform for all marketing practices.

The first element is *consumer insight*, the true understanding of consumer desires, aspirations, motivations, buying, and consumption behaviors. It is now widely recognized that consumer insight—whether it be called the marketing concept, customer orientation, or market orientation—underlies all good marketing and all facets of good marketing planning from the design of products and services to pricing, distribution, and communications. A true understanding of consumer insight begins with knowing why consumers desire products and how they consume them, then moves to the mechanism though which consumers acquire products and services: Purchase transactions. From there, truly consumer-oriented marketing planning finds its direction. Or, stated in another way, it is to the purchase transaction that all marketing planning must align itself.

Consumer insight and *brand strategy* have come to together to form a platform for all marketing practices.

The second element that established a platform for marketing is *brand strategy*. Brands represent the connecting point between what a company offers in the marketplace and what the individual consumes. Brands encapsulate the psychological aspects of product and service offerings, including perceived quality and performance, competitive positioning, and the self-oriented meanings that consumers give to products on a regular basis.

A great deal of attention has recently been paid to brands. Brands represent a psychological point of differentiation that, when used properly, can lead to long-term profitability. One reason for this is that firms increasingly find it difficult to succeed based on product, distribution, or price advantages because all their competitors have available to them the same production technology, distribution infrastructure, labor force, and communication media.

While consumer insight and brand strategy pertain to every aspect of marketing, they are particularly salient at that moment where consumers and brands meet—the time and place of a retail transaction, what we call *marketing at retail*. Marketing at retail includes all aspects of marketing, marketing communications, and retailing that take place at physical locations where products are sold and services are provided. The defining aspect of marketing at retail, and for that matter the moment of truth for all of marketing, is the point of transaction where the customer chooses to make a purchase, takes possession of a product or consumes a service, and pays in real dollars. It is at the point of the retail purchase that all of marketing, in fact all of business, justifies its existence. It is at that point where a product or service is transformed from something that is produced to something that is consumed. And consumption is the only reason for a business to exist.

MARKETING MANAGEMENT TODAY

In some respects, marketing is experiencing an identity crisis. Top managers at many organizations consider marketing a huge cost center that may not deserve the monies allocated to it.

Critics view marketing as little more than selling, advertising, and a host of other rudimentary tactics assembled to support sales efforts. Whereas part of the blame for this perception lies with executives who fail to understand all of the ways marketing contributes to corporate performance, some of the blame also must be shared by marketing itself—and by its failure to assume financial accountability and demonstrate its true contribution to profitability. Companies that do marketing well realize the one defining characteristic that sets marketing apart from all other business functions: The recognition that the entire reason for a business to exist is to create and keep a customer.[1] It is only by doing so that companies achieve profitability.

Among all the departments in business, it is marketing that is responsible for customers. It is customers who are responsible for the revenue flows that support the functioning of businesses. Marketing is the external side of a business that gathers information on customers and competitors, identifies profit-making opportunities, and develops business practices that match corporate offerings with marketplace demands. From this vantage point, marketing makes a contribution to corporate performance that is unmistakable and irreplaceable.

Many of the difficulties taking place in marketing stem from a dramatically shifting landscape both in the marketplace and within organizations themselves. Key among these changes are environmental factors such as the shifting demographic and ethnic compositions of consumers, rapidly developing technologies for market research and marketing communications, and a shifting value system within corporations whereby marketing can no longer exist as a loosely managed cost center but must justify itself for the financial contributions it brings about. These forces are manifesting themselves in the following five predominant ways that are relevant to marketing at retail.

CONSOLIDATION OF RETAILING

As is the case in many industries, retailing is in the midst of a major consolidation whereby a fewer number of larger retail establishments are supplanting a greater number of smaller, independently owned retailers. Wal-Mart, the world's largest company in revenues, continues its global expansion with a retailing model featuring efficient distribution, precise inventory management, and aggressive retail pricing. Major grocery chains continue to merge with large operators such as Safeway, Albertson's, and American Stores, gaining an increasingly national presence. The five largest grocery chains now account for 45 percent of grocery sales, up from 26 percent in 1995. Similar patterns of major chain growth and consolidation are taking place in pharmacies, gas stations, restaurants, and nearly all areas of retailing and service marketing.

The implications of retail consolidation are far-reaching and dramatic. For manufacturers, this means that access to consumer markets is dominated by fewer, larger retailers that, in addition to controlling increasing portions of the distribution channel, are controlling both the means through which consumers are communicated to and the information on purchase behavior.

RETAILER AS MEDIA

In part due to the increasing size of major retailers, stores are becoming a primary form of "media." While traditional broadcast and print media struggle with fragmentation of media markets and an overabundance of media choices for consumers, retailers have emerged as a key source of information and service for the consumer marketplace. Traditional media will always be important because manufacturers must make their brands famous through advertising. But any information that consumers need to make brand choices and learn about product and service performance is better suited for retailer-based communications. The brand TiVo—a digital recording device that can be programmed to capture and record TV shows and paused during viewing—is a case in point. Despite TiVo's abundant consumer benefits and widespread media advertising, sales have been slow. Market research has shown that the brand's benefits are too complex to convey in print and broadcast media. Hence, TiVo marketers have developed in-store product demonstrations to communicate the many benefits of the technology. This is one of many instances in which the retail establishment serves as a primary communication medium.

EXPERIENTIAL RETAILING

Many retailers are transforming traditional stores from places where a shopper goes to pick up a product to where a shopper goes to enjoy an experience. Examples include bookstores featuring a coffee shop and lounge chairs, shopping malls featuring community events and entertainment, and sporting goods and outdoor stores that feature product demonstration and instructional programs. Purchasing takes place in a broader context that includes interpersonal interaction, entertainment, and on-site consumption experiences. What this means is that marketing at retail is no longer just about finding ways to increase the likelihood of purchase; it is also about finding ways to enhance the shopper's experience. As a result, marketing at retail is broadening to include many nontraditional practices that enhance the shopper's experience, not just promote the sale of a product.

DATA AND TECHNOLOGY

During the 1980s, retailing experienced dramatic changes brought on by point-of-sale data from store checkout scanner technology. Although the original uses of that data were for inventory management and centralized pricing, scanner data generated a boom in the level of understanding of consumer brand choice, the impact of price and promotions, and in-store merchandising. This information was one of the contributing factors in the migration of marketing expenditures to marketing at retail. Today, retailing is on the cusp of another revolution in knowledge. This time it is the individual-level purchase data generated by retailer frequent-shopper programs. Purchase transaction data on the individual customer is the finest level of data possible on shopping behavior. Accordingly, great strides are being made in understanding not just the impact of pricing, promotions, and all aspects of marketing at retail, but also the impact of market baskets, cross-time purchasing, consumer expenditures, and store patronage. Over the next few years, retailers will experience continued improvements in their ability to manage customers by selectively offering merchandise and promotions to shoppers based on customer buying patterns. The fact that retailers control the collection and ownership of customer-level purchase data will contribute to the power of retailers and the importance of marketing at retail relative to media-based marketing. Presently, most marketing at retail is targeted either to all shoppers or to broad segments of shoppers in a store. Because of the availability of customer databases, marketing at retail is increasingly gravitating toward customer-specific communications and merchandising. This is a dramatic and sustainable shift in retailing practice, one that puts the retailer further to the forefront of all marketing.

> Over the next few years, retailers will experience continued improvements in their ability to manage customers by selectively offering merchandise and promotions to shoppers based on customer buying patterns.

MEASUREMENT

No topic is of greater interest to marketing today than measurement. Relative to other business areas, marketing has performed weakly with respect to measurement. However, data collection systems now in place are bringing about a control revolution in marketing whereby measurement and financial quantification will be the norm. In scientific and professional fields, advances take place in conjunction with the quality of measures. The improvements now occurring in marketing measurement are bringing about more precise targeting, more relevant communications, and more profitable allocation of marketing dollars. The key areas of measurement include (1) *customer profitability*—the computation of the dollar contribution individual customers make to manufacturer and retailer revenues and profits; (2) *brand equity*—the evaluation of the financial values of brands and the role of marketing communications in generating brand value; and (3) *customer response analysis*—the assessment of the financial contribution of individual marketing tactics—such as coupons, in-store displays, and feature advertising—to revenues, both as independent marketing elements as well as an integrated whole.

MARKETING AT RETAIL AND CUSTOMER MANAGEMENT

At the core of marketing today is a mindset that marketing is above all else about managing customers. This transcends the traditional view that marketing is about managing the functional areas of products, pricing, distribution, and communications.

Managing customers entails market research and consumer insight analysis, strategically oriented customer segmentation, brand positing and targeted distribution, and marketing communications. Within this framework companies can shift their thinking to the performance of customer segments as opposed to product groups.

Much has been written and discussed about a new era of marketing. Whether it is called relationship marketing, customer relationship management, one-to-one marketing, or integrated marketing communications, this new era is fundamentally about managing customers. Although much of this discussion is conceptually attractive and strategically useful, the practice of marketing has lagged behind the promises made by the marketing books and consultants. The reason for this lag has to do with two overarching factors.

First, organizational structures have largely been established from a production point of view to facilitate product development and manufacture, physical distribution efficiency, service delivery, media buying, and additional facets of business, from the perspective of the businessperson. Attempts to shift corporate values toward a greater consumer orientation conflict with the inherent structure of many organizations. Companies are slowly making the changes necessary to manage customers and market segments. Examples include financial services where segment managers are in place, or consumer packaged goods manufacturers who organize brand teams around key retail accounts.

The second difficulty in making business truly consumer-oriented has to do with the measures that businesses use to make decisions. Most companies, by and large, run their businesses based on measures that have very little to do with consumers. The prevailing measures represent the performance of brands, product groups, market areas, regional sales districts, media markets, and so forth. Accordingly, most marketing managers spend their time attempting to maximize the revenue or profit performance of these areas, not the profitability of customers. Customer measurement is the only thing that will make businesses shift toward managing customers. Hence, we are seeing the gradual incorporation of financial measures of customers, largely through retailer and service marketing data and point-of-purchase measurement.

> **Whether it is called relationship marketing, customer relationship management, one-to-one marketing, or integrated marketing communications, this new era is fundamentally about managing customers.**

IMPLICATIONS FOR MARKETING AT RETAIL

Marketing at retail is most powerful when it connects directly to the strategic objectives of manufacturers, service providers, and retailers. The most effective marketing-at-retail practices are those based on the following six strategic foundations.

Know Your Customers

Marketing at retail should be based on market research and consumer insight. The abundance of information available on shopping behavior, brand choice, and customer response to marketing tactics provides a thorough knowledge base for marketing at retail. Brand marketers need to understand the underlying motivations that drive shopping behavior. These motivations go well beyond the acquisition of merchandise and often have more to do with consumer aspirations and self-actualization.

Connect Marketing at Retail to Marketing Strategy

Too often, marketing at retail is treated as an add-on tactical element to a more broadly established marketing effort. Marketing at retail should be conducted with the same strategic focus of marketing communication and channels of distribution.

Integrate Marketing at Retail with Media Communications

A fundamental aspect of integrated marketing communications is that all marketing efforts, through the media and through retailers, should be driven by the same marketing objectives and strategy. In particular, advertising and promotions at the point of purchase should complement communications through the media.

Understand the Contribution Made by Each Tactic

Every marketing-at-retail tactic makes a contribution to the overall marketing effort. For proper planning to take place, each element of marketing at retail must be managed with an understanding of what that specific element can contribute. For example, point-of-purchase advertisements reinforce brand messages, checkout coupons allow for precise targeting based on brand purchasing, and packaging and product displays provide tactile communications not possible through the media.

Practice Targetability

Retailers are increasingly customizing product assortment, store atmosphere, prices and promotions to match customers in narrowly defined geographic markets, particularly with respect to socioeconomic factors and ethnicity. This customization, enabled by detailed information on geodemographics, allows retailers to offer a merchandising mix that suits the needs of local residents and provides some differentiation from nearby competitors. Relative to print and broadcast media, marketing at retail has a particular advantage in this respect because of the countless opportunities to do highly targeted communications and promotions at the point of purchase.

Measure Everything

Marketing expenditures are increasingly being allocated to practices that provide quantified metrics of impact. Precise and timely measures of the impact of marketing at retail ensure continued spending in this area.

SUMMARY

This chapter began by defining consumer insight and brand strategy as the two prongs that define marketing today. Marketing at retail is no different from other facets of marketing in needing to embrace these two concepts. The advantage of marketing at retail is its centrality at the connection point between companies and their customers. The challenge to marketing at retail is to rise above the view that it is merely a set of merchandising tactics to be appended to a brand or distribution strategy. The chapters that follow depict the many areas of marketing at retail where specific practices can be implemented to truly contribute to core marketing and business objectives. This is achieved by leveraging consumer insight to bring forth merchandising practices that connect with shoppers, by representing brand positioning and message strategies at the point of purchase, and, ultimately, by providing the measures that capture the effectiveness of marketing and integrating those measures to all marketing functions.

ENDNOTES

[1] Peter F. Drucker, *Management: Tasks, Responsibilities, Practices* (New York: Harper & Row, 1974; reprint, New York: HarperBusiness, 1993), 79.

"Brand marketers and retailers
who have a true understanding of
P-O-P advertising and consumer buying
behaviors and habits can no longer
ignore the potential for increased sales
and market share."

Consumer Behavior at the Point of Purchase

**J.R. "Doc" Ogden. Ph.D., Chair and Professor, Department of Marketing
Kutztown University of Pennsylvania**

**Denise T. Ogden, Ph.D., Assistant Professor, Marketing
Penn State University Berks/Lehigh Valley Campus**

WHAT IS RETAILING?

Retailing is a set of activities utilized to get products and services into the hands of the final consumer. Typically, retailing is the last activity in the supply chain process. Retailing encompasses not only in-store sales but also sales via the Internet (called e-tailing), through the postal system, over broadcast media such as radio or television, door-to-door, through print media such as catalogs or magazines, and even through vending machines.

In a channel of distribution, the retail setting is often the only time the consumer is exposed to a company or to a company's products and services. A typical channel of distribution is shown in Figure 2-1. Notice that the location of the retail function is between other businesses and the final consumer or end user, making retailers the link between manufacturers and the ultimate consumer.

Figure 2-1
Typical Channels
of Distribution

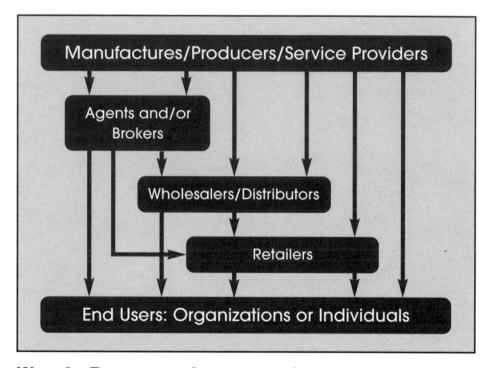

WHY IS RETAILING IMPORTANT?

According to the National Retail Federation (NRF),[1] there are more than 1.4 million retailers in the United States who generate an estimated $3.6 trillion dollars in sales. The retailing industry employs more that 20 million people—that's one in five American workers. To be sure, this is a very important industry.

The large size of the retailing industry and the amount of money it generates make it a a primary source of revenue for marketers. In addition, since businesses and customers come together at the retail level, it is a key element of the integrated marketing communication (IMC) mix.

It should be understood that the majority of retail operations are small businesses. It is also important to understand that "new" retailers are finding innovative and unique ways of offering consumer products to their markets. A trend has been developing that has shoppers moving away from traditional retail stores and toward "nonstore" retailing. This movement can be seen in the growth of major e-tailers such as Amazon.com and in catalog retailers such as Delia*s, Celebration Fantastic, and others. Numerous large-store retailers are creating divisions or departments so they, too, can sell via non-store retailing outlets (e.g., Bloomingdales by Mail, Ltd.).

In addition to the growth of non-store retailing, other organizations are expanding the retail category by offering products through other forms of retailing such as warehouse retailing or supercenters and hypermarkets. *Supercenters and hypermarkets* are actually combinations of traditional retailers with supermarkets or a combination of a discount store and supermarket. Discount mass merchandisers, such as Wal-Mart, Target, and Kmart have also grown in size and sales volume. Discount mass merchandisers such as Costco have actually become discount general merchandisers through the sale of additional products and increased selling areas.

These "new" merchandisers have increased their department numbers to 30 or more departments per store. Additionally, these stores have increased the numbers of *SKUs* (stock-keeping units, which represent separate products or items of merchandise) to as many as 80,000. Costco, on the other hand, carries less than 6,000 SKUs and appeals to families who purchase large-sized goods and prepackaged-or bundled-products.

Lifestyle centers are also gaining momentum. According to the International Council of Shopping Centers (ICSC; www.icsc.org), a lifestyle center "caters to retail needs and 'lifestyle' pursuits of consumers in its trading area."[2] Targeted to upper-income shoppers, lifestyle centers are typically outdoors with a "Main Street" type of ambience, have tenants that sell nonessential items, and have parking available in front of the stores. Although the lifestyle center concept has existed since the mid-1980s, the number of such centers has grown nationwide only during the past few years. Presented as an alternative to the big, enclosed shopping mall, the lifestyle center is typically one-third the size of a traditional regional center in terms of retail square footage. Most lifestyle centers do not have structured parking and are located where land is less expensive in typical urban or suburban areas.

The point-of-purchase advertising industry must understand the challenges associated with doing business in this highly dynamic and changing marketplace. Point-of-purchase professionals have a great opportunity to expand sales, but they must understand the buying behavior of retailer shoppers.

POINT-OF-PURCHASE ADVERTISING'S ROLE

Point-of-purchase advertising is part of the overall promotion mix. It usually falls into the sales promotion category, although there are those who argue it is a standalone function of IMC. As such, P-O-P advertising is used to stimulate sales at the point of sale or point of purchase. Keep in mind that this point of sale may not be a physical retail location but rather could be a cyber-location or could be located on the consumer's television or in a magazine (among elsewhere). There are numerous ways by which one can execute P-O-P advertising, for example, shelf talkers, in-store couponing, counter units, shelf units, banners, in-store demos (both wet and dry), checkout messages, in-store radio, and shopping carts.

Point-of-purchase promotions have been found to have a significant influence on consumer shopping behavior. While many shoppers have brand preference for numerous products, they are not brand insistent or even brand loyal for a large majority of products that they purchase. For example, a Coca-Cola brand loyalist may opt for a store brand of potato chips given enough information at the point of decision or purchase. In addition, individuals who have a brand preference may decide to try a new brand if there is an out-of-stock situation for their usual brand, or if there are sufficient P-O-P advertisements inducing them to switch.

Point-Of-Purchase Advertising International (POPAI) reports that as much 75 percent of buying decisions are made in-store.[3] Marketing research on impulse purchases, conducted to determine how consumers behave, has found many influences on the purchase decision. Factors such as anxiety level, physical surroundings, and whether or not the shopper is alone can influence the purchase. In the past, P-O-P communications suffered because it was difficult to track the effectiveness of P-O-P advertising efforts. POPAI, working in conjunction with the Advertising Research Foundation and Prime Consulting Group, developed measurements or metrics that prove P-O-P advertising increases in-store sales,[4] giving retailers tangible evidence of the effectiveness of P-O-P advertising.

The high number of unplanned purchases creates a substantial marketing opportunity for P-O-P planners and other marketers. This opportunity, coupled with the increased ability to measure the effectiveness of P-O-P, strengthens the argument that perhaps point-of-purchase advertising should be a separate tactical variable in the IMC plan. Brand marketers and retailers who have a true understanding of P-O-P advertising and consumer buying behaviors and habits can no longer ignore the potential for increased sales and market share.

RETAILING AND BUYING BEHAVIOR

The idea of increasing product, brand, or product category sales can be explored by looking at how, why, when, and where consumers shop. In addition, the point-of-purchase expert needs to understand what consumers shop for. Point-of-purchase professionals can then exploit these consumer-decision processes and increase product category or brand sales. According to Jacob Jacoby,[5] consumer behavior is the study of how consumers acquire, consume, and dispose of products and services. Through an understanding of consumer behavior, companies can develop better strategies to attract retailers to P-O-P as well as to influence the final consumer to action. An explanation of the consumer decision process follows.

PURCHASE INFLUENCERS

Retail shoppers are influenced in their purchases by others (group influences) and by personal influences (internal, individual consumer characteristics). These two influences have a major impact on why shoppers select certain types of products or services. It is important to understand these influences when developing point-of-purchase promotions.

Cultures and Subcultures

Among the more important group influences on purchase behavior are cultures and subcultures. Many mistakes have been made internationally because marketers did not understand the dominant, or host, culture. *Culture* refers to the aggregate of knowledge, patterns of behavior, and attitudes that a group of individuals shares. Culture, in one form or another, is generally passed down from generation to generation with modifications made each time it passes. Customs, beliefs, and values help to make up a culture. Language and religion may have a large impact on any given culture.

Subcultures are homogeneous subsets within a society (or culture). National origin, ethnic background, geography, or simply value systems may make up subcultures. Researchers have recently described the population of the United States not as a melting pot but more as a tossed salad, where various subcultures exist (ideally in harmony) but maintain their own identities. According to 2000 census figures, of the nearly 300 million people in the United States, 12,298,500 (or about 4 percent) are Asian or Pacific Islanders. A population of 36,832,800 (or about 13 percent) is African-American. Individuals of Hispanic origin make up 36,354,700 (or about 12.8 percent).[6] In June 2003, the U.S. Census Bureau announced that Hispanics had overtaken African Americans to become the largest minority group in the United States.[7] The Bureau estimates that 90 percent of total population growth from 1995 to 2050 will be among blacks, Hispanics, Asians and Pacific Islanders, and Native Americans.[8] In some major cities, such as Los Angeles and New York City, the "minority" population outnumbers the "non-minority" population. The increase in diversity in the United States highlights the importance of subculture. Because culture helps to shape in-store purchase behavior, it is important to understand its influence on consumer behavior.

Additionally, social class plays a role in helping to explain why consumers buy the products they do. An understanding of where consumers see themselves in terms of social class may give clues as to what that particular consumer may want to purchase (in terms of groups of products).

Reference Groups

Reference groups are important in learning about the consumer's shopping behavior. *Reference groups* are those clusters of society that shoppers refer to or look toward to assist them in deciding what products they should buy (and also where they should make the purchase). An individual's friends or associates, including coworkers, constitute one reference group. Social and business organizations, such as the Elks, the Masonic Lodges, Toastmasters and others, can also be reference groups. If a consumer sees a P-O-P display that shows people who look like her colleagues dressed in business casual attire, she may be motivated to purchase these clothes. In this case the display offers the potential consumer an "invisible" influence that says to the buyer she will "fit in" if she buys these products. The strongest reference group for any buyer is the immediate family. Given any shopping situation, the family exerts an enormous amount of influence. P-O-P specialists must concern themselves with the buyer's immediate family when planning P-O-P executions. In fact, a single in-store shopper may be representing numerous buyers (wife, husband, sons, daughters, etc.). Imagine the situation where the newlyweds with the new baby go to the automobile retailer to purchase a car. The husband is looking at those hot, red Corvettes yet comes home with a family minivan. Who made the purchase decision? Perhaps the baby, but probably the wife.

PERSONAL INFLUENCES

Understanding the consumer motivational processes is important for P-O-P marketers. One of the objectives of P-O-P advertising is to incite consumers to action (making a purchase or increasing their purchase size). To incite the consumer to buy, it is essential to understand why the purchase is being made. The model in Figure 2-2 represents the process consumers use to make purchase decisions.

Needs represents a desire, or, more accurately, the lack of something. If the consumer has an unmet need, for example, hunger, the consumer will look for ways to best satisfy that need. The need may be real or imagined, but it affords the point-of-purchase

Figure 2-2
Consumer's
Motivational
Perception

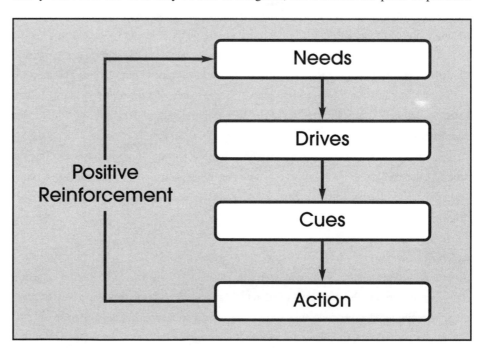

promotion an excellent opportunity for making a sale or increasing a sale. How many times have you been hungry and purchased large amounts of food that you couldn't finish?

The consumer must be motivated to act on a need. The desire to satisfy that need is referred to as *drive*. A drive is anything that causes the individual to act. An individual incited to satisfy a need is driven to that action.

The most important step in this process for the P-O-P specialist is the cues stage. *Cues* are external stimulations that help to propel a customer toward the product. Cues offer the consumer options for reducing or eliminating their drives and satisfying their needs. The cues can be P-O-P advertising displays that provide extra incentives for consumers in helping reduce or eliminate their drive or need.

In a study conducted by Safeway, POPAI, and Unilever Bestfoods,[9] it was found that the combination of new merchandising layouts and P-O-P produced a 90 percent increase in the number of shoppers who interacted with the displays. Merchandising and P-O-P acted as cues to stimulate curiosity. Recent research shows that when motion, another cue, was added to P-O-P displays, sales increased an average 44 percent over sales for the same displays without motion.[10]

Action refers to the consumer's final purchase-decision behavior. What response did the consumer have to the P-O-P cue? Did they purchase? The consumer's purchase is the action that marketers are looking for. The idea behind P-O-P advertising is to increase sales; thus the intended consumer action is the purchase. For example, Eddie Bauer and Indiana University conducted tests to determine whether electronic signage in the form of plasma screens in store windows impacted consumer behavior and store sales. Traffic devices were installed to count consumers walking past the Eddie Bauer stores in the study. Interviews were also conducted to determine recall. Traffic jumped 23 percent in those stores using digital signage compared to the Eddie Bauer stores that did not use the digital signage. In addition, 23 percent of surveyed customers recalled seeing the digital signage in the store window and nearly 10 percent recalled the specific product advertised. Of the shoppers who remembered the product, 46 percent said they would consider buying it.[11] Although these results are encouraging, it is the impact on sales that is important. For Eddie Bauer, sales increased by 56 percent after a nine-week period, thus prompting further investment.[12]

One often-overlooked step in the motivational process is reinforcement. After a consumer action, the consumer will experience satisfaction or dissatisfaction. The consumer who experiences dissatisfaction, or cognitive dissonance, is unlikely to buy the product again, and worse yet, may not buy any of the company's products. Additionally, consumers who are very unsatisfied may choose to shop at another retail outlet. If the consumer is satisfied, their repeat behavior may be assured. If the product is not their preferred product, it will be a purchase alternative with a satisfied buyer.

P-O-P displays that help to reinforce consumers' decisions in a positive direction are extremely valuable to the retailer. P-O-P turns a chore into an experience and offers companies an intimate way to reach their customers.[13] Remember that sales can be made or lost at the point of purchase, so making the shopping experience enjoyable is important to all members of the supply chain.

Decision Point Marketing of Winston-Salem, North Carolina, developed a cross-promotional display for A-1 Steak Sauce. The display allowed the consumer to receive a free sample of A-1 Bold Steak Sauce if they made a meat purchase at the point of sale. This display provides the consumer with reinforcement for their purchase decision by inferring that the company is so sure the consumer will like the product (A-1 Bold), they're giving it away for free. See Figure 2-3.

KRAFT FOODS AND DECISION POINT MARKETING, INC.

Figure 2-3

A-1 free sample

display

Headlines, warranties, and guarantees are some ways the P-O-P specialist can create positive reinforcement at the point of sale. Surveying customers about P-O-P should also be considered. In a study of convenience stores conducted by POPAI and Prime Consulting Group, 79 percent of consumers surveyed reported they were satisfied or very satisfied with their stores' current level of P-O-P advertising. Ten percent wanted more, and 11 percent felt there was too much in-store advertising. Fifty-nine percent reported that P-O-P was somewhat or very helpful in making purchase decisions.[14] Remember that the idea of positive reinforcement is to reduce the amount of cognitive dissonance (or buyer's remorse) that the shopper may experience.

WHAT CONSUMERS PURCHASE

What consumer's purchase is also important when developing effective P-O-P displays. Displays should be developed based upon the types of products being featured. For example, services are very intangible, so P-O-P displays should provide some types of tangible "add-ons." The unisex hair boutique may offer reduced prices on related products such as shampoo or hairbrushes. The P-O-P displays may also provide "evidence" that the new hairstyle (just purchased) is popular, by placing pictures or testimonies of supermodels on/in the display. *Durable* goods must be sold utilizing long-term promises. *Nondurable* goods must be sold utilizing convenience. This type of product, or brand, moves best when brought to the consumer (e.g., at end-of-aisle, eye level, dump tables).

By targeting the consumer's family situation, marketers can take advantage of a shopper's propensity to spend. Family income and patterns of spending should be studied. One important area for study is the *family life cycle*. Families go through a series of stages in spending (the family life cycle). Definitions of what makes up a family life cycle vary slightly; however, behaviors of the individual family units in each of these phases (or stages) are similar. For example, people in the *Bachelor Stage* of the life cycle spend heavily on clothing, while those in the *Full Nest I Stage* spend heavily on child-related products and household operations.

What consumers purchase also depends on the amount of effort they will have to expend (and are willing to expend) in search of a product or service. Major differences exist with convenience, shopping, and specialty products. Convenience products, such as staples, impulse, and emergency products, must be displayed and sold based upon time convenience to the shopper and place convenience. Shopping goods can be either homogeneous or heterogeneous.

Homogeneous shopping goods are big-ticket items that are similar to those of competitors. P-O-P advertising should emphasize competitive pricing for these goods. Effective placement and targeting of shoppers are critical for heterogeneous shopping goods (since these products are perceived as being of higher quality or unique styles, or just basically as different).

Finally, specialty goods (brands, products, or services that a consumer is willing to spend a lot of time and effort locating) should be "featured" within the P-O-P advertising executions.

HOW THE CONSUMER BUYS

Once the P-O-P planner knows the *what* and the *why*, the planner must spend time assessing *how* the consumer shops. Consumers' shopping behaviors vary by the type of product wanted or needed. The key to developing effective P-O-P displays depends on the consumer's experience with the service or product, the cost of the product, and the amount of information the consumer must gather to make an educated and effective buying decision. For example, should the consumer need or want a product he or she is unfamiliar with, and which is on the expensive side, the P-O-P planner must provide significant amounts of information about the product—information that is important to the buyer. For consumers who wish to purchase a product they have had experience with, the task of the P-O-P planner is to excite them to action by reminding them that they liked the product the last time they made a purchase. The consumers may know what they want and may already be planning the purchase. The opportunity here is to increase the size (quantity) or frequency of the purchase. Remember that the consumer is purchasing a product, service, or brand that they have most likely already used.

Consumers today are often pressed for time. P-O-P can make it easier for them to find what they want. When they find what they want quickly, the rest of their time is spent browsing, which often increases their purchase amount.[15] There is also a good chance of increasing sales by creating additional impulse purchases. Impulse purchases, as indicated earlier, are made without a planning process. The P-O-P display, product packaging, and/or branding are keys to creating additional impulse purchases. This is one of the best opportunities for point-of-purchase planners.

At times, when consumers need certain types of information about a product they have limited experience with, the P-O-P display needs both to attract the shopper and to provide just enough information to warrant the purchase. In this particular situation, the

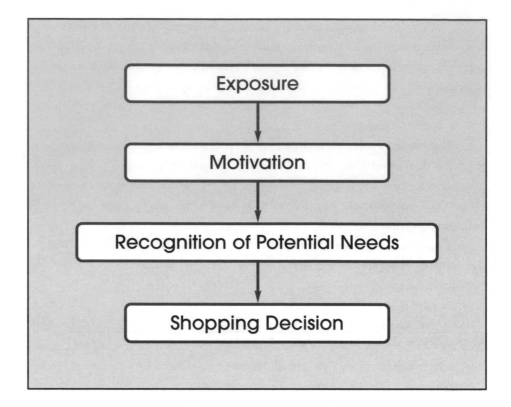

Figure 2-4

Framework of

Consumer Decision

Making[17]

P-O-P display usually needs to have a direct tie-in with the overall IMC program and, most importantly, with the advertising of the actual product or service. This can be accomplished effectively by creating some type of continuity. Utilize the tag line within the P-O-P display, or tie in a continuing central character with the display; perhaps a logo or even a jingle can create the tie-in and, therefore, continuity.

In an in-depth study about consumer in-store decision making, "Where the Rubber Meets the Road,"[16] cosponsored by Point-of-Purchase Advertising International and the Marketing Science Institute, researchers Inman and Winer developed a model of consumer decision making. Overall, the authors suggest a framework for in-store decisions. The framework is presented in Figure 2-4. Inman and Winer suggest that *exposure* to product categories and in-store displays is necessary to create consumer motivation. The study's authors further suggest that there has to be some type of motivation generated to process the in-store stimuli (or P-O-P displays). Once the exposure and motivation are in place, the consumer will have a need recognition (created by exposure and motivation and moderated by prior shopping trip planning). Finally, the consumer makes the shopping decision of purchasing or not purchasing. This framework translates to the full model depicted in Figure 2-5.

It may be helpful to take a look at the model in a little more detail and operationally define some of the terms the authors use.[19] For example, when Inman and Winer discuss the "Category Purchase" type, they are referring to whether the shopper's decision was specifically planned, generally planned, a brand switch, or an unplanned purchase. Additionally:

- "Trip Type" refers to why the shopping trip was initiated (i.e., a major shopping excursion vs. a "fill-in" for just a few products, or an in-between).

- "Display Type and Location" refer to the exact in-store location of the display and the type of display unit being used (e.g., shelf talker, end-of-aisle, shelf).

- "Deal Proneness," as identified by POPAI and the researchers, refers to shoppers' propensity to avail themselves of any products on deal. In other words, did they purchase certain items because they received a discount or other motivation?

- "Feature Proneness" refers to the fact that shoppers did, or did not, utilize FSIs (free-standing inserts), mail circulars, or other types of newspaper inserts in their planning process prior to entering the store.

- "Aisles Shopped" represents the answers consumers gave when queried as to how they shopped—that is, did they shop all aisles, some aisles, or just sections of the store? In other words, what was their shopping behavior once inside the retail store?

- "Purchase Involvement," "Compulsiveness," and "Need for Cognition" are constructs that were measured utilizing scales developed by the researchers. *Purchase involvement* measures how involved the buyers/shoppers were in the purchase decision; *compulsiveness* refers to how prone to impulse purchases the buyers were; and *need for cognition* refers to the shoppers' use of "effortful, systematic thinking": Do they spend a lot of time thinking about all of the information they have gathered and utilize that to help make a decision, or do they make a faster purchase decision?

The rest of the terms discussed by Inman and Winer are self-explanatory.

The Inman and Winer model of in-store decision making provides the point-of-purchase expert with an excellent overview of the in-store process. In addition to the model, the study's findings are very helpful in understanding and planning for consumer in-store purchases. The findings can be generalized as follows:[20]

- "Although both shopping-trip-specific and consumer-specific factors are significant drivers of in-store decision making, shopping-trip-specific factors play a greater role."

- "The biggest effects on in-store decision making were . . . the exposure-related factors of number of aisles shopped and trip type. . . ."

- Fifty-nine percent of purchases were unplanned.

- Unplanned purchases are more likely for end-of-aisle and checkout than for in-aisle.

- "Consumers with a higher level of purchase involvement were less prone to making in-store decisions."

- "Motivation-related factors played a significant role. . . ."

- "In-store decision making is greater for larger households, larger shopping parties, households with greater income, and women."

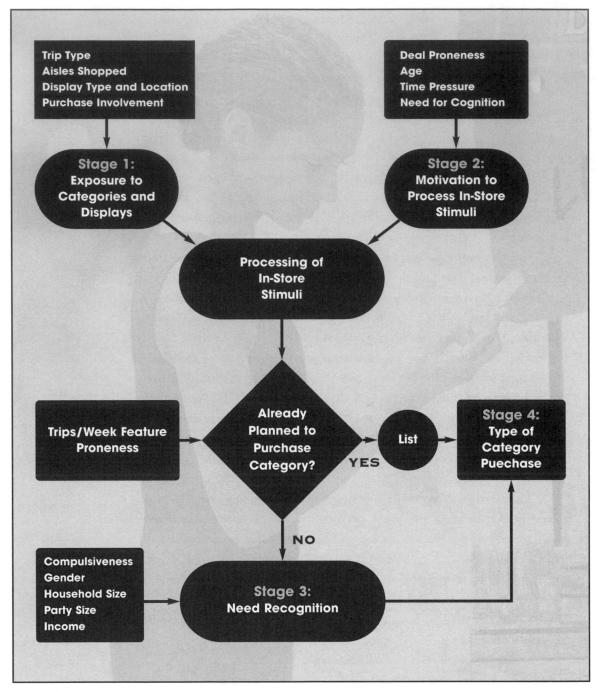

Figure 2-5

Inman and Winter

Model of In-Store

Decision Making

In addition to the above information, the P-O-P planner needs to understand the changes in purchase patterns based upon "time." To exploit the time, or *when* variable, the point-of-purchase planner should plan the displays in conjunction with the consumer's "times." In other words, displays must be in place when the consumer expects them. For example, certain products can be sold during holiday seasons (e.g., candy at Easter, toys before Christmas, champagne before New Year's Eve, beer before the Fourth of July, or greeting cards before Valentine's Day). Social time periods also provide excellent opportunities for "when" to reach the targeted buyers (e.g., gowns before proms, homecomings, or weddings). Cultural events may also provide hints to merchandising (e.g., the opening of the opera season). Furthermore, the school year is a great time to plan displays (back-to-school events, summer vacations, and graduations). Work schedules and corresponding paydays are excellent cues—or motivators—to purchase, and provide clues to displaying merchandise. It is important that P-O-P advertising be planned taking into account the decade (or millennium), year, day, month, hour, minute, second, or whatever time period is important to those buying products at the point of purchase.

Where Customers Shop

As important as all of the above information is regarding consumer behavior, *place*, or *where* a consumer buys, is becoming even more significant. It is important to remember that a lot of retail purchases are made not in the store but elsewhere. In addition to the direct location of a consumer's purchase, point-of-purchase professionals should pay specific attention to the buyer's reason(s) or motivation beyond store or location choice. In-store purchasing (at a physical retail site) is where most consumers today buy products or services. Shoppers enjoy the merchandise selection. They enjoy trying on fashions. Shoppers at retail stores are physically able to make quality comparisons between products and brands. Price comparisons are facilitated at an actual physical site, especially at store cluster sites (such as malls and central business districts of cities and towns) where more than one store carries the same kind of item.

Although consumers can shop in a retail store and also from work (via catalog, the Internet, telephone, videos, DVDs, CDs, direct salespeople, etc.), most retail purchases not made in-store are made from the consumer's home. Home shopping offers convenience and privacy. Most home shoppers can access a store via the methods listed above, which include taking the "store" with them wherever they go, even during long-distance traveling. The point-of-purchase advertiser needs to be aware of these non-store locations and to plan tactical executions that meet or exceed the shopping needs of consumers who use them. The amount of P-O-P activity at these locations will continue to grow, becoming a large part of the P-O-P market.

The majority of the P-O-P planning discussion concerns those purchases made in a typical retail environment. The P-O-P consumer behaviorist should understand that there are purchases made outside of a typical retail store. For example, many shoppers patronize warehouse/discount clubs, such as Costco. When developing P-O-P advertising for such clubs, success depends on an understanding of who the consumer is. In fact, Costco is utilizing more and more brand-marketer-provided P-O-P displays because they have caused a significant increase in sales.

In a study undertaken by J. Patrick Kelly of Wayne State University,[21] the researcher points out that "two-thirds of warehouse purchases are made by one-third of the customers-business customers. This must be considered when displays and P-O-P messages are designed." The consumer behaviorist must understand that business customers go through some of the same processes as consumers, but with some significant differences.

Two of the most important issues for the P-O-P planner are (1) the business buyer is shopping for a company or organization and thus has a list of specific products that must be purchased, preferably for lowest cost possible, and (2) the business buyer is less motivated by emotion than the nonbusiness buyer. Therefore, P-O-P displays set up in the warehouse industry should provide more pricing information and should make the purchase as easy as possible for the buyer (by providing a convenient location, price, and information on the product).

CONCLUSION

The effectiveness of point-of-purchase advertising depends on an understanding of the customer and the customer's in-store behavior. With their understanding of retailing, point-of-purchase specialists can motivate and provide meaningful cues to customers, resulting in increased sales. Because consumer decision making may be brand- or product-specific, it is recommended that brand marketers who utilize P-O-P tactics design and implement research to study specific behaviors of their target market. This research could also be outsourced.

Those involved in the point-of-purchase advertising industry also understand that this type of promotion does not stand alone but is an intricate part of the overall, IMC effort put forth by the client companies. Whether one is using banners, counter cards, interactive computers, in-store television or radio, temporary signs, or shelf talkers depends on the outcome desired by the client for the whole promotional effort. Premiums almost demand a point-of-purchase display, as do sweepstakes and games. Displays can generate new trials or excite consumers to want to own or try new products. Brand extension strategies are easily executed utilizing displays.

The overall issue here is: Point-of-purchase executions must be integrated with all areas of the IMC (promotion) mix and must be based on a thorough knowledge of the customer base and the customers' particular buying habits. This understanding is essential to the continued success of the industry as we move toward new and exciting challenges.

ENDNOTES

[1] "Retailers: Get Bankruptcy Reform to President's Desk," PR Newswire, March 19, 2003.

[2] "Lifestyle Centers—A Defining Moment," *ICSC Research Quarterly* (Winter 2002). Also available at http://www.icsc.org.

[3] Rachel Miller, "In-Store Impact on Impulse Shoppers," *Marketing* (November 21, 2002): 27.

[4] Elizabeth Boston, "Point-of-Purchase Industry Develops Audience Gauge," *Advertising Age*, June 30, 2003, Midwest Region edition, 6.

[5] Jacob Jacoby, "Consumer Behavior: A Quadrennium," *Annual Review of Psychology* 49 (1998): 319–45.

[6] "Sales and Marketing Management: 2001 Survey of Buying Power and Media Markets," (September 2001), Bill Communications.

[7] Maria Elena Salinas, "Latinization of U.S. a Reality," *Seattle Post-Intelligencer*, July 1, 2003, B5.

[8] Julie Moran Alterio, "Does Diversity = Dollars?", *The Journal News on the Web*, March 29, 2002, http://www.thejournalnews.com/diversitydollars/articles/31divbigpicture.html.

[9] "POP Makes Sense Count," *Grocer* (June 14, 2003): 72.

[10] "Motion Moves Product: The Effect of Motion in Displays," (August 1998), Point-Of-Purchase Advertising Institute, 3.

[11] Raymond R. Burke, "Retail Technology: Digital Signage—Promises and Pitfalls," *Point of Purchase Magazine* (April 1, 2003): 22.

[12] Calmetta Y. Coleman, "Eddie Bauer's Windows Add Electronics," *Wall Street Journal*, November 28, 2000, Eastern edition, B10.

[13] Thomas Lee, "Experts Say Point of-Purchase Advertising Can Influence Shoppers' Choices," *Knight Ridder/Tribune Business News*, January 19, 2002.

[14] "In-Store Advertising Becomes a Measured Medium: Convenience Channel Study," (December 2002), Point-Of-Purchase Advertising International, 14.

[15] Miller, "In-Store Impact," 27.

[16] J. Jeffrey Inman and Russell S. Winer, "Where the Rubber Meets the Road: A Model of In-Store Consumer Decision Making," working paper (report no. 98-122), The Marketing Science Institute, October 1998, 6.

[17] Ibid., 6.

[18] Ibid., 6.

[19] Ibid., 6–9.

[20] Ibid., v.

[21] J. Patrick Kelley, *Uses of Point-of-Purchase Advertising Materials in the Warehouse Club Industry: Challenges and Opportunities* (Englewood, N.J.: Point-Of-Purchase Advertising Institute, 1992), 30.

3

"The challenge of designing and delivering superior P-O-P solutions demands an informed, dedicated, and forward-looking team of P-O-P specialists committed to getting the project done on time and on budget."

Introduction to P-O-P Project Management

FRED SKLENAR, CPP, ACCOUNT CREATIVE DIRECTOR
UNIFIED RESOURCES

OVERVIEW

"What is needed to make every P-O-P project successful is complete and thorough participation from all stakeholders. Every stakeholder must be committed to clear and open communication of the project objectives, and all must understand the challenges that may be encountered along the way. "

Barbara Daugherty, Director of Merchandising Strategies and Design, Frito-Lay, Inc.

Every project management book has one major theme: Understand the objectives, have clear goals, communicate those goals to the stakeholders, pay close attention to the details, follow up and evaluate how you did after the fact, and you will have a successfully managed project.

In today's competitive marketing world, the role of a coordinated and synchronized marketing communications program is paramount, especially when it comes together at the moment of truth—when the consumer purchases the product at the point of sale. There is no more critical point in the marketing chain than at that moment in time. In the world of integrated marketing communications (IMC), the consumer's choice of brand depends on a history of associations with the product and/or marketing communications that stimulate the buyer's choice of product.

This chapter deals with management of the point-of-purchase display project from its beginning to its installation at the point of sale.

SCOPE OF RESPONSIBILITY

Consider the brand marketer who has a global responsibility. That marketer must create a P-O-P advertising display in many languages; design for many different retail environments (from mass merchandisers, to supermarkets, to convenience stores); coordinate many vendors around the globe; monitor budgets and production schedules; and meet the demands of each retailer and sales channel. It can be a Herculean task.

For brand marketers who have local or regional chain distribution, the tasks can be no less challenging. Those marketers usually have less to manage, but they also have a smaller staff and budget, and have to be equally creative and dedicated to managing budgets and production schedules.

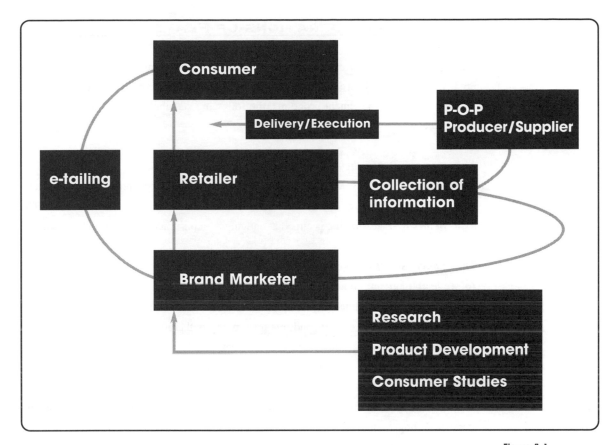

Figure 3-1

Relationship between
the three participants
in a P-O-P display
program

Managing a P-O-P project is not unlike managing any project, large or small, where there are project objectives, multiple parties involved, production and marketing schedules, and budgets. The challenges of managing a P-O-P advertising project, however, are different for the brand marketer, producer/supplier, and retailer. This chapter addresses the myriad of project management issues faced by each of them.

Figure 3-1 demonstrates the relationship between these three participants of a P-O-P display program. Managing a P-O-P project requires participation and interaction by all key stakeholders. The consumer is placed at the top of this chart because the consumer is the ultimate target audience. The management of all elements—from which P-O-P product/displays are executed—may start (at the bottom) with research and product development, but the consumer defines the core parameters.

More importantly, Figure 3-1 demonstrates the flow of information and the order of relations between the retailer, the brand marketer, and the P-O-P producer/supplier. All three are involved in the collection of information that helps define the parameters of an in-store promotional program. It is also important to note that research is not limited to the brand marketer. Retailers are engaged in traditional market research to understand and define their customers, as are producers/suppliers who research the effectiveness of P-O-P.

SPECIAL CONSIDERATIONS OF PLAYERS

During the creation and marketing of products, it is important to consider the parties involved in the P-O-P production process. To achieve better communication and more effective project management programs, the following stakeholders and their roles must be considered:

The customer: Drives the need

The end consumer drives everything—store layout, merchandising, and product placement. Products are designed, packaged, and offered for sale at retail for the end consumer. The focus of all P-O-P advertising is aimed at enticing the consumer to purchase the products.

The retailer: Sets the stage

As we learn more and more about IMC, we can identify how retailers are building themselves as brands independent of the products they offer. All retailers are positioned by the brands and products they carry, and this positioning is therefore transferred to the retailer's brand. For example, Lowe's and Home Depot have built strong, differentiated brands based on the products and brands they offer their customers, and they use that as the platform of their marketing programs.

The retailer, by supporting its own brand in the marketplace, sets the style of the in-store marketing vehicles that are created for their stores. As part of its brand building and support, the retailer engages in marketing its brand through its own advertising and through the creation of private label products. Costco's private label, Kirkland, is applied to practically everything—from socks to ice cream to barbeques.

The brand marketer: Manufactures what the consumer wants

The brand marketer supplies the product, the packaging for the product, the selection of product mix, the promotions, the advertising, the image, the message, and the retail execution of promotional materials known as point-of-purchase advertising.

The brand marketer comprises many different departments, from research and development to sales, all of which are involved with delivery of the product to the consumer.

The producer: Creates the in-store marketing vehicle—the display

The P-O-P display company provides the design, engineering, material specification, manufacturing, delivery, and follow-up, including installation of the retail promotion.

With these roles well defined, where is the challenge in project management? It is to understand the complete process, have a clear picture of the end objectives, and communicate effectively within the framework of the parties involved. We must also understand why each partner in the P-O-P chain is involved.

A project manager involved in any phase of in-store promotion should be aware of the following special considerations regarding the display programs when defining an in-store program:

- *Consumer issues.*
- *Retail channel issues.*
- *In-store category issues.*
- *The type of display or promotion to create.*
- *Effectiveness goals relative to budget availability.*
- *Engineering and durability concerns.*
- *Distribution issues.*
- *Time and delivery issues.*

WHO MANAGES THE P-O-P PROJECT?

At the retailer level, there are often teams charged with strategic store planning (plan-o-grams), existing store resets, new store planning, seasonal planning, and those whose jobs involve day-to-day merchandising. These managers may or may not be considered the "buyers." Buyers are the persons responsible for the choice of product offered at a retailer.

Brand marketer sales teams call on buyers and merchandising managers to offer their products for placement within the retail store. During the P-O-P selling process, retail buyers and merchandisers, sales force managers, and brand marketer merchandising managers usually all take part in planning the retail P-O-P project. Along with the P-O-P supplier, these are the stakeholders that are critical to the success of the project.

In recent years, the producer/supplier has also become increasingly involved with both retailers and brand marketers to assist in managing the design, engineering, production, distribution, and execution at retail of P-O-P displays.

Utilizing the knowledge of each member's expertise and the team approach, point-of-purchase displays and promotional programs have the opportunity to become a unified, cohesive force to achieve the maximum potential within the retail environment.

What Experience Do Managers Need?

Marketing and merchandising managers often have extensive knowledge of their specialty. They typically come from the sales force at brand marketer companies. Having spent time in the field, they have gained experience that enables them to understand the daily challenge at retail. Obviously, knowledge of the target consumer is needed, and most retailers invest substantial sums in establishing, evaluating, and catering to their target consumer. It is the role of the producer/supplier, however, to understand the design, engineering, and manufacturing of P-O-P materials and displays. Coincidentally, many retailers and brand marketers place their own managers with manufacturing experience and/or knowledge in these merchandising positions.

What Knowledge Do Managers Need?

Managers at the retail, brand marketer, and producer/supplier levels must all know the product and the selling environment and must understand the best possible way to deliver the product to the consumer. Some of the best producers/suppliers pride themselves on their ability to research, understand, and develop P-O-P advertising for many different situations. However, the best team approach is for each member to bring his or her specialty to the P-O-P planning process. Retailers know how to deliver what the consumer wants and needs. Brand marketers know how to develop what the consumer wants and needs. Producers/suppliers know how to design, engineer, and produce point-of-purchase vehicles to meet the needs and requirements of both the brand marketer and the retailer to ultimately achieve the goal of delivery of the product to the consumer. Figure 3-2 presents a checklist of special considerations for each team member.

Figure 3-2
Checklist of special considerations of team members in a P-O-P display program

What are the special considerations of the brand marketer?

☐ The brand message—Is it being communicated properly?
☐ Consumer buying habits—How do they affect sales?
☐ Knowledge of the competition—Are we proactive or reactive?
☐ Retailer relations—Do we act with them in mind at all times?
☐ Manufacturing experience—Do I understand time, budget, materials, etc.?
☐ P-O-P integration—Am I using it to its fullest potential?

What are the special considerations of the retailer?

☐ Understanding the ultimate end user: the consumer.
☐ The physical retail environment.
☐ Distribution channels.
☐ Style and type of retailer differences.
☐ Category management issues.
☐ Competition between retailers.

What are the special considerations of the producer/supplier?

☐ It is critical that the producer/supplier have an understanding of, or at least inquire about, all of the above points that are specific to both the product and the environment it is sold in.
☐ Product SPR (suggested retail price), in relation to cost of materials (i.e., budget)
☐ Time schedule and distribution factors.
☐ Materials and manufacturing processes.

How Do Brand Marketers Handle Relationships?

It is critical that brand marketers see their vendors as partners in the process of selling their products. Producers/suppliers welcome the opportunity to be part of the team. As with any purchasing situation, there are conditions where the financial burden of achieving what is needed goes beyond what is practical and feasible. Similarly, the brand marketer is always challenged with selling its product to the retailer. Often, programs are created that provide allowances to each party. For example, a retailer may allow a brand marketer's logo to be placed as the prominent graphic at the top of a display, and also allow the brand marketer's product on no less than 60 percent of the peg hooks on that display, in return for receiving the display at no cost to the retailer. On the producer/supplier side, a brand marketer may agree to purchase a particular volume of displays over a given time period in return for a discounted display price.

In many cases, the retailer will charge slotting fees—specific costs to brand marketers to permit their product to occupy certain locations within the stores. So, in addition to the cost of manufacturing the requested display, the brand marketer will often pay slotting fees or promotional allowances to gain a larger in-store presence through a P-O-P display.

Building positive working relationships between the brand marketer and the retailer becomes critical to the success of both parties: brand marketers need the retailer to reach the consumer. Conversely, the retailer needs brand marketers to supply them with product that is timely and relevant to their customer. By working together, all parties achieve corporate goals.

How Do Brand Marketers Handle the Relationship with Producers/Suppliers?

Typically, the selection process involves choosing the supplier who best serves the brand marketer's needs. Therefore, evaluation of current suppliers and consideration of new suppliers should be a continuous part of the operation. As consumers and retailing change, so do products. It follows that promotional strategies and execution will also be modified to meet the current selling environment and competition.

Producers/suppliers in the P-O-P industry are usually defined by the type of production or type of display they can produce. In selecting a supplier, brand marketers and retailers can consider elements such as location, experience, capabilities, and history, if any, with the company or retail channel. There are no set rules or guidelines for how to choose a supplier except that they must be readily available to produce what is needed, when it is needed, and to produce the desired look.

What Is an RFP?

A request for proposal (RFP) is a formal request for work-for-hire. An RFP is usually the result of meetings between retailers and brand marketers whereby a tentative agreement for delivery of product is contracted and, in general terms, promotional support is required to accompany the display of product at retail. RFPs may seek simply to gather information such as cost of the promotional program and the time it will take to manufacture the promotional displays. Alternatively, they may look for design concepts to meet a unique or sometimes not-so-unique selling situation.

Some requests are detailed and some take the form of simply providing a sample of the product to producers/suppliers and advising them of the location at retail where the product will be displayed, leaving an open door for creativity to run free.

As brand marketers and producers/suppliers manage the design, development, engineering, production, and distribution of the displays, it is critical that they maintain constant communication. Retailers ultimately see most presentations of design concepts before the brand marketer commits to production. They are often very involved in establishing parameters for the displays and typically require full-working prototypes to be delivered to them for approval prior to mass-quantity manufacturing.

HOW DOES A DISPLAY COME TO LIFE?

After a retailer or brand marketer decides to have a display, someone must design it and produce it. Knowledgeable display professionals, in most cases, start their development process by visiting stores—a lot of stores! Understanding consumer behavior and the differences between the types of retail environments is paramount when developing vehicles to help products sell better. We must understand why consumers buy, why they choose to shop in certain sections of a store and not others, why they frequent favorite stores, and what might motivate them to stray from their normal shopping behaviors

POPAI offers seminars and other programs that speak directly to this type of in-store research. Combining formal presentations of real-world statistical data with informal store visits and informational discussions with store personnel aid the P-O-P producer in developing relevant and successful display programs.

DESIGN

The P-O-P firms that specialize in design, development, and engineering of P-O-P are specialists in understanding all of the challenges of creating point-of-purchase displays. These firms may provide turnkey solutions for the client or they may just provide design without any further involvement in the production of the displays in quantity. Some are specialty promotional or advertising agencies that are engaged in various facets of a product's marketing programs. Others may be industrial design firms whose roles include product and package design. As P-O-P displays become more high-tech and require more sophisticated design expertise, brand marketers and retailers are increasingly looking for suppliers who understand the total P-O-P solution—from design through installation.

MANUFACTURING

From the simple shelf dangler to the most complex interactive display, the manufacture of displays and in-store marketing vehicles utilizes some of the world's most-up-to-date and innovative processes as well as some of the oldest and most traditional forms of manufacturing available. Some display companies are producers of stock items and simply modify the mix of their stock elements to meet the custom need of the display. Other companies use a custom-design approach and will utilize any process available to create unique and attractive components for the displays they produce.

As with any marketing effort, a budget and a timeline are involved. Those who manage display projects are responsible for picking and choosing, from the sea of manufacturing operations available, the operations that can achieve the desired aesthetic and can be produced on time and within budget.

The evaluation of a display company should be focused on its ability to service the needs of its customers, its creativity, its experience, its existing client base, how well it can meet the budget, and its track record on past promotions.

WHAT INFORMATION IS NEEDED TO DEVELOP AN EFFECTIVE P-O-P DISPLAY?

Figure 3-3 (presented on pages 52 through 55), the project profile questionnaire, is an extensive list of questions that can help to define the parameters for developing effective displays. Brand marketers and retailers who are responsible for any part of the process should review the questionnaire and create their own lists of questions relevant to them. All of these questions should be familiar to producers/suppliers.

THE TIMELINE

A simple way to clarify the P-O-P design and manufacturing process is to divide it into seven phases: (1) project definition, (2) design proposal, (3) prototype/test/install, (4) manufacturing/production, (5) IMC tie-in, (6) delivery and setup, and (7) post-promotion evaluation.

Phase One—Project Definition

The first phase is to define the scope of the project between the retailer and brand marketer. For example, some products are seasonal, such as candy. Although candy is merchandised throughout the year, candy is sold in larger quantities during the Halloween season. Halloween is an annual event with a set date and, typically, Halloween promotional programs must be in place immediately after Labor Day to maximize the sales opportunity.

Other products such as toothpaste have no predetermined selling season. Promotional program planning for such products should be an ongoing effort, with retailers and brand marketers working together to establish dates for special promotions.

Some brand marketers and retailers begin the process during specific times of the year in order to allow for a proper development timeline; other programs may be scheduled to coincide with store resets, the renovation of existing stores, or the building of new ones.

Phase Two—Design Proposal

Once the P-O-P project and its scope have been identified, the P-O-P manufacturer or producer/supplier will begin work with specific designs and concepts. Regardless of the type of product, the season of the year, or why the display is needed, once the retailer and the brand marketer agree on a creative direction for a P-O-P program, they give display companies about two weeks to develop display concepts.

Phase Three—Prototype/Test/Install

Before retailers or brand marketers invest in a full production run of a display, small-run prototypes are sometimes made and delivered to retail for evaluation. It can take a week to three to four weeks to build just one display, or a small handful of prototypes, especially when there is no tooling available and most of the work is done manually by designer-model makers.

If a prototype display is to be subjected to the hazards of the real-world retail environment, where consumers will interact with it, it must be fabricated from durable materials just as it would be if manufactured in mass quantity. This requires that a display company order the correct materials and hire a knowledgeable prototype maker. The display will be evaluated for both durability and selling success after a predetermined selling time.

If positive results are gathered, full production can be approved. When planning timelines, it must be remembered that the installation of prototypes sometimes requires coordination with installation crews. In addition, coordination may also be required with store management and the brand marketer. This coordination may eat up time, delaying not only the installation of the prototype but also the gathering of results from the display after installation.

Phase Four—Manufacturing/Production

While materials and processes vary, manufacturing production usually averages six to eight weeks. Some programs that require tooling can add six to 12 weeks in front of the actual production, and some smaller-run programs require no tooling and can be produced start to finish (i.e., shipping) in four weeks or less.

Retail distribution of the P-O-P display can take one to two weeks or more. Some programs may be initiated, designed, manufactured, and distributed in under six weeks while others may take more than a year to develop. Because displays are so varied, it would be difficult to give one exact recommendation here. Your P-O-P display professional can better help you with determining lead times based on your specific display needs.

Phase Five—IMC Tie-In

While the display is being developed, the other elements of the IMC plan (i.e., newspaper, direct mail, television, and outdoor advertising) should be developed and coordinated for the timely arrival of P-O-P materials at their destinations. The critical task is to tie together approvals and production lead times so that all elements of the campaign reach the consumer, allowing each element of the campaign to do its job of persuading the consumer to purchase the product.

Phase Six—Delivery and Setup

Once the P-O-P display is manufactured and shipped to the brand marketer's or retailer's fulfillment center, the project may in fact end for the producer/supplier display company. But it is certainly not over as far as the retailer or brand marketer is concerned. However, for those P-O-P firms that specialize in total solutions, including supervision of fulfillment, installation, and P-O-P monitoring, the P-O-P provider may stay on the project for the entire length of the in-store promotion. This post-production phase may take as little as one month or as long as a full year to complete.

Delivery is critical. It is not uncommon that 25,000 corrugated displays are shipped to supermarkets but only 6,000 or so are actually set up and placed in the correct store location. Dozens of personnel and departments within all interested parties must coordinate if displays and other marketing vehicles are to arrive on time and have the chance to sell the product.

Knowledge of the critical processes by all involved will aid in the precise availability of and arrival of in-store marketing vehicles. It is not uncommon for U.S. trucking companies to delay a truck ordered for pickup at a display manufacturer, perhaps because truck availability is at a premium during a heavy shipping season. Similarly, trucks may be held at previous destinations. A shipment may sit for days upon arrival at a retailer's distribution center (DC), waiting for an available open dock for unloading. Because delivery coordination involves numerous people, things can easily slip through the cracks unless all parties understand the pitfalls, coordinate, and exercise caution. If the brand marketer, purchasing retailer, and display company do not clarify all details with each other, shipments can be held up for days or even weeks.

The question of who is going to set up these displays must also be considered. There are service companies whose sole responsibility is to go store-by-store and restock or set up displays. These companies might visit the stores on their account list every six weeks. If a display arrives the day after a visit, it may sit in the back of a store, unopened, for six weeks. (Those who have never seen the back of a supermarket might want to visit one just to see what it is like.) Even if a display was shipped FedEx and signed by a known representative, it will probably be very difficult to find. As one remedy, shipments should be tracked very well and identified on the box with print as big and bold as is possible. For example, Sam's Club requires a 3 x 5-inch or larger neon green sticker with item numbers and other important information about the display's requirements to be attached to a display box so that their personnel can differentiate it from a product box.

Phase Seven—Post-Promotion Evaluation

You will learn in Chapter 5 why it is critical to conduct a project review once a project is completed. The objective of the post-project review is to ensure that all parties learn how to improve the P-O-P promotion planning process.

From the project manager's point of view, the post-promotion evaluation takes on increased importance in building upon a project's success or learning from disappointing results. For some lengthy P-O-P projects, project managers (from all parties) will be continuously monitoring the project during the promotion, to make adjustments during the P-O-P store life. In some cases, temporary P-O-P projects have turned into permanent point-of-purchase programs because the P-O-P display was so effective. However, it does occur that improperly designed or manufactured P-O-P displays must be removed, which is costly to all parties.

It is the role of the project manager to ensure an understanding of and to clarify why a P-O-P promotional program succeeded or failed. The project manager should conduct post-promotion evaluation meetings with all team members to review P-O-P performance, design, advertising, sales (projected vs. actual), and overall promotion objectives.

EXTRA SERVICES

Research and Marketing Know-How

Research and marketing knowledge are essential parts of the core services that P-O-P manufacturers and direct brokers provide. Typically, brand marketers, retailers, and producers/suppliers are all interested in trends relative to consumer-buying behavior. Other areas of research may include how consumers react to certain displays and how effective the distribution and subsequent placement of displays were. Elements that display companies should provide include proof of delivery, field checks for proper assembly, and field research for documentation of retail trends—in addition to maintaining relations with retailers in order to better design with them in mind.

One key element brand marketers and retailers should look for when evaluating P-O-P suppliers is the producer/supplier's knowledge of and usage of marketing within the design and development of displays. Ultimately, displays are a marketing tool—a vehicle to deliver the product to consumers and to motivate and modify the behavior of those consumers. An awareness of human psychology and a familiarity with marketing are essential if a P-O-P provider is to be successful with a brand marketer or retailer.

Installation (In-Store Setup)

One of the key services in the P-O-P industry is the installation and setup of display programs at retail. Typically, companies that specialize in installation services have field teams whose job is to travel from city to city and store to store to custom install and ensure the proper setup of displays. Some of these companies have warehouse and distribution networks, and others simply follow the preset distribution program.

These companies provide a valuable service to retailers and brand marketers by ensuring quality implementation of programs that otherwise may never get beyond the stockroom door. Some producers/suppliers provide this service, but most companies engaged in this activity are not involved in display production.

Merchandising

Similar to the installation companies, some companies specialize in the setup of product in/on displays and are hired by brand marketers to attend to store restocking. Programs exist in which employees of these firms maintain a regular schedule of store visits and are responsible for collecting data on sales and restocking the displays when necessary, sometimes daily.

CONCLUSION

The P-O-P professional plays a critical role in the overall success of a brand marketer's or retailer's business. When you consider that 70 percent of all purchase decisions are made after the customer enters the store, the importance of the right design and proper manufacture of a P-O-P display cannot be overstated. A properly managed P-O-P project is critical to any product's success.

Successful management of a P-O-P project requires that all parties be aware of the latest technologies and trends in P-O-P design and that they be attentive to the challenges of managing a complicated, multifaceted P-O-P project that may be produced for local, regional, national, or global businesses. When P-O-P advertising trends create a need for more creativity or utilization of new technologies, combined with the different selling environments, P-O-P project management must constantly evolve to meet the market needs.

In summary, the challenge of designing and delivering superior P-O-P solutions—whether for the brand marketer or the retailer—demands an informed, dedicated, and forward-looking team of P-O-P specialists committed to getting the project done on time and on budget.

Project Profile Questionnaire

Taken from
"The Power of Point-Of-Purchase Advertising: Marketing At Retail"
Chapter 3: Project Management
Fred Sklenar, Unified Resources
Published by Point-of-Purchase Advertising International (POPAI)

Market Analysis

Target Market			
❑	Convenience	❑	Mass Market
❑	Department	❑	Mom & Pop
❑	Drug Chain	❑	Supermarket
❑	Other:		

Where are the stores located?	
Are any of these stores located outside of the U.S.?	❑ Yes ❑ No
If yes, where?	
Description of store environment:	
Is this retailer historically display friendly?	❑ Yes ❑ No

Placement in store:			
❑	Aisle	❑	Gondola
❑	Ceiling	❑	In-line
❑	Checkout	❑	Lease Line
❑	Endcap	❑	Window
❑	Entrance	❑	Other:

Are any stores local to our office for a field visit?	❑ Yes ❑ No
If no, where is the nearest store location?	

Description of other displays near placement of this display:

Miscellaneous Information:

Figure 3-3   Project Profile Questionnaire

Product Analysis

Product name(s):	
Selling points or features:	
Number of different SKUs on the display:	
Describe differences in SKUs:	
Number of total SKUs on the display:	
Product specifications:	
Samples of product available?	❑ Yes ❑ No
Pending graphics or packaging changes?	❑ Yes ❑ No
List competitor's products:	
❑	National brand name.	
❑	Private label.	

Display Criteria

Type of display desired:			
❑	Banner	❑	Free-standing
❑	Connect to existing store fixtures	❑	Merchandiser (Number of sides:_____)
❑	Counter	❑	Signage
❑	Glorifier	❑	Specialty
❑	Floor	❑	Wall
❑	Kiosk		

Describe details:	
Quantity needed:	
Quantity per store:	
Budget per display:	
How long will the display be in stores?	
Special product layout?	
Merchandising/marketing goal for display:	
Will the product ship with the display?	❑ Yes ❑ No

PROJECT PROFILE QUESTIONNAIRE CONTINUES ON NEXT 2 PAGES

List any special functions (e.g., movement, illumination, special engineering):

Client-specified materials of choice:	
Client-specified materials to avoid:	
Production methods considered inappropriate:	
Graphic message to communicate:	
Placement of graphics:	
Special printing requirements (such as spot colors):	
Special colors requested:	
Are there any logos to use or will they be available?	
Will the client supply final art?	❑ Yes ❑ No
If yes, on disk?	❑ Yes ❑ No
Are there other media tie-ins?	❑ Yes ❑ No
Who will set up the display?	
Instructions needed:	❑ Printed sheet ❑ With photos ❑ Video
Will a separate company be contracted for in-store set-up?	❑ Yes ❑ No
Size recommendations or limitations:	
Is there budget available for tooling?	❑ Yes ❑ No
Does the client have existing tooling that this display must fit into?	❑ Yes ❑ No

Deliverables

What is the client expecting?

❑	Conceptual rough sketches for fax.
❑	Conceptual sketched mounted for client meeting.
❑	Renderings mounted for presentation.
❑	Renderings posted on Web site.
❑	Renderings e-mailed.
❑	Sketch models for digital photos to be posted on Web site.

❏	Sketch models for digital photos to be e-mailed.	
❏	Working prototypes.	
Delivered how and where?		
Work is needed by?		

Approvals

Who will be required to approve the program?		
❏	At the client:	
❏	At the retailer:	
Will the pre-production prototype need to be installed at the corporate offices of the retailer prior to approval for full production.		❏ Yes ❏ No

Shipping/Delivery Packaging

Any special client specifications?	
Shipper size requirements (UPS, FedEx, other expedited delivery companies, fit in sales rep's car, etc.):	
Special printing on carton (code numbers, UPC bar codes, PO numbers, etc.):	
Where will the displays be shipped?	
What carrier is recommended by the client?	
Is floor loading acceptable?	
Special pallet considerations:	
Any previously incurred problems that need to be avoided?	

4

"Sales promotion is

one of the building blocks

of the marketing plan,

along with packaging,

advertising, market research,

public relations, consumer

relationship marketing,

and event planning."

Sales Promotion Planning

ARLENE S. GERWIN, MARKETING DIRECTOR, DIAGEO NA

SALES PROMOTION PLANNING AND POINT-OF-PURCHASE ADVERTISING: GREATER THAN THE SUM OF THE PARTS

This chapter focuses on the unique, combined strength of sales promotion planning and point-of-purchase advertising. Well-designed P-O-P advertising materials such as displays, case cards, shelf talkers, banners, and the like are enhanced by a consumer call to action such as cents-off coupons, recipe booklets, or BOGO's (buy one, get one free). This chapter discusses the importance of sales promotion planning—both short- and long-term— and how sales promotion relates to the other elements of the marketing mix.

Several tools that may aid in maximizing the marketing investment are presented.

SALES PROMOTION PLANNING— AN INTEGRAL ELEMENT OF THE MARKETING MIX

Pity the poor shopper who walks into a retail store and is bombarded by point-of-purchase promotional messages: "Save 50 percent off the suggested retail price of shoes." "Buy a bottle of soda at full price and get another one for free." "Buy two cans of soup and get a free box of crackers."

What do these offers have in common besides confusing the average consumer? They are all P-O-P promotion tools that add value to a product and enhance marketing at retail. Such P-O-P prompts, as poorly conceived as they sometimes seem, encourage the consumer to buy a specific brand, to buy more than one item, or to buy a preferred brand and sample another. In short, they give consumers more for their money by reducing the cost or by providing something for free. Figure 4-1 shows a selection of P-O-P displays presenting value-added offers.

POPAI's P-O-P Advertising Desktop Reference Guide defines sales promotion as "the use of temporary incentives by consumer goods and services companies to change the behavior of their trade (retail) consumers and/or their end consumer."[1] As such, sales promotion is an important element of the overall marketing mix. Companies develop comprehensive strategic plans that incorporate integrated marketing communications campaigns whose overall objectives are to build brands, enhance services, or even build company equity. Thus, sales promotion is one of the building blocks of the marketing plan, along with packaging, advertising, market research, public relations, consumer relationship marketing, and event planning.

When all of the marketing tasks mentioned above are driven by a common strategy and shared objectives, the company communicates with the consumer in a single voice with the consistent creative approach. For publicly held companies, this ultimately translates into building shareholder value and increasing the stock price. The other elements of the marketing mix also add value to a company's products and motivate consumer purchase.

How do these elements differ from sales promotion? To begin, the objective of advertising is quite different from that of sales promotion. Advertising is usually viewed

Figure 4-1   Value added displays for free video rentals and bobble head toys

as a longer-term investment. Over time, advertising builds brand equity by establishing a consistent image or feeling for a brand—a softer sell. Current national advertising campaigns for leading automotive or cosmetics brands, for example, are designed to build brand image and may last several years. In comparison, sales promotions are more immediate, involving a finite time period (during which return on investment [ROI] can be determined), and offer consumers something tangible during that time. The impact of sales promotions is, therefore, easier to evaluate than advertising results.

At the majority of marketing-savvy companies, sales promotion budgets are larger than advertising budgets, attesting to the desire for more immediate consumer response and quicker payback on marketing investment than that provided by advertising investment.

P-O-P PROMOTIONS CONTRIBUTE TO LONG-TERM BRAND BUILDING

Ever since retail establishments came into existence, there has been some form of P-O-P promotion. Carefully hand-painted signs announcing a sale or price reduction can often be spotted in 19th-century photos of country general stores. Figure 4-2 illustrates P-O-P signs in a drugs store window dating from the 1950's, when cents-off coupons were first offered.

Because sales promotion tools are used for a short time period, marketers can be tempted to "shoot from the hip" and develop ad hoc promotions in an attempt to quickly

Figure 4-2

A 1950's retail store front of Eckerd Drug. Notice the P-O-P signs in the windows

move product. This is a dangerous practice that can backfire in the long run. Ill-planned and poorly timed promotions can interrupt the natural consumer product-use cycle, artificially inflate sales volume, and even disrupt normal seasonality trends.

For example, if a consumer has loaded his or her pantry with deeply discounted pet food yet has not increased demand for the food, the consumer's purchases will cease until the supply runs out. The myopic marketer who analyzes only the short-term spikes in sales volume during the discounted promotion period will be disappointed by sales performance in subsequent weeks when sales trends decline and profit erodes.

The more successful P-O-P promotions are those that are developed against a clear set of objectives. For example, a campaign that succeeds in getting consumers to stock up on pet food meets the objective of temporarily removing those consumers from the market, precluding their purchase of competitive pet food brands. This technique is extremely effective, and frequently used, as part of a pre-planned campaign defending against the launch of a competitive brand. It shows how the sales promotion function has evolved from a quick in-and-out tactical effort to a pre-planned, long-range, strategic campaign.

Successful sales promotion programs develop from campaignable, ownable "big ideas" that extend over a minimum of one year and, often, over several years. The promotion becomes intricately intertwined with the brand or service by enhancing its image. The promotion can be refreshed or enhanced as desired, but it continues to be based on a strong creative theme, many times echoed in the advertising creative campaign.

Think of airline frequent-flier programs that have run for several decades. Enhancements are regularly added to further entice the frequent flier to remain loyal to a particular airline. These programs initially offered only free airline tickets and upgrades, but they now extend to value-added offers for hotels, car rentals, travel packages, and even retail goods. See Figure 4-3.

P-O-P Promotion Plans Are An Extention Of A Company's Stratecic Plan

Besides being pre-planned and having long time horizons, effective promotions tie back to the marketing plan. Marketing plans are usually developed annually and specifically detail objectives, strategies, and tactics that support the overall corporate objectives.

Figure 4-3

American Airlines

Advantage Program

extends well beyond

the realm of ordinary

frequent flyer

programs[2]

Equally important is the long-term strategic plan that maps out corporate goals beyond the current year, typically five years out. The marketing plan is revised annually so that it is always current and contributes to the future vision of the strategic plan. Strategic planning is defined as "the consideration of current decision alternatives in light of their probable consequences over time."[3]

In the strategic plan, alternative scenarios are investigated and analyzed. A useful tool is the *SWOT analysis* (*strengths*, *weaknesses*, *opportunities*, and *threats*). Strengths and weaknesses are internally focused, whereas opportunities and threats involve the external environment. Brands and services are virtually dissected and analyzed from all angles to determine what works, what doesn't, and the potential vulnerabilities. Using this mapping tool, smart decisions can be made to determine long-term direction and to address anticipated competitive actions. A SWOT analysis is particularly useful in forecasting competitive actions and planning both offensive and defensive tactics. Figure 4-4 presents the SWOT analysis grid.

Strengths	Weaknesses
Opportunities	Threats

Figure 4-4

SWOT Analysis Grid

Once agreement is reached as to the strategic direction, the marketing plan details other variables that impact a brand or service. This usually includes defining the consumer target audience-those consumers who are the best prospects for the brand or service. The consumer target can be current users, past users, or nonusers. The consumer target audience is defined in both demographic and psychographic terms. It is no longer sufficient to define the consumer by demographics—age, geography, and household income. It is more meaningful to understand the psychology of the consumer—*psychographics*—what motivates him or her to try a product and repurchase it. What are the consumer's likes and dislikes? What values are most important? What motivates a college professor earning $75,000 annually may be quite different from what motivates a long-haul truck driver earning the same income.

What consumer need does the product fulfill? How does the product fill this consumer need better than a competitive product? In addition to defining the consumer target audience, potential markets and channels must be identified. The more realistic and specific the plan, the greater the probability of meeting the objectives.

In summary, have a game plan to follow—usually five years out. That plan should be revised each year so that it is always current—and it must be realistic and grounded in facts.

DEVELOP SMART OBJECTIVES

Objectives, strategies, and tactics are elements of all marketing plans, but these words can be easily confused. An objective is the end goal. It could be to increase sales by 10 percent. A strategy is the action to meet the objective. Using the SMART (strategic, measurable, actionable, realistic, and timely) approach (see Figure 4-5) to marketing ensures that all bases are covered.

Strategic

Measurable

Actionable

Realistic

Timely

Figure 4-5

Develop SMART

Objectives

The strategy to meet the goal of increasing sales by 10 percent could involve introducing a new line extension to an existing brand portfolio. Tactics, in contrast, are more immediate. A free coupon to sample a new flavor is considered a tactic against the objective of increasing sales by 10 percent by launching a new line extension. Sales promotion techniques usually fall under the definition of marketing tactics.

Objective, strategies, and tactics as part of the marketing plan represent a road map of action steps. But the marketing plan also serves as a tool for measuring results. Therefore, a sound marketing plan clearly details how, when, and why programs will be measured. Typically, market research and sales/profit analyses are used. Setting SMART objectives ensures that results can be analyzed. Using this approach as a checklist when writing objectives ensures that success is objectively—not subjectively—defined.

TRADE AND CONSUMER PROMOTION OBJECTIVES ARE CLOSELY LINKED

Promotion objectives fall under two broad classifications—trade promotions and consumer promotions. They share similar end goals but differ as to who is incentivized and how.

Trade promotions are targeted at the middlemen—those responsible for getting goods and services from a manufacturer into a retail establishment. Examples of trade promotions include incentives to authorize new products, distribution-building programs, display allowances, volume discounts, and shelf-expansion incentives. Trade promotions push product into the store—onto the shelf or on display—and are therefore termed *push strategies*.

Consumer promotions, on the other hand, are those programs targeted at the end consumer or purchaser. Accordingly, consumer promotions are termed *pull strategies* since they literally motivate the consumer to pull the product off the shelf or display and out of the retail store. Trade promotions and consumer promotions should be jointly planned to maximize consumer purchases of product that has been pushed into the retail environment.

Consumer promotions usually offer the potential purchaser some type of added incentive structured against the pre-planned brand strategies and objectives. For example, if the stated objective is to generate trial of a new product, the consumer promotion tactic could offer the consumer a free coupon to try the new product. Or the promotion could provide the consumer with a free sample distributed at retail or even delivered to the consumer's doorstep.

In addition to motivating trial, consumer promotions can build demand, build brand awareness, generate an impulse buy, and even motivate multiple purchases. Various consumer-directed tactics can be employed to encourage this type of buyer action, including coupons, refunds, rebates, sampling, and free items, to name just a few. See Figure 4-6. These offers can be delivered via various vehicles, ranging from handing the consumer an incentive at the point of purchase to using printed media such as newspapers and magazines, direct mail, or electronic communication.

As part of a larger, integrated marketing campaign, consumer promotions can also include games, contests, sweepstakes, cross-promotions, and tie-in promotions. Care should always be taken as to how these programs are structured, as laws regulating such activities vary by state and by country.

Point-of-purchase displays serve as a bridge connecting trade and consumer promotions. The most powerful offers are those delivered directly to consumers in the retail environment at the point of purchase. Well-constructed and attractive display units—temporary or permanent—showcase products for easy shopping for consumers with coupons in hand. A consumer might find a

Figure 4-6

Coupons and rebates assist sales at the point-of-purchase

wooden rack filled with wine bottles and free recipe booklets suggesting which wines complement various foods-meat entrees, for example. If this rack is strategically placed near the meat section, the consumer need not search the store for ingredients.

When trade and consumer promotions work in tandem, the push-and-pull efforts reach a state of equilibrium. The trade incentives ensure that the right products are at the right place at the right time. The consumer incentives deliver motivated buyers to purchase the products. Together, these efforts support the corporate objectives by delivering projected sales volume and profit.

JOINT PROMOTIONS LINK BRANDS AND ENHANCE CONSUMER VALUE PERCEPTIONS

Joint promoting, also known as *co-promoting*, is the joining of two brands promotionally and sharing point-of-purchase materials to make the shopper's task easier—and provide twice the promotional impact at half the cost. Two companies are likely to consider co-promotion if an offer will appeal to both companies' target audiences.

Using joint promotions, brands can communicate extended usage ideas, provide new recipes using both brands, or even promote counter-seasonality usage. During the holiday season, when floor display space is at a premium, multibrand promotions proliferate. Soft-drink companies build massive displays, add snack products to these displays, and offer consumer coupons for the purchase of two or multiple items, in effect providing a one-stop-snack-shopping center. See Figure 4-7.

Joint promotions can also give exposure to brands or services outside their normal channel of trade. For example, amusement parks jointly promote with many types of brands. Consumers might gain free admission by collecting soft drink bottle caps. The amusement park promotes the venue in supermarkets and other food stores, and the free offer increases soft-drink sales. Both brands benefit.

Figure 4-7
Pepsi/Frito-Lay Joint
Promotion

FRITO-LAY USA AND MASTERACK DIVISION OF LEGGETT & PLATT, INC.

Brand: _____	Initiation Date: _____
Project No.: _____	Project Contact: _____
Program Elements: _____	Program Period: _____

Background Information	
Brand Strategy	
Promotion Strategy	
Program Objectives	
Research/Analysis Component	
Communication Priorities	
Advertising/Media Campaign	
Target Audience & Mindset	
Competitive Information	
Program Requirements	
Tone	
Call to Action	
Mandatories/ References	
Program Budget	

Figure 4-8

Agency Creative Brief

THE COMPREHENSIVE CREATIVE BRIEF

A creative brief should be developed before plunging into the tactical execution of a promotion. The creative brief is an invaluable tool that provides the agency or design firm with important information for developing the creative concept and recommending appropriate promotion elements in support of the concept. The creative brief is just that—brief—typically one page in length. Limiting information to a single page focuses ideas and forces the synthesizing of the creative rationale. It helps the marketer to think very specifically about what must be accomplished.

The creative brief provides background data, strategies and objectives, timing, communication priorities, legal requirements, and overall tone for the promotion. Budget parameters and a timetable are also developed as part of the brief. Figure 4-8 is a template for an Agency Creative Brief.

PROMOTION ELEMENTS SHOULD BE CAREFULLY SELECTED: ARE THEY ON STRATEGY, AFFORDABLE? CAN THEY BE PRODUCED ON TIME?

Although the marketing plan provides a road map of action steps, a road map offers several routes to reach the ultimate destination. Similarly, there is a range of promotion tactics available to the marketer to meet the objectives and strategies set forth in the marketing plan. Several major promotion tools have been discussed in this chapter. Figure 4-9 summarizes some of these tools.

In many cases, several different promotion tactics can all be strategically sound. If so, the marketer must determine which approach meets the budget parameters and the

Figure 4-9

P-O-P Promotion

Tools Grid

P-O-P Promotion Tools	Objectives	Strengths	Weaknesses
Displays • Permanent • Temporary	• Generate off-shelf product display • Build brand/product awareness	• Shopper convenience • Increases retail volume • Showcases consumer offers	• Retail space limited for displays • Costs • Limited time on floor
Price Reductions • Temporary markdowns	• Motivate consumer trial • Generate multiple purchase • Defend against competitive pricing	• Clears out inventory • Moves old or off-season items	• Not important factor to all potential buyers • Reduces margins
Coupons • Manufacturer • Retailer	• Motivate consumer trial • Generate multiple purchase • Build brand/retailer loyalty	• Instant gratification • Redemption slippage	• Low redemption • Limited appeal to coupon clippers • Inconvenient
Refunds/Rebates	• Motivate consumer purchase • Build brand/product loyalty	• Provides future reward	• Delayed gratification/reward • Not all retailers participate
Sampling	• Generate trial • Motivate brand switching	• Direct to consumer • Instant gratification	• More expensive promotion vehicle • High cost per consumer reached
On Packs/In Packs	• Sampling device • Generate trial of related or different product	• Free item • Instant gratification	• Retailer shelving and inventory issues
Games/Sweepstakes	• Generate consumer excitement • Tie to advertising campaign	• Generates brand PR • Big prizes	• Limited consumer appeal

project timetable. Estimating costs can be a challenge. When coupons, refunds, and rebates are offered, for example, redemption percentages can vary widely. Coupon-fulfillment services can issue redemption reports that provide guidance, but history does not always repeat itself.

The following scenario highlights how a small swing in a coupon redemption rate can have big financial implications. A national FSI (free-standing insert) buy means that 55 million coupons are circulated across the United States in Sunday newspapers. Assume that a 50-cent coupon runs in this national distribution. History shows that a 50-cent coupon on this brand typically redeems at 3 percent. Thus, it is projected that 1.65 million coupons will be redeemed (55 million × 3%). The additional 9-cent processing and fulfillment cost brings the estimated redemption cost to $973,500 (1.65 million coupons × 59 cents).

If the estimated percent redemption is off by only 1 percent—if the coupon redeems at 4 percent, not 3 percent—the actual redemption cost is $1,298,000 (55 million circulation × 4% × 59 cents), which overspends the promotion budget by $324,500. Most probably, the budget for another promotion program will need to be cut to fund this overage. This points to the importance of good forecasting and budgeting, and of having contingency funds identified to cover unexpected expenses.

Realistic promotion timetables are as important as accurate cost estimations, especially when a promotion includes several elements. The marketer must be sensitive to longer promotion lead times for custom-designed items and offshore sourcing. Assume a promotion campaign includes multiple items such as a permanent wooden display piece with a cardboard header card, a corrugated-case display, a premium-dealer loader, posters, shelf-talkers, and a printed sales brochure. If the premium is custom designed and produced offshore, a minimum of six months is required for the design and production process. Similarly, a permanent wooden rack requires longer lead times than printed-paper pieces, for example.

The marketer, working closely with the promotion design and production teams, must develop a realistic timetable leading to all the elements coming together as an integrated program. It is not uncommon to initiate the design and planning of complicated, multifaceted promotion campaigns 12 to 18 months in advance. This ensures that longer lead-time items are produced and delivered on time. A Christmas display delivered in February is worthless.

DETAILED BUDGETS IN ADVANCE ENSURE NO SURPRISES AT THE END

As indicated earlier, promotion budgets are developed as part of the overall marketing plan. The marketer needs to determine how company resources are allocated among the elements of the marketing mix-traditionally the four P's (product, promotion, price, and place). Once an overall budget is determined for the promotion plan, a more detailed promotion budget is developed for the year. The promotion budget is usually segmented into seasonal time periods. Within these time periods, the promotion campaigns are further detailed. Budget categories may include estimated costs for creative development, agency fees, coupon media and fulfillment costs, production and procurement of the elements, shipping costs, and warehousing fees.

When the budget is developed, many costs are still only estimated. The marketer may look at previous promotion costs to more accurately identify the estimates. Obviously, the more realistic the estimates, the closer the budget will match actual costs when the programs are executed.

The promotion budget is also a dynamic tracking tool. The budget template should include a method by which to constantly update estimated costs with actual expenditures. By constantly tracking real costs, the marketer has the confidence of knowing the promotions are on track against projections. When actual costs start exceeding estimates, the marketer can make adjustments accordingly.

The astute marketer knows the importance of contingency budgeting—having funds earmarked for unexpected overages. The promotion arena is not immune to the ravages of Murphy's Promotions Law: Designs that look great on paper often times present unanticipated production complications, not to mention the intervention of natural disasters and ill-timed strikes.

Timing Is Everything: The Promotion Plan Should Be Developed At Least A Year In Advance and Refined Throughout The Year

The importance of advance planning cannot be overstressed. At the outset of a promotion, not all program details need to be finalized, but the marketer needs a road map to illuminate where to go and how to get there. There are many planning tools and software packages to simplify the process. Microsoft Project is a particularly useful project management tool to schedule and track activities as they progress. As a planning and tracking tool, it allows the marketer to report project details, delegate tasks, obtain status updates, and track costs. Simple flow charts or project templates can be utilized, like the example shown in Figure 4-10.

As discussed previously, P-O-P promotion activities and tasks have different lead times relating to complexity, availability of materials, and even offshore sourcing. Promotion planning involves coordinating various activities and tasks at different stages of completion; therefore, multitasking is an important skill for those working on promotions. Hypothetically, a marketer could be working simultaneously on concepts that are in different stages of production, from developing concepts in white-paper format for a program that is a year away from introduction, to recommending elements for promotional programs nine months in advance, to producing elements for programming that is only six months from being introduced. The marketer must juggle many balls in the air at the same time.

Task	Week #	Description	Output Owner
Program Planning			
Program evaluation	45	Review past program evaluation	Business Analyst
Program objectives/strategies		Set goals with quantitative and qualitative measures	Promotion Manager
Concept Development, Program Design, and Program Development			
Complete creative brief	41	Inputs/approvals	Marketing Management
		Brief agency	Promotion Manager
		Budget confirmed	Promotion Manager
Concept brainstorming starts	41	Narrow brainstorm concepts to 2 to 3	Promotion Manager
		Determine channel/account customization	Promotion Manager
Concept approval	37	Marketing management	Promotion Manager
Develop program elements/prototypes	36	Program defined with visuals	Promotion Manager
Estimated costs of elements	36	Estimated budget costs for elements	Promotion Manager
		Identify long lead time items	Promotion Manager
		Issue specs for long lead time items	Promotion Manager
Program approval	30	Program elements, visuals, structure. design approved	Promotion Manager
Communicating the Program			
Communicate final program	24	Communicate program details, costs and budgets	Program Coordinator
In-Market Planning			
Begin account/channel planning	24	Retail planning	Sales Management
		Identify augmentation needs	
Ordering and Producing Materials			
Order long lead time items	24	Approve costs, select vendor	Promotion Manager
		Submit art/disks for production	Promotion Manager
Specs and drawings	20	Specs/drawings to vendors	Promotion Manager
Field inputs orders	19	Input quantity and shipping instructions	Sales Management
Bidding process	18	Sealed bids to vendors	Promotion Manager
		Bidding analysis completed	Promotion Manager
Order consolidation	18	Consolidate orders	Promotion Manager
		Review/revise items	Promotion Manager
Approve costs/quantities	17	Update promotion budget	Promotion Manager
Select vendor	17	Order materials/elements	Promotion Manager
Approve art/mech for production	17	Last chance for revisions to program/elements	Promotion Manager
Art/mech to vendor	17	Submit final art/disks and hold preproduction meeting	Promotion Manager
Start production	16	Art and disk preflight and archive	
		Production proofing	
Delivering and Executing the Promotion			
Ship materials	8	Program elements to central warehouse/collate	Traffic Managers
Promotion materials/sell sheets ship	6	To arrive at least 6 weeks before promotion starts	
Promotion in market	1	Promotion executed	

Figure 4-10   Project Planning Template

BUILD IN FLEXIBILITY, WITH BOTH TIME AND MONEY, TO REACT TO UNEXPECTED EVENTS

Finally, flexibility is important. Promotions can be cancelled unexpectedly when budgets are cut. Competitors may enter the market unexpectedly, forcing defensive plans to be quickly put in place. The astute marketer has an arsenal of tactics waiting in the wings to meet such unplanned circumstances.

ENDNOTES

[1] *P-O-P Advertising Desktop Reference Guide* (Washington, D.C.: Point-Of-Purchase Advertising International, 1999), 25.

[2] American Airlines, AAdvantage, AA.com and AADVANTAGE DIAL-IN are marks of American Airlines, Inc. All other trademarks referenced are trademarks of their respective companies. American Airlines reserves the right to change the AAdvantage program at any time without notice. American Airlines is not responsible for products or services offered by other participating companies. For complete details about the AAdvantage program, visit www.aa.com.

[3] Peter D. Bennett, ed., *Dictionary of Marketing Terms*, 2nd ed. (Lincolnwood, Ill.: NTC Business Books, 1995), 276.

"Some display programs

may seem expensive;

others may seem cheap.

Not until you understand what

you get for the expenditure

can you precisely address

return on investment."

Post-Promotion Evaluation

JIM SPAETH, PAST PRESIDENT
THE ADVERTISING RESEARCH FOUNDATION

WHY EVALUATE POINT-OF-PURCHASE PROMOTIONS?

Post-promotion evaluation enables marketers to realize more of the potential power of P-O-P advertising. For example, recent research from POPAI/ARF (the Advertising Research Foundation) found that certain forms of point-of-purchase advertising worked better for particular brands under specific in-store conditions, with some P-O-P advertising producing sales lifts *twice* the size of others. Do you know what works and what does not work for your brand? Do you know why? If you do not, you may be getting as little as half the value from your P-O-P expenditures that you should.

This knowledge is a competitive advantage that will make bottom-line differences for your brand. In the short term, you can be smarter about where to place P-O-P advertising, what form of P-O-P advertising to use for your brand, and what types of creative will work for you—all of which will make your marketing budget fight harder for you. Over the long term, you can apply greater competitive leverage with fewer dollars.

There is an even more important benefit to utilizing P-O-P properly—coming to understand not just what the effectiveness of each P-O-P ad is, but how it works within the marketing mix: not just how P-O-P drives sales, but *how* it builds brands. The key is to transform promotional events into brand-building campaigns.

Beyond "what" and "how," you also need to know "why" your P-O-P advertising works. That is where breakthrough ideas come from. Simply knowing what has worked in the past enables smart marketers to recreate successful retail advertising campaigns in the future. Eventually, even tried-and-true campaigns become worn out or just plain dated. Where will the most cutting edge ideas come from? Isn't there some great, powerful P-O-P idea just waiting to be conceived? Who will discover it first? Someone who really understands why previous advertisements worked, or someone who is just plain lucky? Quite simply, great ideas all come from a profound insight into the consumer—an answer to the question, "Why?"

THE ADVERTISING PROCESS AND P-O-P

To understand how advertising works, it is helpful to break apart the effects into several different "processing" stages—*exposure, perception, persuasion, purchase,* and *repeat purchase.* See Figure 5-1. P-O-P advertising can be evaluated at any or all of these stages, depending on its particular business objectives (e.g., building awareness or driving sales).

- *Exposure* is the currency of all media, measured as GRPs (gross rating points) or *impressions.*
- *Perception* drives consumer *awareness.*
- *Persuasion* results in *attitude* and *intention shifts.*
- *Purchase* increments are readily valued as *sales.*
- *Repeat purchase*, especially when driving loyalty, is what ultimately results in profitable marketing and *high return on investment (ROI).*

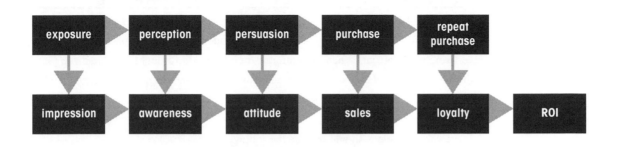

This model can be applied equally as well to P-O-P advertising in traditional brick and mortar retail outlets as it can to P-O-P advertising on e-commerce sites.

One way to think about the effect of a P-O-P advertisement on the consumer purchase decision is to use Frankel's *Purchase Corridor* model. See Figure 5-2. In Frankel's model, P-O-P advertising is represented as the pivotal step in an ongoing process to win and retain customers. In contrast, word of mouth, public relations, in-home media advertising, and other factors may influence brand choice and, more importantly, drive the customer to the store. However, most final brand purchase decisions are actually made in-store, driven in no small degree by the P-O-P material present. Unfortunately, the only post-purchase contact with the consumer may be the monthly bill, which may not be the most effective means of encouraging brand loyalty.

Figure 5-1
Advertising
Processing Stages

Figure 5-2
Customer Corridor
for Cellular
Subscribers[1]

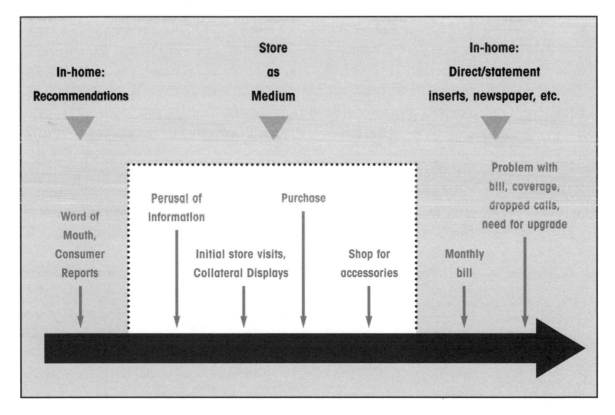

PLANNING THE P-O-P EVALUATION PROCESS

Evaluating P-O-P advertising requires careful control of many details. A recommended best practice for any evaluation process would include the evaluation phase of the P-O-P advertising plan upfront. When evaluation is merely an afterthought (e.g., put into place after the plan is executed), marketplace results can sometimes unduly influence an executive's judgment as to what metric is measured rather than what metric should have been measured.

Evaluation plans should include the following:
- The advertising objective.
- The target audience.
- The expected outcome.
- Performance metrics.
- The criterion for success.
- The experimental design.
- Factors to be controlled.

Advertising Objective. You must have a clear understanding of the advertising objective the P-O-P advertising campaign, which serves as the foundation of an effective evaluation process. Each campaign or event will have its own objective derived directly from the brand's marketing objective and tightly related to the objectives of the brand's other marketing factors, ensuring they operate in concert, not confusion.

Target Audience. The target audience may be defined in standard demographic terms (e.g., 18- to 34-year-old men earning $40K). Or it may be more relevantly defined in terms of purchase behavior (18- to 34-year-old men who earn $40K and buy Brand X). In any event, the target group considered for the evaluation must be measurable and relevant within the context of the study.

Expected Outcome. Defining a quantifiable expected outcome ahead of time could spare a lot of agonizing after the fact. For example, imagine that you have determined the performance of a given advertising campaign and now are trying to determine if that was "good enough" to be considered a success. If a 10 percent increase in brand awareness is achieved, would this now be considered great, just okay, or disappointing? Stating the brand's expected outcome—in this case, defining +10 percent as either great, okay, or disappointing *up front*—ensures the objectivity of your evaluation.

Performance Metrics. Performance metrics used for evaluation may be different from the expected outcome itself. If the advertising objective is to increase awareness, for example, a specific measure of awareness must be selected. If the objective is to increase repeat purchases, a household panel-based measure may be used to estimate the *actual population repeat rate*, defined as the percent of current purchasers who had previously purchased the brand in a specified time frame such as six months, depending on the purchase cycle.

When measuring whether advertising has increased awareness, a surrogate measure is required because marketing research professionals cannot actually measure consumer or respondent awareness, a psychological phenomenon. Instead, they measure how often respondents volunteer the brand name when asked what brands of the product they can think of.

Criterion for Success. Given that these performance metrics will likely be obtained from a sample (a representation of a target population), the results from this sample will provide an estimate of the results from the population, with some sampling error associated with that estimate. So, if the performance metric exceeds the expected outcome, researchers can be only partially certain that performance in the actual population truly exceeds the expected outcome.

How certain depends on by how much the expected outcome is exceeded. For example, if you want to be 90 percent certain, the performance metric will have to exceed the expected outcome by a calculable amount. Statisticians often term the expected outcome the action standard and the amount by which it must be beat the sampling tolerance. The sum of the action-standard and the *sampling tolerance* is known as the *criterion for success*.

Experimental Design. Many environmental and societal factors influence how P-O-P promotions are developed. How researchers evaluate these factors and isolate the one they wish to evaluate is known as the process of planning the *experimental design.* Sometimes this process is simple; sometimes it is complicated. It depends on what the researcher is trying to accomplish, how many factors are involved, and the degree of control the researcher has over the experimental setting.

Factors to Be Controlled. An important element of experimental design, worthy of its own mention, is *non-criterion factors to be controlled.* Suppose you are evaluating the effect of a P-O-P advertisement on repeat purchase. Brand marketers know that price, especially a temporary price reduction (TPR), will also have an effect (along with P-O-P advertising) on the consumer's tendency to repeat purchase. If they wish to isolate the effect of the P-O-P so that brand marketers can really know its contribution to repeat purchasing, researchers need to control for the noncriterion factors of price and TPRs in this example.

The final step for any evaluation plan is gaining buy-in from all of the stakeholders. Those who will use the information, those who can affect the information-as well as those with primary responsibility for the evaluation-must all clearly understand and support the plan. So much can go wrong inadvertently; there is no point in encouraging your own team members to contribute to the risk!

EVALUATION VERSUS OBJECTIVES

Every P-O-P advertisement should have a precise goal or objective. As simple as that sounds, a good deal of P-O-P advertising runs "to support the promotional event" or "to drive sales." While these are both worthwhile objectives, neither expresses "how" the P-O-P promotion is expected to accomplish this. Or, more pointedly: If you don't know how the advertisement will work, it probably won't.

Research requires well-defined objectives as the basis for performance evaluation. This is often the first benefit that accrues from careful evaluation planning. The request for the advertising's objectives often sparks the realization that there are no objectives. If this realization eventually culminates in a carefully conceived advertising objective, the evaluative process has delivered its first benefit: disciplined thinking.

Evaluation must be conducted with respect to the original objectives. Typically, objectives fall into six categories:

- Developing awareness and improving attitudes.
- Generating trial.
- Stimulating an impulse purchase.
- Reminder/repeat purchase stimulation.
- New usage idea/repeat purchase stimulation.
- Brand differentiation.

A brand marketer's objectives may not match any of these exactly, but will probably bear a close resemblance to at least one of them. It is also reasonable for a single P-O-P advertisement to have more than one objective, especially if each objective targets a different group. However, an advertisement—P-O-P or otherwise—that attempts to do everything usually does nothing well. Focus is crucial. We will discuss the evaluation of each objective in greater detail, but first let us consider each one briefly.

Awareness is a simple concept with a variety of very specific definitions. It is the starting point for the relationship between a brand and its consumers. The consumer "knows of" the brand. In the absence of any other difference, consumers will usually choose the brand they know. (Unless, of course, what they know is negative.) It is the very first rung on the brand trust ladder. As modest as it seems, it is one of the most common advertising objectives and one of the jobs advertising does best. Beyond mere awareness, P-O-P can also engender positive attitudes toward the brand. If these attitudes differentiate the brand from others, the brand might become part of the consumer's *consideration set* (e.g., those brands that they would consider purchasing) or even become a preferred brand. The target audience is usually anyone who could be a potential buyer. The specifics will vary for any given marketing program. A common target audience definition would be current product category purchasers.

P-O-P advertising's potential for generating awareness should not be overlooked. No other medium has the ability to intercept the consumer at exactly the moment when the product is in front of the consumer, and when *purchase intent* is the primary motivation for being in the store. This is the one moment when the consumer is most likely to be attentive to messages about brands in the category.

Generating trial is a relative concept. It is simple enough for a new product: "trial" is the first time a consumer purchases the product. Of course, brand marketers can complicate matters with free samples to generate trial, or special trial sizes and special trial offers.

While these typically blur the boundaries between someone who has purchased the product and someone who has not, there is something qualitatively different about a consumer
who has paid real money to obtain a real package of the brand. The consumer may or may
not ever repurchase; the product experience has a lot to do with that. The brand marketer's
objective is now to win a larger share of a consumer's future purchases by moving the promoted brand into the target audience's active consideration set.

The target is anyone in the market (ready to purchase) for the given product category during the given shopping trip. P-O-P advertising that grabs the consumer's attention
and excites the consumer's imagination can motivate the consumer to add the advertised
brand to their consideration set and to actually make a purchase. P-O-P advertising can be
pivotal in generating trial.

Brands with a long history will experience consumers entering or leaving the brand
franchise at various times. For example, a former regular buyer may have switched years
ago to another brand. Winning this consumer back would be considered generating retrial.
This provides a new opportunity for the brand marketer to fulfill the basic objective of trial
discussed above—winning a larger percentage of the consumer's future purchases.

Impulse purchases—or buying on a whim—can come in many forms. Trial is often
an impulse purchase, but all impulse purchases need not be trial. When P-O-P actually
expands the number of shoppers *in the market*, it is usually generating impulse purchases.
Impulse purchases are extremely important to certain types of products. Every shopping
trip offers the potential for an impulse purchase. Effective P-O-P advertising increases the
incidence with which such purchases are made by calling attention to the brand and communicating its benefits in a persuasive manner.

Reminder advertising, the role of which is *repeat purchase stimulation*, is an
engine for shared maintenance and growth. The targets for reminder advertising are current brand buyers in the market to replenish their supplies. This is important to bear in
mind both in planning the evaluation and in developing the advertising itself. Brand marketers know that a current buyer of their brand is far more likely to repurchase than someone who has never purchased their brand before. They also know that totally loyal buyers
(e.g., consumers who stick to one brand and accept no substitutes) are an extremely rare
breed. Most people have a set of brands that they consider acceptable (i.e., a consideration
set) and will purchase from this set each time they are in the market.

Several factors exist to encourage these consumers to continue to purchase a particular brand over competitive offerings: ongoing satisfaction with the product; better distribution across stores; more shelf facings; presence of a display; a price promotion; and,
of course, P-O-P advertising. Putting a brand on display or making it somehow more
noticeable than other brands is a proven method for gaining a greater share of purchases.
P-O-P advertising contributes to this by providing the brand with a voice with which to
shout to consumers, "Here I am!" In comparison to other media, P-O-P advertising is by
far the best means of communicating an optimally timed brand-differentiating message.

Finally, P-O-P advertising also serves a unique role in a brand's marketing communication strategy as it serves as a bridge between the physical presence of the brand, either in the form of packaging or display, against the prior investment in an image-focused advertising message. It brings it all together at the moment of truth. This is in contrast with price promotions, which, while frequently effective in driving volume, can sometimes communicate a lack of value to consumers. Price promotions can imply that the only reason to buy the brand is because it is cheaper.

New usage idea, or other extended use advertising, is a different *repeat purchase stimulation* tool. Unlike the trial, retrial, or reminder strategies discussed above, the target in this case may or may not be current brand buyers ready to replenish but, instead, shoppers in the market to meet a need that the brand is not currently thought of to fulfill. For example, consumers may be shopping for desserts but not considering fresh fruit as a dessert option, even though they consume fresh fruit on other occasions. Point-of-purchase advertising can present the brand as suitable for a need or an occasion for which the consumer might not have previously considered it. This "occasion-specific" advertising is often accomplished through in-store sampling or integrated with out-of-store advertising. P-O-P advertising may actually work to help the shopper recall previous advertising through the mental process known as "imagery transfer." If the P-O-P advertising is compelling enough, it can create a new use for the brand, and if the brand fulfills the consumer's new expectations, a new source of volume is created.

Brand differentiation is the primary source of every brand's power. Consumers purchase a brand more often, and frequently do so at a higher price, because to them it is unlike the other brands in personally relevant ways. The attributes that differentiate a brand must be communicated and magnified if they are to break through the clutter of thousands of commercial messages bombarding each of us daily to leave a lasting impression that affects our future brand choices.

Two factors known to be extremely important in determining the effectiveness of advertising are (1) target audience and (2) saliency. P-O-P advertising addresses the consumer with a known interest in the product category (in the target market) at a time when the consumer is in the market to purchase (high saliency). No other medium can offer that advantage. Calling on the net impression of the total campaign and focusing it at the optimal moment—the purchase occasion—generates a powerful response among consumers, even if the brand is not purchased.

MEASURING P-O-P ADVERTISING EXPOSURE

An exposure to P-O-P advertising is defined as *opportunity to see (OTS)* the advertising. In practice, this means the advertisement was available to the consumer, who may or may not choose to attend to it. This is the definition against which all other media are held accountable. Market researchers can *operationalize* exposure to P-O-P advertising by counting the target audience traffic in front of the P-O-P. An exposure is also called an impression, and the total of all impressions generated is called *gross impressions*, which is expressed as a percentage of the target audience population, or *gross rating points (GRPs)*.

The gross ratings points delivered by P-O-P advertising can be substantial, as shown by the Simmons Market Research Bureau shopper data estimates for 2003 presented in Figure 5-3.

RETAILER	SHOPPERS PER MONTH	GRPs PER MONTH
Wal-Mart	610 MM	296
Sears	114 MM	55
Toys R Us	50 MM	24
Kroger	138 MM	67
Publix	62 MM	30
Shop Rite	32 MM	16

Figure 5-3
Gross Rating Points
for Leading Retailers

Exposure can be measured either in real time (i.e., as it actually occurs), by observer counts, or by a video recording of the location for future counting. Other measurement techniques may also be used, including infrared or other automatic means of shopper detection. Regardless of technique, the goal is counting the number of shoppers in front of the P-O-P advertising. Counting all locations at all times would be impractical, so a sample of stores, locations, and times should be selected on a random probability basis such that the sample is as representative of the total target population as possible.

In most instances, any form of direct counting may be too costly to justify on an ongoing basis. A technique that may prove more practical is to apply a count of total store traffic to a flow model of the percent of shoppers visiting each store section or location. This flow model must be based on actual measurement of consistent shopper patterns and have demonstrated high reliability. Flow models use measured traffic patterns to identify the typical percentages of total store traffic to visit each specific location within the store. They can be simple or complex; the key is that they reveal reliable shopping patterns that we can count on as total store traffic rises or falls. Once the model is developed and proven reliable, total store traffic counts can be applied to the percentages to estimate traffic at each location within the store.

MEASUREMENT OF INTERNET EXPOSURE

E-commerce Web sites represent a unique opportunity for measuring exposure. Every visitor can be logged and tracked. Each page viewed is logged by the site and can be counted with a good degree of precision, although there are some limitations to the current state of the art. Since pages accessed from proxy servers are not recorded by the main site's server log, exposures for these pages will be undercounted. On the other hand, pages not fully downloaded, abandoned, or timed out are assumed to have been visible to the consumer and are typically overcounted. Finally, pages downloaded by robots, spiders, or the Web site's own staff must be deducted from the count. Although assessing exposure on the

Internet is still in its infancy, many third-party auditors are stepping in to correct for these errors and providing a greater level of precision.

MEASURING AWARENESS AND ATTITUDE SHIFTS FROM P-O-P ADVERTISMENTS

Some consumers exposed to P-O-P advertising will pay no attention and therefore will not process the brand message. Others will pay attention, attend to some aspect of the message, and at least be reminded of the advertised brand. By definition, these consumers experience an increase in *brand awareness* and *advertisement awareness*. Some of these consumers will be persuaded in the manner that the advertisement was intended to persuade. Such persuasion actually changes the consumer's mind in some relevant way such that they experience an *attitude shift*.

	Supermarket	Mass Merchant	Fast Food
Average Visit Time (minutes)	54	51	7
Number of P-O-P Elements	493	400	25
Estimated Attention Per Element (seconds)	0.65 – 1.00	0.76 – 1.20	1.70 – 2.50

Figure 5-4

Customer Attention

by Retail Channel[2]

The battle for the shopper's attention is considerable, as indicated by the statistics presented in Figure 5-4. Because awareness and attitudes cannot be observed, they must be inferred through interviews. Interviews may be either (1) aided, in which a list of brands is read to the respondent, who indicates which brands are known to the respondent, or (2) unaided, in which the respondent recalls brands without the aid of a list. Since unaided awareness is a more challenging test, generally much lower levels of recall will be obtained as compared to aided awareness. Because of this, unaided awareness tests are especially suitable for well-established brands that are not just seeking confirmation of their familiarity but want to understand if they are "top of mind." In fact, some brands look specifically at a literal top-of-mind measure (e.g., first brand mentioned) in response to the unaided brand awareness question. Reaching "top of mind" indicates the brand has moved up in the consumer's consideration set toward being the preferred, first choice.

A P-O-P advertiser can measure the following through these interviews:

• Top-of-mind brand awareness.

• Unaided brand awareness.

• Aided brand awareness.

• Top-of-mind advertising awareness.

• Unaided advertising awareness.

• Aided advertising awareness.

The awareness measures chosen should match the objectives of the advertising. Variations on these themes can be developed to meet special needs.

Attitude questions are less standardized, dictated directly by the advertising strategy. The respondent's attitudes toward all the relevant brand attributes are probed using a battery of questions. Sometimes these questions are posed as statements, with the respondent asked to record the degree to which the respondent agrees or disagrees with each statement. Another common method is to have the respondent rate the brand on several attributes using a rating scale. In sum, there are many useful approaches to measuring consumer attitudes.

There are many ways in which these interviews can be conducted, but a key factor to keep in mind is that the respondents should not be led or influenced, even unintentionally. Respondents can often pick up very subtle cues, often telling the researcher what the researcher wants to hear and thus not capturing how the respondent actually feels. One guideline is to avoid sensitizing the audience to the brand name. A novice researcher might first ask several questions in an attempt to assess consumer attitudes toward the test brand, followed by asking the same consumers which brands they are aware of. Unwittingly, the novice researcher has just introduced a history bias to the survey (by introducing consumers to the test brand in the form of the question) and will falsely report a 100 percent awareness level.

FIELD EXPERIMENTATION

A bigger problem arises due to the daily onslaught of marketing messages. How do you know if the awareness gains or attitude shifts are really attributable to the P-O-P promotion alone? There are two techniques to confirm this; when they are combined, they can isolate the marketplace impact of P-O-P advertising.

Pre-post testing requires measuring awareness and attitudes, against the same target population, *before* P-O-P advertising is present and then again after the P-O-P advertising has been removed. You will want to sample people exposed to the P-O-P advertising, which may be feasible in the post-wave showing of P-O-P advertising. However, to avoid a history bias (i.e., exposing consumers to P-O-P advertising), the researcher must control which consumers are exposed to the P-O-P advertising before it is placed in the store.

One way to solve this problem is to recruit people to visit the store while being careful not to sensitize them to the brand or even the category you are testing. This is commonly done by asking questions about several categories in the pre-test, with the test brand or category being only one of several options under examination. Alternatively, you can also conduct entry ("pre-test") and exit ("post-test") interviews at stores where the P-O-P advertising appears. Note that, when interviewing people from the general population, you should screen for a random sample by asking the respondents about their most recent shopping trips. Respondents who visited stores that featured the test P-O-P advertising should then be chosen as part of the sample, and given the full questionnaire.

When you cannot confirm whether the respondent has been exposed to the test P-O-P, you must also factor in the distribution of the advertising to precisely understand its effect, as the measured effect can be more or less diluted, depending on its distribution level. For example, assume a specific P-O-P advertising program results in a brand awareness increase of 10 percent among those exposed to it. But if the P-O-P advertising is present in only 50 percent of the stores in the market, researchers would have to adjust downward the advertising effect to reflect this distribution. The adjustment required in this case would be as follows: *A 10 percent lift in awareness x 50 percent (vs. 100 percent) distribution would result in an overall awareness lift of 5 percent for the market.*

Another situation to be aware of is when the respondent makes claims of awareness in the pre-wave (e.g., when consumers claim to remember P-O-P advertisements that simply were not present). People get confused and "remember" things that have not happened but seem familiar. This is called a *ghost* level of awareness and is one of the key reasons for including a pre-wave as part of a P-O-P advertising best practices evaluation.

The point of these examples is that numerous factors can influence P-O-P advertising results, and the researcher must account for all of them.

Post-exposure-only measurements can also be very misleading. A good case in point: A large packaged-goods company in the vegetable category introduced a new line of frozen, microwaveable products. Post-wave research conducted by this company revealed a high awareness level among their target consumers (e.g., 74 percent surveyed were aware of the new brand). This would have been great news for both the agency and manufacturer, except that pre-wave levels were very high as well, indicating a significant level of ghost awareness (67 percent) and dampening the impact of the post-wave results!

Finally, all pre-post designs suffer from their inability to handle dynamic situations. If respondent awareness increases for reasons unrelated to the P-O-P advertising, a pre-post study would observe the increase and incorrectly attribute it to the P-O-P advertising, potentially missing more relevant explanatory variables.

Test-Control

Frequently, a better approach is test-control. In this design, respondents who recently shopped stores with ("test") and without ("control") P-O-P advertising are interviewed. If consumers in the two panels of stores are well matched (e.g., the *only* difference between stores is the single variable being tested—in this case, exposure to P-O-P advertising), then any change (or *lift*) in awareness or attitude toward the brand can be confidently attributed to the P-O-P advertising alone. The researcher can refine this comparison by interviewing only people who can be confirmed as having been exposed to the P-O-P in test stores, and those known not to have been exposed in the control stores. All methods discussed above for pre-post can be applied here as well. Finally, exit interviews outside of both the test and control stores can also be used.

Once you have both exposure and awareness data, you should compute *conversion ratios*, or the percent of those exposed to P-O-P advertising who consequently become aware of it. It is also useful to compare attitudes among consumers aware of the advertisements to those unaware. By comparing these ratios to historical norms or other expectations, brand marketers can begin to understand if awareness gains and attitude shifts are driven by level of P-O-P advertising exposure *or* by the P-O-P advertisement's ability to capture and hold the shopper's attention and communicate attitude-shifting information. Some P-O-P advertising may have little *lasting* attitudinal impact, but strong, *immediate* impact on purchase behavior. Discriminating among these communication goals is essential to effective P-O-P advertising, as will be discussed in the following section.

LABORATORY TECHNIQUES

A range of laboratory-type techniques can also explore various aspects of how P-O-P advertising works. These include the following:

Environment Rooms. Respondents can be recruited into *environment rooms* filled with brands in conjunction with alternative P-O-P materials and asked to rate each brand. Given proper sampling, differences in consumer ratings of the brands can be attributed to the P-O-P advertising.

Eye Tracking. *Eye-tracking* research literally monitors eye movements during real or simulated shopping occasions and reveals what specific elements of the P-O-P advertisement shoppers attend to.

Video Snakes. The eye-tracking approach can be mobilized in the store in the form of *video snakes*—cameras hidden in hats (worn by shoppers) that may reveal the following: where shoppers are looking as they shop, the amount of time spent at a given P-O-P display, interaction with the display, and finally (and hopefully) the purchase.

Visor Cams. These devices combine both eye-tracking and video-snake techniques.

Tachistoscopes. These devices reveal the advertisement to respondents for finely measured split seconds to quantify readability.

Simulated Virtual Shopping. *Simulated virtual shopping* systems enable consumers to take a self-guided tour through store environments using 3-D computer simulation. More traditional techniques such as hidden cameras and following shoppers in the store can also reveal much about how a given advertisement works.

These qualitative techniques composed of small, informal samples—while often insightful—can be challenging to interpret and dangerous to the project. These studies should be balanced with a complementary, reliable, quantitative measurement such as a survey based on a projected sample.

MEASURING P-O-P ADVERTISING-DRIVEN BEHAVIORAL EFFECTS

If shoppers are prescreened to have a purchase intention and are persuaded by P-O-P advertising at that time, the likelihood is high that they will purchase the P-O-P-advertised brand. Whereas the previous stages of the advertising process can be measured more or less directly, purchase behavior effects cannot. It may seem paradoxical that observable behavior cannot be as readily ascribed to the P-O-P advertising as can a change in awareness or attitude. The fact is that there are many reasons why a given consumer purchases a given brand at a given point in time—and that market researchers must be vigilant to identify all of those reasons, and their contributions, before they can be confident they have isolated the unique role of the P-O-P advertising.

The preferred method for isolating the impact of P-O-P advertising is to evaluate the impact from a reading of two matched sets of stores, as mentioned above. Assuming a best practices framework, variables to be matched include sales (or share) of test brand; sales (or share) of major brands in category; sales of total category; promotions and price of test brand and major brands in category; item distribution of major brands; and demographic environment (if available). A comparison between the two sets of stores during a prespecified test period should show little difference in the values of those measures. After adjusting for any sales difference during the pre-test period, the sales difference observed during the test period can then be confidently attributed to the P-O-P advertising alone.

This method physically controls for all factors other than the P-O-P advertising itself. Sometimes these other variables cannot be matched in advance, or they become unmatched during the evaluation. In this case, the match can be achieved mathematically through a covariate analysis. This statistical procedure analyzes all of the ups and downs in sales along with the presence or absence of all of the factors influencing sales to tell us the influence they each have on consumer purchase behavior. This technique allows the analyst to sort out the impact of the P-O-P advertising from among all of the other factors even if the test was not perfectly matched. The combination of well-matched sets of stores and a covariate analysis covers all bases. It is a "belt and suspenders approach" and is considered a *best practice*.

With the availability of frequent shopper data, it is now possible to select matched stores, which provide not only store sales data but also consumer purchasing behavior data. Such data can be analyzed to assess the change in consumer behavior that results from P-O-P advertising.

For example, did the advertising attract more new buyers to the brand than would be expected without the P-O-P advertising? Was the quality of those new buyers higher, exhibiting stronger repeat purchasing? Because these data are drawn from a single chain's frequent shopper panel, researchers must limit analysis and interpretation to those consumers for whom they have a complete purchase history for the category under study. In other words, those consumers must be loyal to the set of stores where researchers are tracking the consumers' purchasing data.

If researchers are missing a significant portion of a consumer's category purchasing because it occurs in stores that are not part of the panel, the researcher may draw incorrect conclusions. Fortunately, this problem is remedied by drawing a proper *static sample*—that is, a sample of consumers whose purchasing behavior has been recorded completely and consistently throughout the analysis period.

EVALUATION OF INTERNET P-O-P ADVERTISING

Using the Internet as a testing medium, it is possible to set up matched consumer panels where one group ("test") is exposed to the advertising and another group ("control") is not. For a meaningful analysis, the two groups must be matched in terms of demographics and pre-test purchase behavior. When it is not possible to set up matched panels, such as when the evaluation is begun after the fact, a covariate analysis or marketing mix model can be developed using the data "as it fell." As with the covariate analysis employed with matched panels, this is a process of statistical decomposition, sorting and sifting apart the effects of all of the various influences on purchase behavior. This type of analysis is limited by the degree of variation found in the data. The matched panel design creates two (or more) dramatically different scenarios—with and without the P-O-P advertising—and provides a cleaner, more certain interpretation of the result.

UNDERSTANDING WHY

These quantitative, behavioral sales and purchase data analyses tell us whether the P-O-P advertising has impacted the consumer and the consumer's purchase behavior. It is often even more valuable to understand why. There are other supplementary techniques that can answer this question, such as observational research that enables you to "see" the P-O-P's ability to draw attention and to motivate behavior, as discussed above.

Exit interviews provide the opportunity to ask the purchaser and nonpurchaser alike, "why?" They also provide a way to separate trial from repeat purchases and to identify impulse purchases or other details of the purchase decision itself. In-store audits can determine the level of proper P-O-P advertising execution, which is directly related to overall impact levels. In addition, comprehensive store audits can identify other factors that can and do impact overall program performance.

For example, in a fast food retail environment, a promotional game achieved less impact than the identical program did only one year earlier. Upon further analysis of the store environment, it was determined that a plausible causal factor explaining this reduced performance was the inclusion of more offers during the second program. Thus, it was concluded that while execution rates were essentially equal to the previous year, the introduction of additional messages competing for customers' attention reduced the impact of the promotional game.

Kodak has employed a useful technique to answer the "why" question. Respondents are recruited to a store to visit a custom-designed display and to speak aloud their thoughts while looking at it. They may be asked to describe the display, as long as prompts are not leading. This technique can be used retrospectively as well as concurrently (e.g., in the presence of the actual display). In a related technique, respondents can also be shown videos of other shoppers interacting with the display. Respondents are then asked to explain (project) what is going on.

LONG-TERM BRAND BUILDING WITH P-O-P ADVERTISING

While P-O-P advertising is often thought of as short-term or trade promotional in nature, there can be longer-term benefits. These benefits depend on the type of brand message communicated and on the type of targeting employed. If the objective is, in part, to communicate a relevant brand-differentiating message, the researcher may expect longer-term effects than if the message is simply one of brand presence or price.

This relevant, brand-differentiating message can work in two ways: First, if it brings a new buyer to the brand for the right reasons (e.g., motivated by superior product performance) rather than because the brand was on deal (e.g., on price reduction). In this case, it is assumed this buyer may continue to purchase the brand long after the initial purchase stimulated by the P-O-P advertisement.

Second, if the message is compelling enough it may persuade the consumer that the advertised brand is worth more than competing brands, motivating the consumer to pay a higher price for the advertised brand. These effects can be observed at three levels: (1) in terms of the strengthening of positive, relevant, differentiating brand attributes; (2) in the high repeat purchase patterns of the P-O-P-induced purchaser; and (3) in the reduced sensitivity to price variability among those same purchasers (although verifying this requires development of an analytical model before it can be quantified).

RETURN ON P-O-P ADVERTISING INVESTMENT

Was the P-O-P advertising campaign worthwhile? Answering this question requires returning to the objectives and considering the value returned against each of them. If exposure or communication was a specific objective sought, its value can be estimated in terms of cost per thousands (CPM) earned by comparable media. If awareness or attitude shifts were sought, the levels achieved by the P-O-P campaign can be evaluated in terms of the expected cost of achieving such gains via other media. If purchase effects were sought, the sales revenue generated and variable income generated by those sales can be calculated directly. If longer-term effects were detected, they can be estimated in terms of the lifetime value of the consumers that were won. Return on investment for each of these advertising objectives is simply the ratio of the value obtained to the cost of the campaign, minus 1, times 100. Some programs may seem expensive; others may seem cheap. Not until you understand what you get for the expenditure can you precisely address the value question with authority.

Statistics provided by William A. Cook, PhD, Senior Vice President, Research & Standards, The Advertising Research Foundation.

ENDNOTES

[1] Ben DiSanti, "Measurements and Analysis for Better Consumer Promotions" (presented at the Promotion Marketing Association/Institute for International Research Conference on Measurements and Analysis for Better Consumer Promotions, New York, N.Y., Sept. 18-19, 2000).

[2] Ben DiSanti, "RCP: A Retail P-O-P Planning Model" (presented at the Category Management and Research at the Retail Frontline Conference of the Advertising Research Foundation, New York, N.Y., Oct. 27, 1998).

"With the proper design,

displays become an

effective part of

the client's overall

merchandising strategy."

P-O-P Advertising
Design and Creativity

LARRY HAUGEN, CPP, PAST CHAIRMAN, POPAI

**CURTIS WEEMS, SENIOR VICE PRESIDENT, SALES AND MARKETING
THE MILLER GROUP**

Purpose Of P-O-P Advertising Design

Design is one of the most important elements in the display industry. Price, service, and delivery are important, but without good design, displays can often be rather useless—a wasted expense. With the proper design, displays become an effective part of the client's overall merchandising strategy.

In a very broad sense, the major objective of a display is to help clients sell more product, and the goal of the designer is to create a display that will meet the clients' needs. In developing a display program, the client's advertising, promotional materials, sales literature, and packaging should come together at one point—the display. Regardless of how a consumer comes into contact with a product, whether from media advertising, collateral sales material, or by any other method, the display should reinforce the consumer's familiarity with the product and its campaign.

The design-planning process is critical to the successful execution of a display program. To understand this planning process, we will review the events leading up to the installation of the P-O-P advertising display in the marketplace, including these six key steps:

1. Input from the client, design director, product manager, or director of sales promotion.
2. Interaction between the client and the account executive and design staff.
3. A series of sketches (e.g., computer drawings) to provide proper direction: rough sketches for structural design only, followed by sketches that indicate of graphic design.
4. A physical structural sample, the first prototype, and then subsequent samples if changes are required.
5. Finished comp—the final structural sample with graphics and surface treatment applied.
6. The assembled display, ready to take on its task in the marketplace.

Client Input

Although it is not necessary that clients design the display, they must provide enough input to help the designer create the ideal display for the situation, based on considerations such as objectives, budget, quantity, theme, or tie-in with other media. Unfortunately, P-O-P advertising design is often executed in a vacuum. All too often, the designer is not given enough time, information, background, or understanding of the product or the intended channel of trade to create a proper design. Ideally, all parties will understand the project "deliverables" that identify all of these considerations. Good business practice dictates that these project deliverables be clearly defined and included in a project specifications agreement. (See Chapter 3.)

The design process starts with a brief of the project objectives; a photo retrospective of the client's products and its competitors in the retail environment; and a pre-design meeting with the account executive, the estimator, the project manager, and the production manager. A pre-design meeting enables everyone to understand the issues that must be addressed before starting the project. The designer, perhaps in collaboration with other in-house designers, often presents preliminary concepts to the account executive prior to presenting them to the client. The designer and the account executive should then compare these concepts with existing designs in the field to determine which concepts would best satisfy the client. To illustrate how well the designs meet the design objectives, the producer should present the design to the client accompanied by a restatement of the objectives and the selection of the competitive photo retrospective. At this session, the producer should also present estimated, preliminary pricing, lead times, materials, production processes, and tooling—all of which indicate the producer's capability to deliver the program. If the client gives a "go ahead" for the project, new timelines, final costing, and installation and logistical issues are then adjusted (from the original project specifications) to meet any changes the client specifies.

It is important to remember that a well-conceived display should not be over designed or under designed: it should be in balance with its intended use. The object of the merchandising display is to focus the consumers' attention on the product so it is not competing with all of the other products in its category.

TECHNIQUES TO EXECUTE A DESIGN PROJECT

There are many techniques in the development and presentation of design concepts. One of the most valuable creative planning tools is brainstorming, where members of the design and manufacturing team can interact in a free-flowing exchange of ideas and concepts. (There are no bad ideas in a brainstorming session.) Depending on the client relationship, clients may be included in these meetings. The goal of such initial creative sessions is to "think outside the box" and generate new concepts that better meet the client's needs.

Thumbnail sketches by designers help zero in on various strategic directions and allow team members to respond to these preliminary design concepts. Because they are loose and inexact in form, thumbnails are quick and effective in determining a creative direction. Thumbnail sketches can be further refined and rescreened before being presented to the client. The client has an opportunity to consider, adjust, modify, and generally shape various ideas into a design that meets project needs. This process illustrates the dynamic collaborative effort by the client and the P-O-P advertising designer.

Computer Rendering

The role of computer rendering has grown to the advantage of the P-O-P design process. Although computer rendering has become a fundamental tool for P-O-P advertising design, it is important to realize that the use of specialized 3-D software programs does not speed up design at the front end. It takes about as much time to do an initial rendering by computer as it does to execute an initial design by hand.

However, the computer does enable the designer and client to make modifications, review color variations, and test design concepts before prototypes are produced, thereby saving substantial sums on rerendering by hand. Most significantly, computer renderings enable the client to clearly visualize the recommended P-O-P advertising display before spending additional sums on building costly mock-ups. An additional key advantage is the ability to visualize the P-O-P advertising display in the selling environment before installation. A photo of an in-store environment can be merged with a computerized rendering to view the designs in a lifelike situation. How well a design works aesthetically can often be determined via this technique, again saving the client valuable time and money.

Several years ago when L'eggs Hosiery decided to launch a new brand, Color Me Natural, L'eggs gave its display suppliers only six weeks to design, engineer, and build a prototype and produce a new spinner display for the product. Using a computer-aided drawing program, the P-O-P advertising designer produced three different concepts. Five different store environments were then photographed and merged with the design to simulate how these three displays would look in-store. One display was selected, and a decision was made to move immediately into production, thus eliminating all production prototyping and testing.

The result was a display utilizing vacuum forming, wire, and silkscreen printing, produced in six weeks from start to finish. Although this hurry-up schedule was not the optimum way to produce a display, using a computer to pre-test concepts in-store substantially reduced the lead time required to produce the display, while eliminating the cost of prototype testing. Although, in this case, the process was not detrimental to the client's interests, the selection of materials and production processes was greatly limited.

Utilizing In-House Design

In addition to prototyping and production, most producers provide clients with in-house display design. These in-house design departments usually have the ability to manage and transfer files electronically from Mac- or PC-based systems. Computer technology enables the designer to use a variety of existing resources or to access previously produced work that can then be adapted to create a design that meets the client's criteria. Artwork can then be accessed or incorporated into a particular design to give an idea more "panache" or to allow the client to better understand the concept. Because the design can be managed in a more dynamic manner without increasing the time needed to complete it, such techniques, among many others, enable the producer to respond more quickly to client needs, often saving the client money.

Design Schools

Many excellent design schools worldwide provide special training in numerous creative disciplines such as industrial styling and design, graphics, modeling, or structural or packaging design. While most schools do not provide training specific to point-of-purchase advertising, they offer an excellent source of creative ideas. By developing a relationship with a design school, the client or the producer can gain a creative resource that extends far beyond their company's creative department. Not only does this extend a company's creative abilities, it also gives design students training experience.

The Internet

As a creative resource, the Internet will grow as a servicing medium for producers/suppliers and clients. It provides a medium where design ideas can be exchanged between clients and producers in real time. By setting up a password-protected suite for a client, a producer can provide designers, account executives, clients, and any other parties who need to be included a place to review and make design modifications online. Input can be provided via the Internet from any part of the world by those engaged in the project. This can speed up project development and reduce costs involved. Nonetheless, clients and producers must not as a result reduce the time spent on understanding and planning for the project.

As the global demand for P-O-P advertising grows, more and more design projects will necessarily be influenced by designers in multiple countries. Internet usage will reduce review time, increasingly enhancing the ability of globally dispersed clients and producers/suppliers to communicate in real time 24 hours a day.

FORM FOLLOWS FUNCTION, OR VICE VERSA

In every design school, the subject of "form follows function" is treated as one of the fundamental precepts of design. Form follows function is an established law of design and, as such, there is often a strict adherence to this principle. "Form follows function" dictates that the basic principle in product design is that a product meets the needs of the consumer in ease-of-use, performance, "clean-ability," and longevity. Additionally, the form, shape, and look should complement and enhance the product's primary function.

However, in display design it is not uncommon (depending on the promotional need) that function follows form. For example, a beverage bottler might want to use a 6 × 3-foot bottle to hold stock to promote a product. The designer would begin by scaling-up the bottle and then developing space that will work within the dimensions of the bottle display. On a very rudimentary level, function follows form. As always, it is critical that the designer understand as many aspects of a project as possible (e.g., merchandising objectives, the product, and the environment in which the display will be deployed). Creative display design is almost always a delicate balance between "form follows function" or, in some cases, the other way around.

Although the aesthetics of a retail display attract the consumer, it is imperative that it also inform the consumer as to a product's benefits and/or features. Consumers are most likely to spend money on products they understand how to use, that will make them feel good, and that will improve the quality of their lives. A display should persuade the consumer that the product will meet these objectives. The client will then subject such a display to a multitude of financial and logistical considerations, including cost, sales budgets, transportation, retail environments, setup, and removal, all of which will help determine which elements of the original design are included in the final display and how they are executed. Although a display's objective is usually just to generate retail sales, a client's desire to have a "killer-looking" display—to match the style of the product, for example-may supercede the financial and logistical considerations listed above. In this case, the need to grab attention at retail is so paramount that function follows form.

OBJECT LANGUAGE

Design school students often hear the term "object language" by their second or third year; they will hear it mentioned frequently. The premise behind object language states that a consumer should be able to look at a product, any product, and determine what the product does and how to operate it. For example, one can look at the shape of a toy ball and deduce that it rolls and can be tossed. Depending on the coloring, one may be able to infer the targeted age group, that is, bright colors with stars for the younger set and solid colors for an older audience.

The retail displays of many products neither attract the consumer nor in any way communicate the product's purpose. The retailer or the brand marketer of these products is apparently relying on the product to do all the work. In most cases, the result will be underpromotion of the product at retail, resulting in fewer products being sold. On the other hand, many products have displays so effective that the consumer can recognize the product and understand what it can do, solely from the display. In such cases, products often "fly" off the display, resulting in a most successful in-store selling campaign.

In the highly technological and fast-paced retail environments of today, the theory behind object language becomes even more important as a design and promotional tool. Consumers who can quickly understand the features, benefits, and value of a product are more likely to buy that product than any product they must decipher. Besides attracting the consumer, well-designed displays communicate how the product works, what it can do, and why the consumer who needs it should buy it now. By taking object language into account, the designer, retailer and brand marketer will more often be able to dispel doubt at the point of purchase, allowing consumers to decide to buy the product on the spot rather deciding not to buy it, because they don't know what the product can do or how it will improve their life.

A successful display will be as intuitive as possible—consumers should need little or no instruction to interact with the display. They must instantly understand important information about a product's features and benefits. Icons, directional signage, illustrations of product use, color, shape, sound, odor, texture, and many additional elements serve to make a product or display more intuitive.

DESIGN SETS P-O-P ADVERTISING APART FROM MEDIA ADVERTISING

Design and creativity in the P-O-P advertising industry are much different than in other areas of the advertising world. The designer of P-O-P advertising displays must think not only of graphic design and clever ad campaigns but also of the underlying structural design. The structural design must be incorporated into the overall display design so that the finished product is a complete, flowing piece. The display must also catch the eye of the consumer and differentiate the featured product so that the client sells more product.

Many areas of P-O-P advertising design require the skills of diverse design disciplines. Most structural designers are from the industrial design field, but some very good designers are from fine arts, particularly the sculptural design field, where artists are taught to think in 3-D and that sculptural designs can and should look good from all angles. This is true in P-O-P design also. Displays should look good from all angles and views, so that in the marketplace they will be pleasantly imposing and not an eyesore that would distract from the positive attributes that the display is meant to portray.

DESIGN CONSIDERATIONS

At least 12 structural design considerations are involved in the design of display structures. See Figure 6-1. The following sections discuss those considerations.

Structural Design Considerations

1. Strength
2. Economy
3. Appearance
4. Integrating Graphics
5. Accommodating Product
6. Telling a Story
7. Creating a Theme
8. Size Restrictions
9. Versatility of Uses
10. Attracting Attention
11. Assembly
12. Floor Life

Figure 6-1

Strength

Strength is a major design consideration, especially for displays intended to be in the marketplace for more than a short time. If the product on a display is heavy, the display must be able to bear such a weight for an extended period. In some applications, displays receive unusual and frequent abuse, such as constant bumping, opening, and closing. In retail stores in which floors are regularly mopped, temporary displays constructed of corrugated material can quickly become damaged unless precautions are taken. The base of the display can be treated with a wax application, plastic feet can be added to hold the corrugated portion off the floor, or casters can be added. (The caster option offers the added advantage of making the display portable.) For permanent displays, bumpers, edge banding, metal guards, or other protective features may be added.

It may be necessary to include additional materials to ensure that a display achieves the appropriate level of strength to support a product. Metal tubes or wood slats to help support product shelves may be added to corrugated displays. It may also be necessary to upgrade the strength of the corrugated board from 200# test to 275# test. Displays can be designed in corrugated to bear almost any weight, but there is a point at which it makes sense to begin with a stronger material as opposed to adding other material components to strengthen a corrugated display function that was improperly designed from the outset. Strength is also required when displays are to be moved on a regular basis, especially when loaded with product. Very simply, displays must be built stronger to last longer. See Figure 6-2.

Economy

The next structural design consideration is economy, the key to which is maximizing display effectiveness and minimizing cost. This can be achieved by allocating enough time to consider material and production alternatives. See Figure 6-3.

Figure 6-2

Display designed to accommodate a large quantity of products

Appearance

A display that elicits a strong visual feeling consistent with the retailer's channel of trade while fitting pleasingly into the marketplace enhances the product. To create an appearance of quality, the product must be placed in an environment where it "looks good." Using an effective variety of materials can help achieve that emotional response. Thoughtful integration of both materials and design not only strengthens the physical element of the design but enhances the appearance of the design as well. See Figure 6-4.

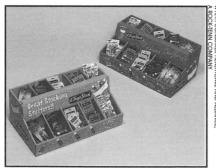

Figure 6-3

Economically designed display

Figure 6-4

Display using a variety of materials to enhance design

Figure 6-5

Display that integrates

graphics and product

as part of the display's

design

Figure 6-6

Display that

merchandises

product within its

packaging

Integrating Graphics Into Structure

The next design consideration is the integration of structure and graphics. The two must work together to create the right appearance. If the design is created with both structure and graphics in mind, ideally the consumer will see only one, integrated, P-O-P advertising display. Graphics can enhance structure, and structure can enhance graphics. The display must be designed to accommodate the product, fitting it in such a way that it looks like it belongs-a perfect fit. The product must be framed, not hidden. See Figure 6-5.

Accommodating The Product

The added consumer benefit resulting from an integrated look is that each product appears to be featured. When possible, have the actual product available for the consumer to touch and strive to create attractive ways of merchandising a product within its package. Never let the display overpower the product. A fundamental axiom of the point-of-purchase designer is always to allow the product to emerge as the "star" of the display. See Figure 6-6.

Storytelling

Storytelling is one of the most compelling forms of persuasion. With very few words, the structure of a display can tell a story of the product or service-its features and its successes-by creative use of shape or color. See Figure 6-7.

Figure 6-7

Display that

tells a story

SMURFIT-STONE DISPLAY GROUP FOR SPALDING SPORTS WORLDWIDE

Creating A Theme

Creating a theme can be an additional design consideration. Seasonal themes can be supported by brief holiday messages and strengthened by the basic colors of that season. Themes can also be created that relate directly to the product. A display that merchandises pickles could look like a giant pickle barrel. A display that merchandises automotive motor oil could be designed to look like a pickup truck or an Indy racecar. Themes can draw the consumer into a feeling of being connected to the product. A golf cart is an excellent way of creating a theme for merchandising golf balls. See Figure 6-8.

Figure 6-8

Display that creates a theme

Size Restriction

Size restriction is another structural design consideration. Display space in the marketplace is nearly always at a premium and, therefore, designing displays that fit into a restricted amount of floor space is the trend within the P-O-P design industry. Going up instead of out is far more acceptable to most store managers, especially if the display leaves void areas that create an open, airy feeling.

Figure 6-9

Two variations of a display designed to use space efficiently

Revolving displays are another way of economizing on space because they allow for the merchandising of significantly more product in a restricted amount of space. Smaller retailer formats (such as convenience stores) have a great premium on floor space and strongly insist on space efficiency. This can be accomplished through the use of tall, slender displays; sidekicks; and ceiling-hung units such as mobiles, danglers, and overhead merchandisers. See Figure 6-9.

For the larger P-O-P design customers such as discount stores, pallet displays make sense because, while they normally occupy a 40 x 48" footprint of retail floor space, they are densely packed with product and in many cases are stackable to double up on the mix of product in the same amount of floor space. The billboarding of products on the pallet displays projects a strong image for the product and, without even indicating it, the massive amount of product on the pallet display seems to shout "on sale."

PERSONAL PRODUCTS AND SMURFIT STONE DISPLAY GROUP

THE SHERWIN-WILLIAMS COMPANY AND INNOVATIVE MARKETING SOLUTIONS, INC.

Figure 6-10

Display that uses size to attract attention

Versatility

Yet another structural design consideration is the versatility of a display. A display that exhibits versatility is one that functions as a counter display and, with the simple addition of a display base, becomes a floorstand display.

Attracting Attention

Attracting attention is the major goal of a P-O-P display. It can be achieved in many ways. One is by sheer size. Displays that take up lots of floor space and that tower into the air are very difficult to miss. See Figure 6-10. Another way to attract attention is through the use of color. Certain colors, such as red, are very "attracting." It is important to use colors that make sense with the product being displayed. Blues and greens, for example, are not good choices when merchandising some food products, such as meat, but work well when merchandising products such as soft drinks or outdoor products (e.g., suntan lotions and beach toys).

Figure 6-11

Display that uses sound to attract attention

The right graphics can help attract attention. Bold copy, colorful photography, and crisp illustrations all do their part in the display design. Attracting attention means standing out from the crowd: "Here I Am Buy Me!"

Additional ways to attract attention include the use of lights, motion, or sound—anything that may catch the consumer's eye. Flashing lights can make a display sparkle like a Christmas tree. A giant-sized version of the product turning on top of a display can draw attention from across the store. A display with a built-in sound device can provide information about a product's features and benefits. See Figure 6-11.

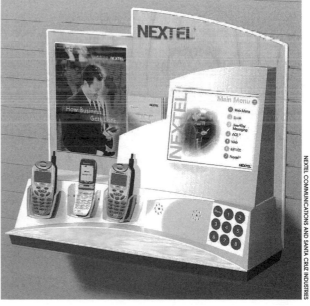

NEXTEL COMMUNICATIONS AND SANTA CRUZ INDUSTRIES

Figure 6-12
Display sent to
retailer partially
assembled and
filled with product

Ease Of Assembly

Ease of display assembly or setup in the marketplace is another design consideration. There are many ways to design displays that "fly together" (where the display parts and pieces are easily assembled with little or no complicated instructions). Retailers generally prefer displays that are partially or even fully assembled. See Figure 6-12. Simplicity and the elimination of confusion are key. Assembly instruction sheets for retailers should be simple and easy to understand. A good approach is to use sketches or photos with identification letters or numbers, and as few words as possible.

Floor Lifespan

Figure 6-13

Permanent display

The final design consideration is the length of time a display can be expected to function in the marketplace. How long a display will be used is often determined by where the display will be located (e.g., on a jewelry department counter or on a mass retailer's floor). Most often the final retail location determines the type of materials that can be used in the design. Displays may be expected to function for three to five years, or just three to five weeks or less.

The display's expected lifespan and location have a major impact on the type of materials to be used. It is important to think in terms of the proper materials. Displays intended to last a year or more will usually be designed in permanent materials such as wood, wire, metal, or plastic. See Figure 6-13. Displays with a relatively short life expectancy of eight weeks or less are usually designed in more lightweight materials such as chipboard or corrugated. See Figure 6-14. Displays intended to last for six to nine months fall into a category called "semi-permanent." They often use a combination of lightweight and permanent materials. See Figure 6-15. For example, plastic channeling

WYETH CONSUMER HEALTHCARE AND SMURFI/STONE DISPLAY GROUP

may be added to the edge of a corrugated display to avoid damage, or a lightweight vacuum shell may hold a chipboard prepack. Some displays are designed to sell out a full turn of product in only one weekend in a busy marketplace. See Figure 6-16.

Choose Compatible Design Materials

While a creative mind is helpful in making the material decisions discussed above, common sense and an eye toward overall profitability must ultimately prevail when the final P-O-P advertising design decision is made. Besides choosing materials that work well with the products, it is necessary to choose materials that work well with each other. Although some woods and metals work well together, others do not. Wire components and fabrics can complement each other, just as glass and wood, glass and metal, or glass and plastics work well together. The variety is virtually endless and the possibilities exciting.

The successful designer continuously experiments and is constantly on the lookout for new materials to combine with existing materials. Creating the right feeling with materials is not always easy. It is important to get to know the product, the marketplace where it is available, the department or category in which it is sold, and the demographics of the typical consumer who purchases the product. It is extremely important to choose materials that meet budget requirements and will be delivered in time to meet the production schedule and promotion deadline.

Figure 6-14

Temporary display

Remember the primary objective of P-O-P advertising is to attract attention: The goal of the chosen materials is to make the P-O-P advertising display attractive. There are countless materials available to design just about any display the mind can envision. But the materials must be made to work together through proper design principles and creativity.

PEPSI-COLA AND NEW DIMENSIONS RESEARCH CORP.

DELL LABORATORIES (CANADA) INC. AND ARRAY

Figure 6-15

Semi-Permanent

display

Figure 6-16

Display designed to sell out in

a short period of time

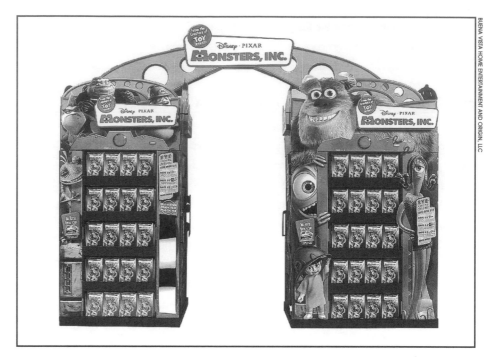

Figure 6-17

Display incorporating structure, product, and graphics

BASE THE DESIGN ON IMPORTANT FACTORS

What comes first: the graphics, the structure, or the budget? They should all come together in a seamless process that concludes: This display works; it makes sense; and it communicates the client's message. The display should first attract the attention of the consumers but should then force the consumer to concentrate his or her attention on the product or service that the display is selling.

The graphics should be tied sensibly to the product, via color, type styles, and composition: Even the structure can be designed to make a statement about the product. All displays can be made more attractive through the use of good graphics tied to a very basic structure. Never say, "Oh well, it has to be a cheap display anyway, because we don't have any budget to work with." The important consideration is that even if the display has to be cheap in an economic sense, it doesn't have to look cheap in the visual sense. Combining even the most basic display appearance with some visual structural tricks and quality graphics can mean the difference between a mediocre promotion and a masterpiece promotion. See Figure 6-17.

It is easier to design a quality display program when the graphics and structure are designed simultaneously. If you have a graphic approach in mind at the beginning, strive to tie it into a structure that enhances the graphics. If you start with a structural design, then incorporate graphics that achieve a synergy between these two fundamental aspects of point-of-purchase design.

Graphics and structure should ideally come together as "one" to create a display that is structurally sound and pleasing to the eye. It must also be graphically pleasing and informational. The cost difference between a second-class and a first-class display is often very small. It is important that the designer, the account executive, and the client clearly understand the project objectives and the design tradeoffs.

The driving philosophy behind successful P-O-P advertising recognizes that displays are not just racks to hold product in the marketplace, but that they are tools that constantly remind the consumer: "Here I am. Here is what I'm all about. Here is why I'm better than Brand X. Buy me!"

Conclusion

A point-of-purchase advertising display can be flat or in full-round sculpture. It can use every technique to reach people through any of their senses—color, light, motion, sound, touch, and even scent—to attract attention and to help convey its message.

A client asks for a display that will accomplish specific objectives. The client has certain parameters—quantity, budget, and usually a time schedule. The designer then develops a display that will meet all of these requirements. Unfortunately, some of the requirements are contradictory. Certain features that might be included to increase attention value may raise the unit cost beyond the level permitted by the budget. The time schedule may be too tight to permit the acquisition of materials that are not readily available. Perhaps using a stock extrusion rather than a custom extrusion can reduce cost. If this were possible, would the change reduce the effectiveness of the finished display? The designer must draw on experience to resolve these challenges.

The designer must take ideas and transfer them to paper in a manner that is understandable to a client who may have a limited visual imagination. The designer should understand human nature and know how to make a design more appealing, knowing what is and is not acceptable in different retail environments. The type of display designed to sell food products in a crowded supermarket would not be appropriate in a jewelry store. Displays, even for identical products, must fit the environment for which they are intended.

Finally, the designer must know his or her material and production limitations. The designer must understand what can and cannot be done with a wide variety of materials such as chipboard, corrugated, wood, wire, and plastic. The designer should consider how displays are shipped and assembled and the other characteristics that will enable a display to command a unique and compelling presentation in the marketplace.

Because the P-O-P advertising industry and retail environment are constantly evolving, working with P-O-P advertising displays is a challenge for any designer. Not only are new materials continually becoming available, but price ratios are never constant. What was impractical yesterday is imminently within reach today. P-O-P advertising displays have a permanent role in contemporary marketing and advertising.

"Since 1959, POPAI's

OMA awards contest

is the premier award for

recognizing the most innovative

and effective in-store and

at retail displays."

POPAI's Outstanding Merchandising Achievement Gallery

POPAI's Outstanding Merchandising Achievement Awards Contest

This section showcases a variety of point-of-purchase advertising displays that received POPAI's prestigious Outstanding Merchandising Achievement (OMA) award in 2003. The brand clients, and companies that produced the displays, are listed with their award levels—gold, silver, or bronze.

Since 1959, POPAI's OMA awards contest is the premier award for recognizing the most innovative and effective in-store and at retail displays that lift sales and make products memorable and enticing to consumers. The entries are judged by a prestigious panel of brand marketers, producers, and retailers. The first round of judging is done online, where judges review submitted images and case history forms, and the second round of judging is done in person, where judges evaluate the actual displays to formulate a final score. Scores are based on the display's ability to increase sales, obtain retail placements, and work strategically to position the brand at the point of sale. Over 700 cutting-edge P-O-P displays vie each year for OMA awards. This is the industry's largest and longest running awards contest.

The displays shown here illustrate the wide degree of creativity, design, and function for P-O-P displays. More detailed information, including a list of materials used and brief case histories for each of these displays—plus thousands more—is available in the POPAI Creative Gallery online at www.popai.com.

GALLERY

BEER

Bacardi Silver Bottle Glorifier
Grimm Industries, Inc.
Anheuser-Busch
Permanent · Bronze

Pilsner Urquell USA Program
Everbrite, Inc.
Pilsner Urquell USA
Permanent · Gold

Bud Holiday Sleigh Spectacular
Anheuser-Busch · Anheuser-Busch
Semi-Permanent · Bronze

Coors Original
Process Displays, Inc.
The Integer Group
Permanent · Silver

Bud Bowl/Olympic Interchangable Spectacular
Anheuser-Busch · Anheuser-Busch
Semi-Permanent · Gold

Bass Beer Backbar display
Rapid Displays · Diageo/Colangelo Synergy Marketing
Temporary · Bronze

BOOKS, COMPUTERS, STATIONARY

Pencil Fun Merchandiser
Great Northern Corporation – Display Group
Banta Packaging and Fullfillment Services/Menasha
Temporary · Bronze

Microsoft 2 FT Custom Unit
Harbor Industries, Inc.
Microsoft Corporation
Permanent · Gold

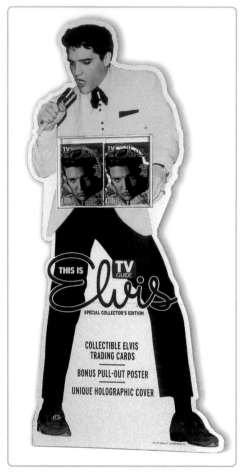

T.V. Guide's Elvis Merchandiser
Taurus Display Corporation · T.V. Guide
Temporary · Gold

Intel Pentium 4 Processor – M "Yes" Campaign
Rapid Displays · Intel Corporation
Semi-Permanent · Silver

Staple's 4 Sided CD Stomper/After Burner Display
Justman Packaging & Display · Avery Dennison
Temporary · Bronze

GALLERY
COSMETICS

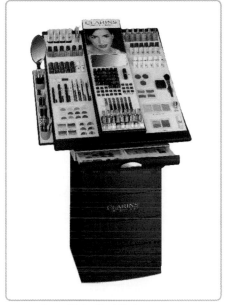

Make-Up General Tester Stand Clarins
Diam International · Clarins
Permanent · Gold

CoverGirl Target Holiday '02
Alliance, A Rock-Tenn Company · Procter & Gamble Cosmetics
Temporary · Bronze

Counter Tester Purple Rain Lancome
Diam International · Lancome International
Semi-Permanent · Gold

CoverGirl Wal-Mart Spring Endcap '02
Alliance, A Rock-Tenn Company
Procter & Gamble Cosmetics
Temporary · Bronze

Color Station Estee Lauder Make-Up Tester
Diam International · Estee Lauder
Permanent · Silver

GALLERY

RETAIL STORES
C-STORE, SUPERMARKET, DRUG STORE, MASS MERCH, OTHER

Walgreens Power End
Masterack Division/A Leggett & Platt Company
Pepsi-Cola
Permanent · Bronze

Energizer Port 2
Trans World Marketing · Energizer
Permanent · Bronze

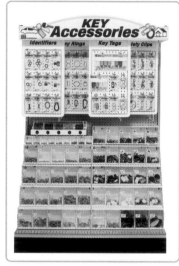

The Accessorizer
PFI Displays · Hy-Ko Products
Permanent · Silver

360 PowerZone Cooler
Masterack Division/A Leggett & Platt Company
Coca-Cola
Permanent · Silver

Gillette Brookshire Checkout Display
New Dimensions Research Corp. · Duracell
Semi-Permanent · Silver

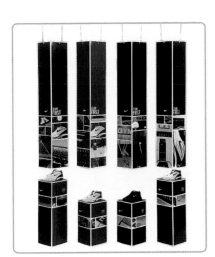

Finish Line Men and Women's Basketball Window
Rapid Displays • Finish Line
Temporary • Silver

<u>Display of The Year Award</u>

io Personal Digital Pen Interactive Endcap
Protagon Display Inc. • Logitech
Semi-Permanent • Gold

Eclipse Flash Strips
Counter Display
Henschel-Steinau, Inc.
The Wm. Wrigley Jr. Company
Semi-Permanent • Bronze

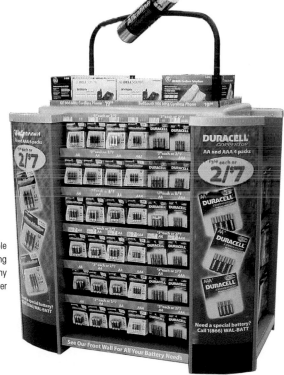

Walgreens Battery Table
AGI Schultz Merchandising
Walgreen Company
Permanent • Silver

Wal-Mart Power Station
New Dimensions Research Corp. • Duracell
Temporary • Bronze

GALLERY
ENTERTAINMENT

Microsoft Xbox Interactive Display
DCI Marketing ▪ Microsoft
Permanent ▪ Silver

Big Idea Penguins 4
Rapid Displays ▪ Big Idea
Temporary ▪ Silver

Sony Psych Launch
Trans world Marketing ▪ Sony Electronics
Semi-Permanent ▪ Bronze

Xbox Blinx Standee
Rapid Displays ▪ Microsoft Corporation
Temporary ▪ Gold

Cinderella II Dreams Come True Half Stack
Smurfit-Stone-Cameo Container
Buena Vista Home Entertainment
Temporary ▪ Silver

Elvis 30 #1 Hits Merchandising Program
Einson Freeman Inc. ▪ RCA Music Group
Temporary ▪ Gold

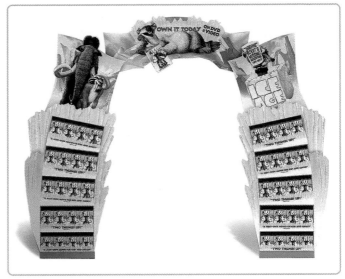

Ice Age Canadian Arch
Smurfit-Stone Display Group ▪ Twentieth Century Fox
Temporary ▪ Bronze

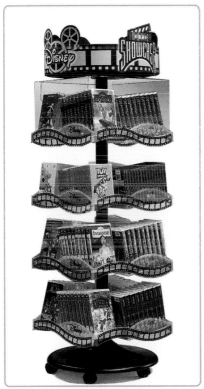

The Disney Monstrous Winter Spectacular Spinner
The Niven Marketing Group ▪ Disney
Permanent ▪ Bronze

Disney Toys R Us
Design Phase, Inc. ▪ Buena Vista Home Entertainment
Permanent ▪ Gold

GALLERY
FRAGRANCES

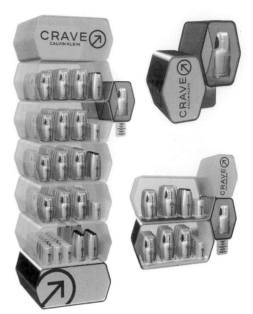

Calvin Klein Crave Fragrance Launch Program
The Royal Promotion Group, Inc. • Unilever Cosmetics International
Permanent • Silver

Elizabeth Arden Green Tea Display
Smyth Displays • Elizabeth Arden
Temporary • Gold

Lancome Tresor Fragrance
Counter Unit
Diam International • Lancome
Permanent • Bronze

Coty Rimmel Fragrance Millenium Tester/Merchandiser
Diam International • Coty Rimmel
Permanent • Bronze

Coty Rimmel Fragrance Promotional Counter Display
Diam International • Coty Rimmel
Semi-Permanent • Bronze

Calgon Plug-In Display
Pride Container Corp., a member of The Strive Group
Coty, Inc.
Temporary • Bronze

GALLERY
GROCERY

Sunkist Go Nuts Pistachio Display
Justman Packaging & Display · Paramount Farms
Temporary · Gold

General Mills – Signature Breads Program
DCI Marketing · General Mills
Permanent · Silver

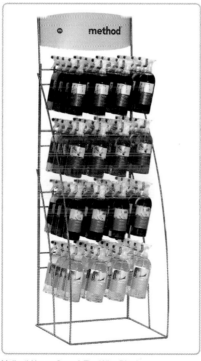

Method Home Care 4 Tier Wire Display
Rapid Displays · Method Home Care
Semi-Permanent · Gold

Cat Treat Variety Display
Smurfit-Stone Display Group · Nestle Purina Petcare Company
Temporary · Silver

GALLERY
HAIR AND SKIN CARE

Chapstick Powerwing
TMI/RDI (Riccarr Displays Inc.)
Wyeth Consumer Healthcare
Permanent · Silver

Roc Counter Display
Smurfit Stone Display Group · Personal Products Company
Temporary · Silver

Alterna Enzymetherapy Merchandiser
Rapid Displays · Katherine Frank Creative
Permanent · Gold

L'Oréal USA Couleur Experte Hair Kiosk
Array · L'Oréal USA
Semi-Permanent · Gold

Kerastase Solaire Counter Display
Diam International · Kerastase
Permanent · Silver

GALLERY
HEALTH CARE

Wyeth Consumer Healthcare Cough/Cold Unit
TMI/RID (Riccar Displays Inc.)
Wyeth Consumer healthcare
Permanent • Bronze

Listerine Pocket Paks
Front End Counter Unit
Rand Display International
Pfizer, Inc.
Permanent • Bronze

Display of The Year Award
Tylenol Floor Display
Artisan Complete
McNeil Consumer Healthcare
Temporary • Gold

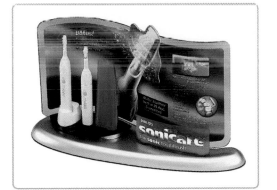

Phillips Oral Healthcare Sonicare Club Display
Gage In-Store • Phillips Oral Healthcare
Permanent • Silver

Claritan Launch
Floor Display/Powerwing
Henschel-Steinau, Inc.
Schering-Plough Healthcare
Temporary • Silver

GALLERY
HOME AND GARDEN

Display of The Year Award

Black & Decker Project Place
Alliance, A Rock-Tenn Company
Black & Decker
Permanent · Gold

PPG/Menards Stain Display
Frank Mayer & Associates
PPG Architectural Finishes
Permanent · Bronze

Dutch Boy Twist & Pour
Merchandising Program
Cormark, Inc.
Sherwin-Williams Company
Semi-Permanent · Bronze

Grainger Nascar Lighting Products Display
Great Northern Corporation-Display Group · Grainger Inc.
Temporary · Bronze

Bruce Hardwood Floors Vista Selling System
Harbor Industries, Inc. · Armstrong Wood Products/Bruce Hardwood Floors
Permanent · Gold

Bic/Luminere 24pc Counter Display
Triangle Display Group Division of
Menasha Packaging Co. LLC · Bic Corporation
Temporary · Silver

GALLERY
LIQUOR

Jack Daniels Holiday 2002
Rapid Displays ▪ Brown Foreman/DraftWorldWide
Temporary ▪ Silver

Robert Mondavi Winery
Luxury Brand 4 Case Display
Ruszel Woodworks
Robert Mondaxi Winery
Semi-Permanent ▪ Gold

Redwood Creek Island
Vintage Wood ▪ E & J Gallo Winery
Permanent ▪ Bronze

Moet & Chandon Holiday Display
MBH Presentations, Inc. ▪ Schieffelin & Somerset
Temporary ▪ Bronze

Khalua Holiday Bottle Pole Display
Bish Creative Display, Inc. ▪ Allied Domecq
Temporary ▪ Silver

GALLERY
MULTINATIONAL

Dove Shampoo Freestanding
Display (Audi)
Armo POP, S.C
Unilver de México S.A. de C.V.
(HPC Division)
Semi-Permanent · Silver

Xbox Interactive Floorstand
APTO Frank Mayer · Microsoft-Mexico
Permanent · Gold

Campbell's Shelves for V8 and Splash, Clock
APTO Frank Mayer · Campbell's de México, S.A. de C.V.
Semi-Permanent · Bronze

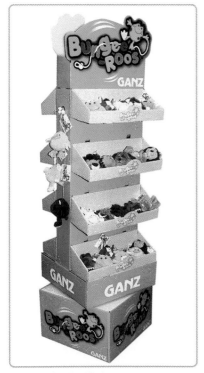

Nestle' Island Display
Meridian Display
& Merchandising
Nestle' Puerto Rico
Temporary · Bronze

Bungeroos Rotating Display
Smurfit-Image Pac Display Group · Ganz
Temporary · Gold

GALLERY
PERSONAL PRODUCTS

Timberland Kids New Product Boot Display
RTC Industries ▪ Timberland
Permanent ▪ Silver

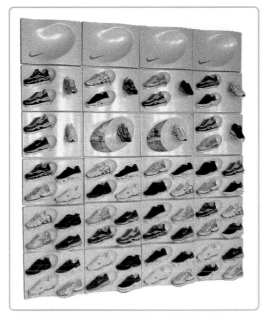

Nike Women's Footwear Wall
Cormark, Inc. ▪ Vehicle 3P
Permanent ▪ Gold

Rogers V101 Floor Display
Artisan Complete
Rogers AT&T Wireless
Temporary ▪ Bronze

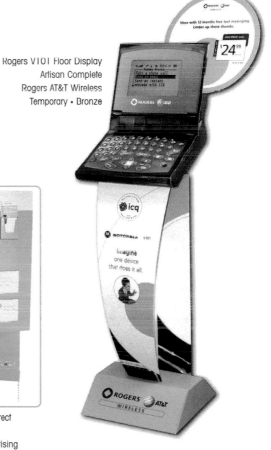

Adidas FootAction USA Tmac Banner
Rapid Displays ▪ Adidas America
Temporary ▪ Silver

AT&T Wireless Indirect
Cylinder Standee
WhiteRunkle Advertising
AT&T Wireless
Semi-Permanent ▪ Bronze

GALLERY
SNACKS

Pepsi Gillette Stadium Display Builder
Tracy Locke Partnership · Pepsi Bottling Group
Semi-Permanent · Bronze

Coca-Cola Ice Pail Cooler
Masterack Division/A Leggett & Platt Company
Coca-Cola
Permanent · Bronze

Dentyne Ice Hotel
Applied Merchandising Concepts, Inc
Adams Division of Pfizer
Semi-Permanent · Gold

Pepsi Memorial Day
Rapid Displays · Pepsi-Cola
Temporary · Bronze

Anheuser-Busch 180 Ten Case Bin
Baird Display · Anheuser-Busch
Temporary · Silver

Jolly Rancher Active Counter Display
Artisan Complete · Hershey Canada Inc.
Permanent · Silver

Trident Franchise Family
Alliance, A Rock-Tenn Company
Adams, a division of Pfizer
Semi-Permanent · Bronze

Keebler Halloween
"Haunted Elfin Manor"
Launch Creative Marketing
Packaging Corp. of America
Temporary • Gold

Pringles Wal-Mart
Checkout Powerwing
Array
Procter & Gamble CDA
Permanent • Silver

Pepsi-Cola Race Car
Bedframe/Merchandiser
The Display Connection
Pepsi-Cola
Semi-Permanent • Silver

Kraft Foods Back
To School Bus
Smurfit-Stone Display Group
Kraft Foods-Nabisco
Temporary • Gold

Keebler Cheez-it Shop Around Display
SMP Display & Design Group • Keebler Company
Permanent • Bronze

GALLERY
TOBACCO

Pall Mall Motion Spinner
Rapid Displays • Brown and Williamson
Semi-Permanent • Bronze

Winston S2 Spinning Swoop
ImageWorks Display & Marketing Group, Inc.
RJ Reynolds Tobacco Company
Semi-Permanent • Gold

Dunhill Metal Pack
Display Counter
Shorewood Display
Lane Limited
Temporary • Bronze

Kool Lightning Packs
Benchmarc Display, Inc.
Brown & Williamson Tobacco Corporation
Permanent • Gold

Salem Lighter Display
CorrFlex Display & Packaging • RJ Reynolds Tobacco Company
Temporary • Gold

GALLERY

TOYS AND ACCESSORIES

The Sweet Magic Kitchen
Interactive Shelf Display
Darko, Inc.
Fisher-Price
Permanent • Bronze

Rechargeable Battery
Floor Display
Artisan Complete
Energizer Canada Inc.
Temporary • Gold

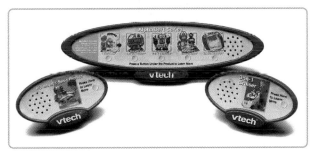

Audio Displays for Vtech
Design Phase, Inc. • Vtech Electronics of North America L.L.C.
Semi-Permanent • Gold

Publications International
Interactive Book Kiosk
Henschel-Steinau, Inc.
Publications International, LTD.
Permanent • Silver

Kodak Picture Kit Floorstand
Mechtronics • Eastman Kodak Company
Semi-Permanent • Bronze

SPORTS EQUIPMENT

Cobra Golf 36 & 18 Metal Wood Displays
NIR Incorporated · Cobra Golf/Acushnet
Permanent · Silver & Bronze

FootJoy 8 Dozen Glove Floor Display
Henschel-Steinau, Inc. · Acushnet Company
Temporary · Bronze

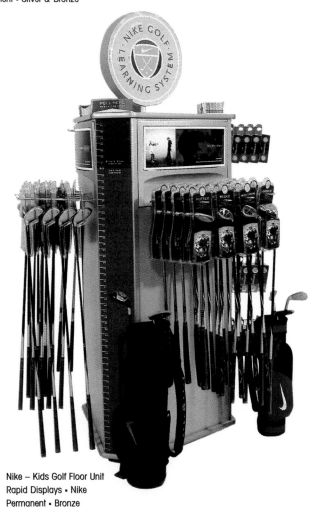

Nike – Kids Golf Floor Unit
Rapid Displays · Nike
Permanent · Bronze

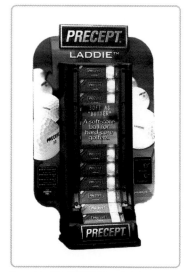

Precept Laddie Golf Ball Counter Display
Gage In-Store · Bridgestone Sports USA
Semi-Permanent · Bronze

GALLERY
TRANSPORTATION

Hyundai Literature Display
R/P Creative Sales, Inc.
Hyundai Motor American
Permanent • Bronze

Kumho Tire Display
Meridian Display & Merchandising
ST & P Communications
Temporary • Bronze

Hyundai Motor America Dealer Showroom Display
Innovative Marketing Solutions, Inc.
Hyundai Motor America, Inc.
Permanent • Silver

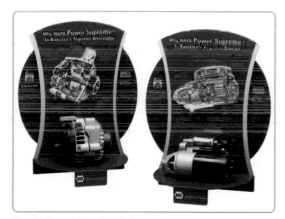

Napa Starter and Alternator Display
Rapid Displays • Napa
Permanent • Bronze

Infiniti Paint and Fabric Display
DCI Marketing • Nissan North America
Permanent • Gold

GALLERY
SERVICES, SIGNAGE, AND SALES PROMOTION

McDonald's 100 Years of Disney
Rapid Displays ▪ McDonald's/IMS
Temporary ▪ Gold

Blizzard® Cup Identification/Directional Sign
The Howard Company ▪ International Dairy Queen
Permanent ▪ Silver

ABSOLUT Vodka – Candle Menus
G2 Worldwide ▪ The Absolut Spirits Company
Temporary ▪ Gold

Pucker Neon
Everbrite, Inc. ▪ Jim Beam Brands
Permanent ▪ Gold

"The challenge for

the display producer is

to understand the entire

spectrum of point-of-purchase

display manufacturing processes

so that they may make

better decisions to meet

the customer's needs."

Display Production
Methods
and Materials

EDWARD C. WHITE, CHAIRMAN
E AND E DISPLAY GROUP

INTRODUCTION

If you ever have the opportunity to visit a manufacturer of P-O-P advertising displays, you will be impressed at the engineering and manufacturing complexities required to construct these displays that play one of the most powerful roles in the movement of goods around the globe.

The challenge of understanding the manufacturing process of either simple or complicated displays is underscored by the vast array of different designs, production methods, and materials utilized by the P-O-P industry to build eye-catching and effective point-of-purchase advertising displays. This chapter discusses these complexities and presents the challenges faced by both manufacturers and producers of point-of-purchase advertising displays.

This chapter covers two major elements affecting P-O-P advertising design:

• Different processes and materials that are used in manufacturing displays.

• How designers and manufacturers chose the specific process or material to produce each display.

While the point-of-purchase advertising industry in not generally regarded as a high-technology industry, it is a "volume-tech" industry. It utilizes an array of different materials and industrial design methods to create P-O-P advertising displays in large quantities that are distributed around the world. P-O-P design and manufacturing teams must know how to apply various technologies and design methods in the manufacturing process to successfully and efficiently produce these displays in large quantities.

For example, it is not necessary to understand the chemical makeup of certain plastics to use them. The plastic manufacturers provide clear guidelines on the best adhesives, or the best temperature to mold plastic, or the type of saw blades to use in processing their materials. The challenge facing point-of-purchase advertising display companies today is to utilize these materials in creative and innovative ways so that can they can provide P-O-P clients/customers the competitive edge they need in the marketplace.

ANALYZING THE DISPLAY PROJECT

There are many ways to manufacture a P-O-P advertising display and achieve similar results. The process chosen by the manufacturer may be based on several factors:

• Quantity.

• Budget per display.

• Tooling cost.

• Aesthetic appearance desired.

• Manufacturing capabilities of the producer.

• Designer's knowledge of different processes.

The quantity required and project's budget will quickly start directing the producer toward the manufacturing processes that are feasible given the resources available. This would also include the tooling cost, which is amortized over the quantity of displays ordered to arrive at the total cost of the display.

Another defining factor is the aesthetic appearance specified by the client. If the desired look is soft and feminine, the processes and materials that will help achieve that look are selected to appeal to these emotions. Display producers know that some plastics, such as polypropylene, have an industrial look when processed, while others, such as frosted acrylic, can be fabricated to convey an elegant appearance.

Another reason to choose a specific processing method could be that the manufacturer has the capability to produce the display component in-house instead of outsourcing to another manufacturer. Of course, a designer may select a manufacturer and process simply because of familiarity or comfort in going in another direction.

DECIDING WHICH PROCESS OR MATERIAL TO USE

Someone once said, "Necessity is the mother of invention." Today, that statement could be restated as, "Cost cutting is the mother of invention." It is true with any of the P-O-P production processes and materials covered in this chapter. The challenge facing point-of-purchase designers today is that customers are demanding displays be produced more quickly and at a lower cost. When cars were first invented, they were cumbersome, slow, and broke down often. Now they are fast, comfortable, and may be driven 100,000 miles or more without major repair. Machines used in processing displays have progressed in the same manner; many have computerized adjustments and operations that allow quick setups and much higher accuracy.

Answering the following questions will help narrow down the type of materials and the processes used in the manufacturing of displays:

1. What is the aesthetic look desired?

The desired appearance will depend greatly upon the product, retail setting, and promotional theme. The overall aesthetic look one is trying to achieve will help to determine the materials and manufacturing processes considered in designing and producing the display.

2. In what setting will the display be used?

A department store, specialty gift store, sporting goods shop, and pet store all require different design parameters. Some retailers draw upon their experience and specify which materials they want a manufacturer to use in building their displays. In some cases, they could be concerned about durability, while in others a consistent look across stores is the objective. In situations in which multiple manufacturers are producing modular portions of the display system, coordination among suppliers and maintaining close tolerances across the "display components list" are essential.

3. What is the desired life span of the display?

To what elements will the display be exposed? Direct sunlight, moisture, heat, and cold are environmental factors that could have an impact on the effectiveness of the display. A display that looks battered or faded, suggesting that the product itself may be old or not fresh, can actually discourage a consumer from purchasing the product. How much physical contact will the display need to endure? How long will the retailer allow the display to remain in the store without requiring a "new" or fresh look?

4. What is the client willing to spend?

A display is a sales tool and must justify its existence by a return on the original investment. Will the display be used for a weekend promotion or for several years? The amount of product expected to be sold from the display will need to be calculated with these questions in mind. The percentage of advertising cost allotted to the product sold will determine how much money can be invested into the display. This budget then helps determine what manufacturing process and/or materials can be used. Determining a justifiable cost up front helps the designer and producer create a display that will meet the customer's needs within a desired budget.

5. What quantity of duplicate parts is going to be produced?

The total quantity of displays produced may not determine the manufacturing process as much as the number of duplicate parts. For example, only 500 of a certain display are going to be produced. If one of the components, such as a shelf or bracket, is used 20 times on a display, 10,000 such parts are required. A quantity of this volume may allow a more automated and cost-effective piece of equipment to be used.

QUANTITY AND BUDGET

The quantity of displays required by the client will have a large effect on what type of manufacturing process is used. Many small-quantity orders are frequently hand-fabricated and assembled. The tooling cost for small orders may not be very expensive but, when amortized over the small quantity of displays produced, tooling costs can add up to a sizable percentage of the total cost of the display. On large-quantity orders, manufacturers will utilize high-speed equipment, when possible, to save time and money. High-speed equipment can require a substantial investment in tooling. Yet when compared with a slower manufacturing process, the tooling will pay for itself with a substantially lower cost per part.

HOW VOLUME EFFECTS UNIT COST AND TOOLING COST

The examples in Figure 7-1 illustrate the effects that quantity and tooling can have on the cost of a display.

The brand marketer who needs only 100 displays and a relatively small quantity would have to spend a total of $25,000 to achieve their P-O-P advertising display requirements. Increasing the quantity ordered to achieve a lower per unit cost per P-O-P piece

	WIRE DISPLAY	PLASTIC DISPLAY
Quantity:	100	10,000
Tooling Jig Cost:	$100 – $200	$100,000 – $200,000
Manufacturing Method:	Spot-welded	Injection-molded
Tooling Costs Amortized over Quantity:	$1.00 – $2.00 (per display)	$1.00 – $2.00 (per display)
Cost of Unit:	$250 each	$25 each

Figure 7-1
Effect of Quantity
and Tooling on
Display Cost

may just not be an option for the smaller company. National brand marketers can increase their selling margins by selling through multiple channels, thus lowering their P-O-P production cost per store.

MANUFACTURING PROCESS OVERVIEW

There are many manufacturing methods available to produce a point-of-purchase display. Most display companies build their business around one or two basic material groups and limit the scope of their manufacturing processes to developing expertise in these materials. There are only a small number of display companies that can manufacture in-house utilizing a wide variety of materials. The production processes listed in the following sections have been around for several years. Technology has helped in increasing productivity, lowering cost, and improving the quality of displays produced. Modern technology has also enabled the display producer to mass-produce complex forms that simply were not feasible previously. As production technology continues to evolve, it will offer the P-O-P industry more ways to mold, cut, glue, decorate, and assemble an advertising display.

PLASTIC-PROCESSING METHODS

It would be impossible to give a detailed description of each of these processes in the space allotted to this chapter. However, after reviewing the brief descriptions of the process and guidelines on when certain processes are used, you will have a basic understanding of why a manufacturing process is used.

Following are descriptions of some of the basic methods used to mold or shape plastic:

• *Fabricating:* Cutting, heat bending, gluing, and assembling sheet plastic into a display by hand. The plastic is formed by using a hot wire or a quartz lamp with a thin hot light directed at the area to be bent As the plastic begins to soften, the sheet of plastic is clamped in a jig and bent by hand to the proper angle. The parts can then be glued together or assembled to develop the display. Graphics can then be added by screen printing, hot foil stamping, or mounting with offset lithography labels. Hand fabricating of plastic displays is commonly limited to small quantities because it is time consuming.

Figure 7-2

Four-station rotary

vacuum former

Figure 7-3

Display with vacuum

formed trays and base

with steel tube column

Figure 7-4

Spectra 500-ton

injection molder

• ***Vacuum Forming:*** Heating either a sheet or roll of plastic until it is pliable and then formed by pulling a vacuum through the mold so that the plastic conforms to the shape of the mold. Vacuum forming stretches the sheet of plastic; depending on how much it is stretched, it will vary in thickness in different areas of the part. The mold can be made out of wood or epoxy for short runs but usually is made in cast aluminum for longer runs Tubes are cast in the mold to allow water to be run through them to keep the mold at a constant temperature during the manufacturing process. Without the water cooling the tubes, the mold would absorb heat from each sheet of plastic formed on it, and eventually the hot mold would keep the plastic from cooling and solidifying to the desired shape. See Figure 7-2 for a picture of a vacuum forming machine and Figure 7-3 for a display produced using vacuum forming.

• ***Pressure Forming:*** Similar to vacuum forming, but with a pressure box added, to improve the level of detail and texture attainable through ambient air pressure alone. Along with pulling a vacuum through the mold, additional air pressure is applied to help push the plastic into tight corners or around text or logos for a better impression. Pressure forming can also help in maintaining the overall consistency of the thickness of the part.

• ***Injection Molding:*** Heating pellets of plastic until they can be injected into a two-part mold under tons of pressure. The plastic is allowed to cool, and the mold is separated to remove the part. If the same amount of plastic is injected into the mold each time, the results will be identical parts that can be molded in close tolerance. Molds are usually milled out of thick, heavy tool steel. Because of the molds' cost, this process is usually used for large-volume runs. See Figure 7-4 for a picture of an injection molding machine and Figure 7-5 for a display produced using injection molding.

• **Rotational Molding:** Pellets of plastic are placed in a two-part clam-style mold cavity. Usually, the machine has three or four arms with one or several molds on each arm. The arms are rotated first into a furnace where the mold is rotated slowly. The plastic pellets melt and coat the inside of the mold. The arms are then rotated. While one arm will be filled with pellets, one arm will be in the furnace and the third arm will be sprayed with water to cool and solidify the part. The arms are rotated again where the part is removed, and more pellets are placed in the mold. The most common materials used in this process are polypropylene and polyethylene. These are tough plastics that are resilient and can withstand water, chemicals, and exterior conditions. See Figure 7-6 for a picture of a rotational molding machine and Figure 7-7 for a display produced using rotational molding.

Figure 7-5

Injection-molded

display

Figure 7-6

Three-station

rotational molding

machine

Figure 7-7

Rotational-molded

polypropylene

display

Figure 7-8

A row of profile

extruders

WELEX INCORPORATED

DAYSPRING CARDS AND E AND E DISPLAY GROUP

• **_Profile Extrusions:_** Plastic pellets are heated until they are melted and can be extruded or pushed through a die in the profile shape desired. The continuous profile is then run through a water bath, sprayed with a water mist, or allowed to cool with ambient air. During the cooling process, the extruded part may be helped to hold its shape with cooling blocks. The extruded profile is then cut to the desired length. The part can be extruded to any length, but the width and height of the part is limited by the size of the extruder's barrel and how much plastic it can push out. Profile extrusions can be produced in clear or opaque plastics and in an unlimited number of shapes. Extrusions have been used as decorative trim, protective trim, support columns, shelving, shelf lips, shelf dividers, and plastic slatwall, to name a few. Figure 7-8 depicts a row of profile extruders and Figure 7-9 is a display produced using plastic extrusions.

• **_Flexible Mold Casting:_** A two-part plastic resin is mixed, which starts a catalytic reaction where the plastic begins to solidify and harden. Before the resin hardens, it is poured into a flexible mold. After the resin hardens, the mold is pulled back and the part is removed. This is a slow process used mainly for small-quantity or very complex parts. The molds are relatively inexpensive.

Figure 7-9

Display with plastic extruded columns

and clear heat bent acrylic pockets

WHICH PLASTIC PROCESS IS BEST TO USE?

Because of the flexibility of manufacturing with plastics, the options seem almost endless and sometimes confusing. Figure 7-10 offers an overall comparison of the different process costs. Note that the figures are guidelines and can vary according to the size of the part, the complexity of the part, and the material used. It is very similar to asking, "How much does a car cost?" Well, are you asking about a Volkswagen or a Mercedes? However, it is possible to give some ranges so that one has a benchmark to compare processes for choosing one over another.

Figure 7-10

Plastic Processing

Methods and Costs

PROCESS	TOOLING COSTS	QUANTITIES	PART PRICE	CYCLE TIME
Injection Molding	$20,000–$250,000	10,000–1,000,000	$.25–$2.00	30–60 seconds
Vacuum Forming In-line or Roll	$5,000–$25,000	25,000–1,000,000	$.50–$2.00	5–45 seconds
Profile Extrusions	$2,500–$5,000	2,500–100,000	$.25–$2.00	10–30 feet/minute
Vacuum Forming Sheet	$2,500–$5,000	250–10,000	$2.00–$25.00	1–2 minutes
Pressure Forming	$5,000–$7,500	1,000–10,000	$2.00–$25.00	1–2 minutes
Rotational Molding	$4,000–$12,000	2,500–20,000	$5.00–$100.00	10–15 minutes
Plastic Fabrication	$50–$150 jig	100–1,000	$20.00–$300.00	10–60 minutes
Flexible Mold Casting	$150–$350	100–500	$2.00–$25.00	30–60 minutes

Note: The above figures are very rough guidelines and can vary according to the size of the part, the complexity of the part, and the material used.

PLASTIC MATERIALS

Plastics have been developed with different characteristics to fit different needs. Acrylic looks like glass, and styrene looks like granite rock. Metallic fleck can be added, or the surface can be printed to look like wood. Described below are some of the basic plastics, which can be modified to take on several different appearances. These are general categories, without going into the chemical compounds.

> **Styrenes:** Styrene plastics used for display components are usually opaque. Color pigments can be added to obtain almost any color, including fluorescent. There are also translucent and clear styrene plastics, which tend to be brittle. For example, some textured fluorescent light fixture covers are injection molded out of translucent styrene. Plastic compounds can be added to styrene to increase its resilience.
>
> • *ABS (acrylonitrile butadiene styrene):* Styrene with a "rubber"-type compound added, ABS has "very good" resistance to breakage.
>
> • *HIPS (high-impact polystyrene):* Less expensive than ABS but less resilient, HIPS has "good" resistance to breakage.
>
> • *Styrene:* Economical, more brittle, good for low-impact uses.

Acrylics: Acrylic can be purchased in pellets or in sheet form and is often used as a substitute for glass. Acrylic is much lighter and, if broken, is much less a safety hazard in comparison to glass. Traditionally, acrylic sheets have been clear, white, or black. Now they can be obtained in a multitude of opaque and translucent colors. In the past few years, translucent color pigments have been added to achieve a neon fluorescent appearance, and a green tint has been added to acrylic to emulate the look of plate glass. Suppliers continue to develop new acrylic resin mixtures, one of the newest being a speckled acrylic with a granite appearance.

Break-Resistant Plastics:

- *Polycarbonate:* Well-known under brand names like Lexan® or Tuffak®, polycarbonate can be opaque but has been used in a clear form to replace acrylic. It is extremely tough and resists breakage.

- *Polyethylene:* A very resilient plastic used for high-interaction applications, polyethylene has a low-luster surface and is difficult to glue or decorate. It has a waxy feel. Most quart oil bottles and gallon milk containers are molded from polyethylene.

- *Polypropylene:* A very durable plastic that is resistant to moisture and chemicals, polypropylene has a high luster surface and can be glued, painted, hot-foil stamped, or decorated in other ways.

- *PETG (polyethylene terephthalate glycol):* A very resilient plastic that can be clear or opaque, PETG can be sawed, drilled, screwed into, and even stapled through. It is more flexible than acrylic and may need to be formed to achieve the rigidity desired. One-liter beverage bottles are produced out of PET, which is a very similar material.

WOOD-PROCESSING METHODS

Technology has also improved production efficiency in processing wood. Computer-programmable saws, routers, drills, and specialty equipment are commonly used. This automatic equipment cuts, drills, routes, rotates, and trims with great speed and accuracy. The following are some of the processes used in producing a wooden display.

- *Cutting/Shaping:* Wood can be cut or shaped with traditional table saws, band saws, panel saws, and routers. Figure 7-11 and Figure 7-12 show computerized saws and routers that allow for multiple sheets to be cut at one time at remarkable speeds. CNC (computer numerically controlled) equipment can often be programmed to do multiple processes. Some equipment is essentially a robot with cutting tools that can rotate on five axes. Other equipment has multiple heads that change bits or cutters automatically and can cut, shape, or drill at any angle. Instead of cutting out parts and then moving them to another workstation where holes are drilled in them, then moving the parts to another workstation where the

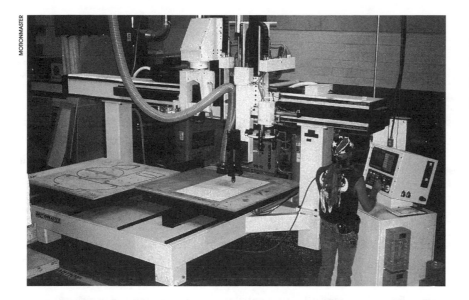

Figure 7-11

Five-axis Computer

Numerical Control

(CNC) router

edges are shaped, the computerized equipment will do all of this and deliver a completed display part.

In the past, to process 100 displays, all the pieces would be cut and manufactured and then assembled. Now, with computer-programmed equipment, all the necessary parts for one or more displays can quickly and efficiently be cut, routed, drilled, and then assembled. Depending on the size of the order and the complexity of the display, this can be an efficient way to produce an order.

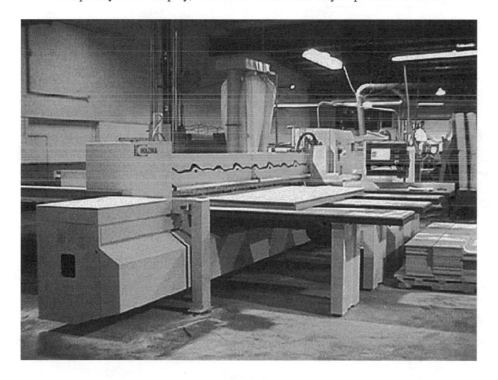

Figure 7-12

Computerized-panel

saw—a built-in

computer helps

calculate the best

utilization of the

material

• *Fabricating:* Natural wood or wood composites are favored materials to work with because of the ease of fabrication. Standard wood-working equipment can be used to drill, nail, screw, and staple or glue components together. Wood can also be combined easily with other materials, such as steel and plastic, with the same fasteners.

• *Finishing:* Wood can be stained, painted, curtain-coated, sandblasted, textured, or covered with low- or high-pressure laminate. The edges can be laminated with edge banding or covered with plastic or rubber "T" molding, or aluminum moldings, or cut with a rounded or decorative shape. "T" molding can be seen on the edges of many lunchroom or restaurant tables.

WOOD MATERIALS

Wood has been used in manufacturing displays since the late 1800s. Some of the first displays produced were the carved wooden Indians that held plugs of tobacco and cigars. Wood is a versatile material that can be obtained in a variety of formats including natural solid woods, laminated plywood, or wood chips compressed into particleboard, fiberboard, or hardboard. Today, many displays and store fixtures have their basic structure built from wood or wood composites that are either painted or covered with a high- or low-pressure laminate. The following are some of the wood and wood composites used in displays today.

Figure 7-13
Display produced
from MDF

THOMAS NELSON PUBLISHING AND E AND E DISPLAY GROUP

• *Particleboard:* Small chips of wood bonded together with a resin. The most common size is a sheet 49 × 97 inches, from $1/4$ up to $1\text{-}1/2$ inches thick. Some mills will run sheets up to 60 × 144 inches. The surface is smooth but has very porous edges that do not paint well. Particleboard is economical and most commonly used for support structures on the interior of a point-of-purchase display. It can be obtained in low-, medium-, and high-density grades. Low-density particleboard is more likely to be used in shipping crates than in a display.

• *MDF (medium density fiberboard):* Fine particles of wood bonded together with a resin. The surface is smoother than particleboard and can be sawed, drilled, glued, and painted like regular hard or soft woods. MDF is more expensive than particleboard but substantially less expensive than natural woods. Although MDF has a higher density than particleboard, its porosity still makes the edges difficult to paint. Double-refined MDF was developed to provide an edge that accepts paint better than regular MDF. MDF is available in 49×97 inches up to 60×120 inches, in thicknesses of $1/4$ up to 2 inches. A very dense and heavy MDF board is made especially for producing slatwall. A lightweight MDF that cuts the weight of regular MDF almost in half is used when weight is a design issue. See Figure 7-13 for an example of a display produced with MDF.

• *Hardboards:* Similar to MDF but less dense and produced in thicknesses of $1/8$ to $3/8$ inch, and available in 48×96-inch sheets. Hardboards can be "tempered" or impregnated with a resin that hardens the board and produces a smooth surface that is less absorbent and can be painted. They can be obtained with one or both of the surfaces smooth. Hardboards are often run through a perforator where $1/8$- or $1/4$- inch holes are punched on 1-inch centers. The perforated board is then used in displays to hold peg hooks.

• *Plywood:* Multiple layers of thin wood laminated together at 90-degree angles to form a very strong board that is resistant to warping. Plywood can be purchased with a fir outer layer or with a veneer of birch, oak, cherry, or other special woods.

• *Natural woods:* Nothing beats the beauty of natural woods. Popular woods used in displays include oak, maple, poplar, pine, and birch

METAL-PROCESSING METHODS

Cutting: Just as in the case of plastic and wood materials, computerized equipment is helping to advance efficiency and quality in the metal-forming industry. Large computerized "nibblers" can punch holes or stamp out shapes or cut a complex pattern out of sheet metal. Lasers are also used to cut repetitive shapes, graphics, or logos in a display panel. A design that previously could have been cost-prohibitive is now affordable with the use of a computer-controlled cutter or laser. In most cases computerized equipment requires programming. As a result, the equipment is used primarily for large-quantity repetitive projects. In the future, as computerized equipment gets easier to program, it will be used for short-run orders also.

Forming and Fabricating: Besides the traditional punch presses, press brakes, and wire benders, computerized equipment has been developed to produce parts with little or no special tooling. Parts for a wire display with multiple bends can now be programmed and produced without expensive tooling or jigs. Metal parts can be fastened together by rivets, nuts and bolts, screws, or special fasteners. Certain metals can be bonded together by heating the parts until they melt together. This is called spot (or resistance) welding. Other welding methods use special gasses and/or filler materials to adhere parts together and include

• *Brazing*—used on brass, copper, or bronze

• *TIG (tungsten inert gas) or gas tungsten arc welding*—used on aluminum and stainless steel and in close-tolerance carbon steel work

• *MIG (metal inert gas) or gas metal arc welding*—used on aluminum or steel, wire-fed for fast production welding

• *Stick arc welding electrodes*—uses a handheld welding rod for small-volume jobs.

Computerized welding robots have been designed to do repetitive step welding for producing wire baskets and wire grids.

Finishing: There are several ways to finish metal displays, including plating with zinc, nickel, brass, or chrome. Parts can also be chemically etched, embossed, or textured to develop a brushed aluminum look or repeat pattern. There are several ways to paint metal parts. Parts can dipped in paint, wet sprayed, or electrostatic powder-coated.

Electrostatic-powder coating is the process of charging the metal part with one electrical charge and the powder with the opposite charge. The powder paint is sprayed onto the metal component. The metal part attracts the paint like a magnet. The coated part is then passed through a heat tunnel where the powder paint melts and bonds to the part. In this process less of the painting material is lost or wasted than in a wet-paint process. Depending on the part, this can be a more efficient and environmentally friendly method than spraying with a conventional wet spray system. Textures, "duo tones," and metallic finishes have been developed for powder coating to add a new look and dimension to metal displays. Wood parts can now also be electrostatic powder-coated.

METAL MATERIALS

Metal used for display components comes in all shapes and sizes. Basic metal components include:

• *Sheet metal*—plain, coated, textured, or perforated

• *Flat stock*—bars of steel

• *Wire*—purchased precut to length or in coils, a few thousands in diameter up to $1/4$-inch diameter

• *Rod*—$1/4$ inch in diameter and larger

• *Tubing*—round, square, D-Shaped, or special formed.

Most of the above metal components can also be purchased with baked-on enamel, preprimed to accept paint, or plated with several coatings.

PAPER-PROCESSING METHODS

Temporary displays are produced with a wide range of manufacturing processes. The first stage is usually to print or mount a preprinted label to the paper substrate. Next, the printed parts are die cut, folded, and glued or stitched. Some displays are partially or fully assembled and packed into a shipping carton. Other displays are shipped out unassembled, to be assembled either in the store or at a fulfillment center.

The following methods describe different processes used to produce a fiberboard or corrugated paperboard display.

Printing Methods: Printing presses are divided into two major categories—sheet fed or web. Sheet-fed presses print on precut sheets loaded into the press. Web presses print on a roll of paper and then either cut it into sheets at the back end of the press or rewind the paper into a roll again. This roll can then be processed and made into corrugated board.

• *Offset Lithography:* Offset lithography is the method used to print books and magazines. The same presses print graphic sheets that are glued to paperboard or plastic for display signage. The printed sheet is often referred to as a "Litho Sheet," or as a "Litho Label" if it is to be laminated to a substrate. Graphics for displays are generally printed on 60# to 80# paper or on an SBS (solid bleached sulfite) board from .010 thick to, for some presses able to handle it, up to .030 inch thick. Offset lithography is based on the fact that water and oil do not mix. Water is applied to the printing plate with a roller. An oil-based ink is applied to the plate with another roller. The image on the plate repels the water but attracts the ink. The ink on the image is transferred to the paper. To print a full-color image, four translucent colors are used—cyan, magenta, yellow, and black. The translucent colors are printed in overlapping dot patterns. The result is thousands of shades of color. The dots are so small (330 dots per inch) that they are very difficult to see without a magnifying glass, blending together and perceived by the eye as a full-color image. This method is referred to as "four-color process" print-

Figure 7-14

Display using offset printed lithography sheets laminated onto corrugated paperboard and foam board

HALLMARK CARDS AND E 3ND E DISPLAY GROUP

ing. Most sheets printed for displays are "overprinted" or coated with a varnish or clear coat to protect the ink. Without this protection the ink can be scuffed or marred when transported or handled. Ultraviolet (UV) light inhibitors are often added to the clear coat for added protection against fading due to sunlight. See Figure 7-14 for a display produced using offset lithography.

• *Flexographic:* Flexographic printing uses a water-based ink with pigment suspended in it. There are both sheet-fed and web flexographic presses. The ink is pumped from a reservoir up to an ink fountain. The ink is transferred by rolls to either a raised image or an etched roller and then to the paper substrate.

• *Rubber Letterpress:* Letterpress ink is a paste about the consistency of whipped butter. The ink can be an oil, glycol or soy base material. The ink is transferred from an ink fountain by rubber rollers to raised image printing

Figure 7-15

UV Silkscreen printer

with micro adjustment

plates and then transferred onto the paper stock. Printing plates were initially cut or molded from rubber. Today many plates are produced from a light-sensitive photo-polymer compound. Light hardens the area exposed and areas not exposed to light are washed away leaving a raised image.

• *Ultraviolet:* UV inks are cured or dried when exposed to an intense UV light. The ink can be applied on a letterpress or screen printer.

• *Screen Printing:* Screen printing was originally called "silk screening" because it was done with silk. Today, nylon or another synthetic fabric is attached tightly to a rectangular wood or aluminum frame. The fabric's pores are coated with a light-sensitive gel. After the gel dries a negative or positive film image is laid on the screen and exposed to an intense light. The gel hardens except in the area of the image. Water is used to wash out the gel in the image area, leaving the porous fab-ric. A rubber squeegee is used to pull thick ink across the screen. The ink is forced through the porous graphic areas and onto the substrate. See Figure 7-15 for an example of a screen printing machine.

Die-Cutting Methods: Die cutters are basically large cookie cutters with sharp-edged steel rule used to cut out the display components. They are divided into two basic sys-tems—flatbed and rotary. Sharp cutting rule is used around the perimeter to cut out the object. Smooth scoring rule is used to create scores or creases where the material will be bent. Small, sponge-rubber blocks are glued to the die board. In the cutting process, the sponge-rubber blocks are compressed. As pressure is released, the sponge rubber blocks help push the material away from the die after it is cut.

• *Flatbed Die Cutters:* Cutting and scoring rules are embedded into a flat sheet of plywood in the shape of the part to be cut. The die board is then bolted to the die cutter. The material is positioned on a platen or flat sheet of steel. The cutting die is pressed through the substrate with tons of pressure while in contact with the steel plate. This creates a cookie-cutter effect, cutting the display part out of the material.

• *Rotary Die Cutters:* Cutting and scoring rules are embedded into a preformed round plywood cylinder. Rotary cutting rule has serrated teeth and acts as scissors. The cutting die cylinder is bolted onto a rotating shaft of the die cutter. Another cylinder is brought into contact with the cutting rule. As the material is fed through the rotating cylinders, the material is cut with a sheering action.

Folding/Gluing/Taping/Stitching: Display components often must be folded and then held in that position. Display bases are folded into a tube, and the seam or "joint" is glued, taped, or stitched. There are wide ranges of machines to automatically or semiautomatically fold display parts. Some folding machines apply cold adhesives, "hot melt" glue, or tape to paperboard.

PAPER MATERIALS

Cardboard: The word "cardboard" is used as a generic term but actually refers to a category of papers. These papers, initially designed for specific industries (e.g., automotive, soft drink, folding cartons, or packaging), have been utilized by the display industry. Figure 7-16 is a short list of some of the paper boards used in producing displays.

Figure 7-16

Common types of paperboard used in P-O-P displays

BOARD TYPE	THICKNESS RANGE	MATERIAL	COMMON USES IN P-O-P DISPLAYS
Chipboard	.010 – .060	Recycled newsprint	Easels, backs of signs
Beverage board	.010 – .030	Recycled newsprint with a white clay surface	Easels, backs of signs
Solid bleached sulfite	.008 – .030	Virgin paper, bleached white and calendered	Die-cut signs, table tents, countertop displays, standees (a smooth surface that is printable)
Poster board	.030 – .125	Recycled Kraft paper with different top layers	Signs, standees
Solid fiber	.020 – .125	Recycled industrial-grade paperboard, laminated to desired thickness	Standees, signs, support parts (often laminated with an offset-printed label)

Corrugated Paperboard: Laymen often refer to corrugated paperboard as "cardboard," as in a "cardboard box." The word "corrugated" comes from the fluted inner liner that gives the board thickness and strength. Corrugated paperboard, also referred to as "corrugated" or "corrugate," can be constructed in many ways. There are different combinations of paper types, flute sizes, and multiple layers to achieve different characteristics.

Figure 7-17 lists the major types of corrugated paperboard used in displays. "B" flute is the most commonly used board for displays. It is strong enough to hold most products, yet still has a good surface for printing. To obtain an even better printing service, "E, F, and G" flutes were invented. However, as the flute becomes thinner, much of the strength is lost and the designer is limited to the size of the display that can be constructed from it without adding more material. The different flutes can be combined to produce special boards. Standard combinations used in displays include B/C, B/E, and E/F. The smaller of the flutes gives the best surface for printing. The larger flute gives the board more rigidity.

Figure 7-17

Common corrugated paperboard flute sizes

FLUTE	THICKNESS	COMMON USES
A flute	$1/4$	For heavy-duty shipping cartons
C flute	$3/16$	For regular shipping cartons
B flute	$1/8$	For most displays
E flute	$3/32$	For small countertop displays and product cartons
F flute	$1/16$	Also called "Micro Flute," for signage and product cartons
G flute	$3/64$	For special effects, can be offset-printed and embossed

CONCLUSION

Although several manufacturing processes and materials have been reviewed in this chapter, only the basic methods and materials used in display design and construction have been discussed. It is important to realize that most displays are manufactured out of multiple materials, utilizing multiple manufacturing processes. To better anticipate the ever-changing demand of the consumer for something new and different, display producers must constantly research new materials or new ways to combine existing materials to catch the eye. In the time it takes to read this chapter, someone will have developed a new way of producing a display or combining new technology with current productions methods to manufacture point-of-purchase displays more quickly. Or, a designer will have discovered a new way to use an existing material. The challenge for you—whether you are a display buyer, a producer, or are in P-O-P display sales—is to understand the entire spectrum of point-of-purchase display manufacturing processes so that you can make better decisions to meet your customer's needs.

"Technology providers are constantly coming up with more bells and whistles. Some are enthusiastically adopted while others fail to deliver on the promise and wind up in the technology pawnshop. With so many choices, and so much hype, how do you know which is which?"

Evaluating Retail Technologies

JEFF SANDGREN, PRINCIPAL
SANDGREN CONSULTING

IN SEARCH OF SOUND SCIENCE

With the accelerated pace of technological advancement showing no sign of abating, any publication that includes an appraisal of the "latest and greatest" retail technologies is doomed to become outdated within a year or two of its appearance. Nevertheless, emerging technologies are an undeniable part of the industry's landscape; they cannot be ignored. Accordingly, rather than attempting to provide a comprehensive appraisal of all new retail technologies, this chapter recommends a framework for considering them and illustrates that approach with some of the currently promising offerings.

There is a story that legendary guitarist Chet Atkins was playing in the studio when someone in the control room said, "Man, that guitar sounds good." Atkins overheard the comment in the talkback monitor, put down his guitar, and asked, "How does the guitar sound now?" In the symphony of point-of-purchase advertising, with CPG manufacturers composing the score and retailers hosting the actual performance, technology provides a wide array of useful instruments—but it is still up to the musicians to make the music.

Technology providers, like instrument manufacturers, are constantly coming up with more bells and whistles (and strings). Some are enthusiastically adopted, because they improve a key area of the business. Others, though they seem promising, often fail to deliver on the promise and wind up in the technology pawnshop. But with so many choices, and so much hype, how do you know which is which?

Figure 8-1

Primary Considerations for Evaluating Technologies

1. Priority of Problem Addressed
2. Potential End-User Benefits
3. Whole Solution Cost
4. Return on Investment
5. Competitive Advantage Gained
6. Proof of Performance/Value
7. Compatibilities/Synergies
8. Workarounds/Best Practices
9. Criteria for Success/Metrics
10. Process Reengineering Impacts

THREE KEY TESTS OF EMERGING POINT-OF-PURCHASE TECHNOLOGY

This chapter addresses the above question in two ways: Three key tests—the People Test, the Pull Test, and the Payback Test—are proposed for evaluating new offerings, and four examples of emerging technologies are provided for application to the about-to-be-real world.

To fully evaluate a new P-O-P technology, many factors must be considered. Figure 8-1 lists ten. While all of these considerations are important, this chapter outlines three essential tests that any new technology must pass—those focused on people, pull, and payback.

THE PEOPLE TEST:
P-O-P TECHNOLOGIES THAT IMPROVE THE IN-STORE EXPERIENCE DESERVE PRIORITY

Manufacturers control funding, retailers control real estate, and shareholders direct priorities—but consumer preference drives all. At the end of the day, it is the shoppers, responding with their purchasing dollars, who determine what sounds good and what sounds flat.

As a result, the most promising opportunities often are those intended to improve the consumers' shopping experience. HDTV plasma screens are among the new, in-store technologies that present product commercials and additional consumer-driven programming to attract attention to the brand marketer's selling message. Interactive kiosks also provide consumers with user-friendly experiences and enhance their shopping choices.

Whether it is discovering exciting new products, special offers, bargain prices, or simply the reassurance of a trusted brand, the key events that add up to a positive in-store experience form the essential foundation for customer preference and loyalty—to brands and to retailers. As such, these same elements of the in-store experience represent to their retailers and brand marketers a potentially sustainable source of competitive advantage. The power of point-of-purchase advertising derives directly from the sensory and functional presence of the media at that precise moment in time when the shopper decides to trade money for selected goods.

The Pull Test: "Pulling" Enabling Technologies Will Solve Priority Problems; "Pushing" New Technologies Into Best-Fit Applications May Backfire

"Science for science's sake" has rarely been a compelling argument for retail technology adoption. But when retail problems happen to overlap technology-based opportunities, it is easy to become infatuated with the "cool factor" of the technology and lose sight of the whole solution. In this situation, the technology may be "pushed" down to end users—like pushing a square peg into a round hole. As someone once observed when viewing a new technology, "That's a great cure. Too bad there's no disease." With numerous challenges, such as cost pressure, supply chain management, poor at-retail compliance, media under-valuation, and increasingly demanding consumers to consider, the industry simply does not have the time or resources to dabble in the technology du jour. The most effective and successful implementations come when the dynamic is reversed: when a high-priority business need instead "pulls" a best-fit technology to resolve the problem. So the second test for considering a new technology has to be: What important problem will it solve?

EMERGING TECHNOLOGY EXAMPLE NO. 1:

Reducing Out-of-Stocks

Before we move to the third test, let us consider a common retail problem: out-of-stocks. This problem has been scrutinized in a number of studies, including those by the Food Marketing Institute (FMI) and the Grocery Manufacturers of America (GMA), which have revealed the following:

• Out-of-stocks averaged 8.3 percent overall in a 2002 study, up slightly from 8.2 percent in 1993. Sales losses from out-of-stocks average 4 percent.[1]

• Shoppers often respond by switching brands, or stores, to acquire the desired items. Retailers lose the sale 43 percent of the time; manufacturers, 31 percent.[2]

• Promoted items have twice the out-of-stocks of nonpromoted items. (P-O-P displays contribute to-and suffer from-this problem.)[3]

Since these conditions all contribute strong negative effects to the shopper's in-store experience, out-of-stocks clearly passes The People Test. Therefore, what solutions should this problem "pull"? First, let us eliminate the obvious non-technology solution of simply increasing overall inventory levels. This is a poor solution, because it would increase inventory carrying costs, which in turn would mean either lower profits to the retailer or higher prices to the consumer.

To determine potential technological remedies for out-of-stock losses, we must first examine the primary causes. According to the FMI and GMA studies referenced above, the primary causes of out-of-stocks are (1) poor ordering and/or forecasting, (2) upstream supply chain factors, and (3) having the stock in-store but not on the shelf/display. Figure 8-2 presents possible solutions and the technologies that might be "pulled" into service as remedies.

Figure 8-2
Causes of and
Potential Solutions
for Out-of-Stocks

Cause (Percent of Problem[4])	Possible Solution	Potential Enabling Technologies/Kowledge
Poor ordering (47%)	Better reporting and forecasting	Analytic software systems, CPFR* systems
	More accurate promotional lift data (to enable better peak demand forecasting)	Lift studies (e.g., POPAI's), compliance monitoring
	Improved order support systems	Automated reorder systems, improved mobile scan/order applications
Upstream supply chain factors (28%)	Improved supply chain management	Radio Frequency Identification (RFID) supply chain tracking
	Remediation alert systems	Point-of-Sale (POS) velocity monitoring, compliance monitoring
Stock in-store but not on shelf/display (25%)	Fully integrated space management, combining shelf and secondary display data	Lift studies, compliance monitoring, CPFR systems
	Better in-store inventory management	Perpetual inventory systems, RFID receiving systems
	POS scan movement alerts	Intelligent POS velocity monitoring
	Better P-O-P inventory monitoring	Shelf/display stock sensors
	Better labor forecasting	Labor scheduling systems

With the size of the problem so large, the customer impact so significant, and so many emerging technologies arising as potential solutions, why is it still a problem? The three commonly cited reasons are (1) a lack of commitment to solve it, (2) a constantly changing environment, and (3) payback on the solution cost. The latter is especially important, and leads us to the third test.

THE PAYBACK TEST: TECHNOLOGIES SHOULD DELIVER A QUICK PAYBACK ON THE WHOLE SOLUTION COST

Even companies with intractable problems rarely have the option of throwing money at their problems. Capital is always precious, so any solution—especially a technology-based one—is typically expected to pay back the investment quickly, so as to replenish the capital pool for other opportunities and quickly create a long-term enhancement to profitability. In other words, buyers don't expect to pay for solutions; they expect the solutions to pay for themselves—quickly.

"Whole solution cost" is an important term. It refers to the fact that the acquisition cost of the technology is often just one part of the total solution cost. When calculating payback, it is essential to consider the whole cost structure in the way that accountants look at "total cost of ownership." The sticker price on a new car, for example, is just one part of the whole solution cost. Finance charges, insurance, fuel, maintenance, and toll charges all figure in to the whole solution of achieving the freedom of travel.

The same approach holds true for point-of-purchase advertising solutions. Electronic displays with changeable content, for example, offer numerous applications for in-store communications with customers, but the whole solution cost will be more than just the acquisition of the displays. Electricity and communications hookups must be factored in, as will retailer charges for the use of valuable space. Moreover, the changing content itself has to be developed or sourced and repurposed, and coordinated carefully with the overall promotional campaigns. All of this takes time and money. To return to the guitar analogy, it is not enough just to buy the instrument. The critical investment is in learning how to properly play it.

So how do the concepts of people, pull, and payback stack up against the real world? Let us illustrate this approach with a prominent example of an emerging technology, RFID, and evaluate the solution's viability.

EMERGING TECHNOLOGY EXAMPLE NO. 2:

RFID at the Point of Purchase

Any survey of newsworthy retail technologies in 2003 had to include Radio Frequency Identification (RFID) near the top of the list. Radio frequency (RF) technologies use radio waves in certain wavelength bands to effect wireless communication between objects. RF technologies have been important in retail solutions for many years, notably performing the following tasks, among others:

• Enabling greater productivity with wireless handhelds for now-untethered employees.

• Protecting against loss with Electronic Article Surveillance (EAS) tags.

• Enabling quicker checkout with RF payment tags such as the Exxon-Mobil SpeedPass(tm).

• Achieving 100 percent point-of-purchase shelf-price integrity with wirelessly updated electronic price displays.

Auto-ID technologies use RF, infrared (IR), or other electromagnetic or optical means to identify objects with minimal human intervention. The heart of RFID is the combination of RF and Auto-ID technologies into small tags, programmed with unique identification codes, to enable objects to be "seen" when they pass within a prescribed proximity to an RF reader. The RF reader detects the identification code in an RF signal from a tag. The signal is emitted from a battery-powered "active" tag, or is reflected from a "passive" tag.

In the latter case, the energy from the RF reader's signal is modified by circuitry within the RFID tag, and this modified signal, which then carries the tag's unique ID, is reflected back to the reader. Although active tags are more powerful and functional, passive tags are less expensive and often last longer. Tags can potentially be placed on palettes, cases, display, personnel, or, eventually, even individual items.

EMERGING TECHNOLOGY EXAMPLE NO. 3:

RFID Compliance Monitoring

An additional scenario with which to illustrate the People/Pull/Payback Test approach is the likely near-term point-of-purchase use of RFID with an application targeted against poor compliance in P-O-P execution. As many studies, including ongoing POPAI studies, have documented, P-O-P promotional compliance remains dismal. Audits typically show execution in the 30 to 40 percent range, sometimes as low as 20 percent. Solutions based on human audit have not been widely accepted; concerns focus on speed, accuracy, and reliability. Many industry leaders see a fully automated implementation as a more desirable and valuable solution.

Not surprisingly, RFID provides an excellent technological foundation for such a solution. One Chicago-based company, Goliath Solutions, working closely with POPAI and a number of manufacturer

When will RFID matter? Maybe sooner than you think. Two key indicators are that (1) standardization is already well under way and (2) Wal-Mart is in the game.

Standardizing RFID

In 2003, RFID had taken center stage. Technology think tanks like MIT's AutoID Center were germinating a bumper crop of emerging solutions using a new breed of electronic tags that will identify objects throughout the retail supply chain and, someday, out into the world beyond the retailers' walls. More importantly, emphasis appropriately has been placed on establishing standards to enable enterprise-wide interoperability of applications and to protect infrastructure investment against obsolescence or upgrade difficulties. These standards for RFID constitute the framework for an Electronic Product Code (EPC), an electronic sibling to the familiar printed Universal Product Code (UPC) seen in barcodes on all manner of objects. Significantly, the AutoID Center is working with the Uniform Code Council, Inc. (UCC) and EAN International to form AutoID, Inc., a not-for-profit organization that will develop and oversee commercial and technical standards.

Wal-Mart and RFID

Wal-Mart is driving its top suppliers to use RFID case- and palette-level tagging by 2005, with others to follow soon afterwards. Although aimed initially at routine warehouse shipping/receiving containers, this policy will almost certainly have implications for pre-packed shippers—by early 2005. This fact constitutes a serious heads-up for the point-of-purchase industry.

Early in 2003 news focused on Gillette's pilot study of smart shelves (shelves equipped with RFID reading functionality) to monitor RFID tags on individual items at test stores including Wal-Mart. Wal-Mart subsequently announced that it was focusing its resources on case and palette initiatives, and specifically not on item-level RFID. Although many considerations were involved, probably the most important was the expected superior payback on case and palette tracking.

and retail industry leaders, is developing just such a solution. Their plan calls for a nationwide deployment of RF readers in selected retail chains, all communicating with a central database, which will continually monitor key areas of the retail floor for a specific type of RFID tag. These tags, each with a unique ID, will be affixed to the P-O-P displays during manufacturing and/or distribution. Once the central system knows which tags have been deployed (and on what pieces of P-O-P), it will compare that list to what is actually "seen" in the store. Timely exception reports will then provide accurate, detailed audits of in-store execution, including time installed, time removed, and perhaps even the physical location within the store-all without the potential inaccuracies of human auditing.

How does RFID compliance monitoring stack up against the three key tests?

People: The almost-invariable sales lift associated with P-O-P advertising clearly establishes it as a plus for shoppers. Therefore, better-executed in-store point-of-purchase advertising clearly enhances the overall shopping experience.

Pull: Numerous studies have confirmed the long-standing vexation that manufacturers feel when a large portion of their precious promotional funds is used to purchase chain-wide P-O-P that ends up largely unused. Human audit services have been proffered but never fully assimilated. Clearly this is a problem in need of an automated solution.

Payback: Pricing and payback for RFID are yet to be demonstrated, but early indications are positive. First, the value proposition is significant. Cost savings from reduced waste offer a desirable hard savings; incremental sales and margin from improved execution add enormous potential value for both retailer and manufacturer; and the analytical value of finally being able to accurately attribute improved sales to actual execution should deliver tremendous strategic benefits. Second, the investment itself appears affordable. Design emphasis on low infrastructure and tag cost should enable pricing that provides a quite favorable return on investment against the potential value.

EMERGING TECHNOLOGY EXAMPLE NO. 4:

Item-Level RFID-Payback and Consumer Concerns

Because of the large number of tags required, item-level RFID has a much more difficult payback. While it appears there will be limited near-term deployments, mainly outside the United States and for selected high-value items (e.g. apparel), large scale deployment of item-level RFID will be constrained by payback considerations until tag costs are significantly lowered. This is several years away. Additionally, the People Test on this solution must also acknowledge privacy concerns. Consumer groups such as Consumers Against Supermarket Privacy Invasion and Numbering (CASPIAN) are increasingly voicing concerns over the need to protect consumer privacy before item-level tagging is implemented. These concerns may also have played a significant role in the decision to slow the Gillette on-item RFID test. So, although some meaningful problems could potentially be addressed by affordable, properly implemented, item-level RFID, Payback and People Tests will continue to challenge item-level applications in the near term.

ADDITIONAL NOTABLE EMERGING TECHNOLOGIES

Following is a brief look at additional significant trends in emerging solutions.

Planning Technologies: Enterprise Optimization

Collaborative design and versioning applications are enabling faster, more efficient, more predictable, and more effectively tailored design development. Image-asset management systems have evolved into enterprise-collaborative planning and execution systems for Advertising, Merchandising, and Promotion (AMP) processes (for example Connect3's Velocity system). This level of technical integration will help enable better business process integration and so help give manufacturers a more consistent marketing approach across the whole marketing mix.

Communicating price remains a key, and sometimes difficult, element of point-of-purchase messaging. Retailers of all types are implementing price and promotion optimization systems. These systems help ensure optimum synchronization between price and promotion communications. Gartner/RIS Market Research states that 47 to 60 percent of retailers will have fully implemented these systems by 2004-05.[5] POS-synchronized electronic price displays remain challenged by payback in the United States, where most retailers would require the cost of implementing the technology to drop to the point where it can be paid back more quickly by simple labor savings (from reduced price change activities). Adoption is accelerating more rapidly in Europe, with retailers like the Metro Group, as evidenced in their "Future Store" Initiative.

Digital Printing Technologies: Anything, Any Size, Anywhere

Digital printing has had a revolutionary effect on the printing industry, reducing setups, improving throughputs, and creating new efficiencies. It is estimated that the large format digital printing market is growing at twice the rate of the overall printing industry.[6] In addition to wider formats, higher speeds, more varied substrates, improved image quality, and new inks continue to expand the print horizon. Additional advances should be expected in image capture devices, image processing software, image output devices, media, inks and toners, and finishing systems.

Digital Display Technologies: Improving Visual Interaction

Electronic displays of visual images and item-specific information are becoming increasingly prevalent. Dynamic display technologies will continue to enhance the in-store experience as new capabilities are pulled in and leveraged to better serve end-customer needs and preferences. Static print imagery is not going away in our lifetime, but its virtual monopoly over in-store visual communications will increasingly yield to more dynamic and effective visual tools. Thin displays with new, electronically driven inks have already been tested and are expected to be available in the next few years. Plasma displays should continue to become more affordable solutions for selected in-store advertising applications.

Shopper-Interactive Technologies: Personalizing the In-Store Experience

Kiosks, while not as widely implemented as once expected, continue to find niche applications in areas like photo, cosmetics, and home improvement. Personal shoppers have evolved from early designs that were primarily shop-and-scan applications, into systems like Shopping Buddy, using hardware from Symbol Technologies and software from Cuesol, Inc. These systems provide a new level of personalized customer service, allowing shoppers in supermarkets to receive customized promotional offers while they shop, or even receive notification when photos, prescriptions, and deli orders are ready.

Payment Technologies: Merging P-O-P and POS

Changes such as self-checkout and Speedpass(tm)-type payment options are becoming increasingly common, both in number of stores deployed and in percent of shoppers using, demonstrating shopper willingness to adopt new technologies in order to streamline their in-store process. As customer payment options grow, especially through the utilization of wireless communication devices, the traditional delineation between the tender-oriented focus of traditional POS and the merchandising-oriented focus of traditional P-O-P may blur—or it may sharpen into a hybrid of the two: a consumer-oriented point-of-response, strikingly similar to online retailing in which selection of products and tender of payment are accomplished at the same place and virtually the same time.

ENCORE:
MAKING NEW SOLUTIONS SOUND SOLUTIONS

In conclusion, one last argument for the importance of the three key tests deserves mention: Virtually any company has three groups of people to please—customers, employees, and shareholders. The three proposed tests align closely to those groups:

- The People Test focuses on satisfied, loyal customers;
- The Pull Test looks toward productive, unhampered employees; and
- The Payback Test is directed at ensuring happy, well-rewarded shareholders.

Although numerous other considerations may be made, a poor evaluation in any of these three key areas is likely to result in problems and disappointments.

Finally, this chapter would be incomplete without noting that all of these technologies will add to P-O-P's slice of the pie. Well-designed, well-implemented, technology-based solutions will continue to be a source of process improvement, positive customer differentiation, and competitive advantage. As these technologies continue to enable point-of-purchase advertising to mature into an even more viable and cost-effective media, forward-thinking companies will continue to reap the rewards.

As Chet Atkins might ask, "How does it sound now?"

ENDNOTES

[1] "Retail Out-of-Stocks: A Worldwide Examination of Extent, Causes, and Consumer Responses," (October 2002), Grocery Manufacturers of America/The Food Marketing Institute/CIES–The Food Business Forum, viii.

[2] Ibid., 20.

[3] Ibid., 15.

[4] Ibid., vii.

[5] "Revving Up Revenue Optimization," (January 2004) LakeWest Group, LLC, 5.

[6] CAP Ventures, *CAP Stats*, November 4, 2003, http://www.capv.com/home/CAPStats/CSArticles/2003/11.04.03.html.

"Although copyright law gives

the copyright owner the exclusive

right to the work and subsequent

reproductions of that work,

the immediate question is:

'Who owns the copyright in

a point-of-purchase sketch,

design, prototype or model?'"

Trade Practices and Intellectual Property

DAVID W. SCHULTZ
PAST CHAIRMAN, POPAI

Establising and Monitoring Trade Practices

All advertising media—broadcast, print, outdoor, and point-of-purchase—as well as advertising agencies, adhere to certain trade practices. These trade practices have typically been developed and maintained by the various trade associations such as the American Association of Advertising Agencies, the National Association of Broadcasters, and Point-Of-Purchase Advertising International (POPAI).

These industry trade practices should not be confused with state and federal laws that deal with advertising. Federal laws take precedence over state laws, which vary from state to state. In recent years, both federal and state governments have become increasingly concerned about monitoring advertising trade practices.

The advertising community has generally felt that as individual associations have established stricter trade practices for their members over the years, there is less need for federal and state governments to oversee the advertising industry. Like most professions—including law and medicine—the advertising industry would prefer to be self-governed.

A member company that finds itself in violation of its association's code of ethics or bylaws will generally find itself censured by that association. The censure can include any or all of the following: (1) loss of certain membership benefits for a specified period of time, for example, voting rights, committee privileges, and trade show exhibition rights; and (2) notice in the media-including industry publications-of the violation.

Point-Of-Purchase Advertising Trade Association

The P-O-P advertising industry's professional association is Point-Of-Purchase Advertising International, headquartered in Washington, D.C. Founded in 1936, POPAI is one of thousands of trade associations located in the metropolitan Washington area.

Like many trade associations, one of POPAI's stated goals is to serve as an advocate for its particular industry while promoting the highest level of professionalism within that industry. POPAI's elected leaders and professional staff have served as resources for government agencies and congressional committees. Continuing education programs for its members, including a formal Certified Point-of-Purchase Professional (CPP) program, are an example of the association's commitment to higher professional standards.

The association has established industry ethics and expects its members to comply with the following standards:

- Abide by all federal and state laws while maintaining the highest level of integrity and honesty;
- Communicate clearly and comprehensively all relevant company policies prior to entering into a business relationship, including pricing and ownership issues; and
- Possess awareness of and adhere to P-O-P industry trade practices and standards as issued by POPAI.[1]

POPAI maintains a number of committees and task forces that meet throughout the year, including one that deals solely with trade practices and intellectual property. Over the years, the Intellectual Property Committee has met with the U.S. Justice Department, the U.S. Patent and Trademark Office, the U.S. Copyright Office, and with federal and state officials familiar with trade practices and intellectual property issues.

The purpose of these meetings has been (1) for POPAI officials to clearly understand the different jurisdictions between these government agencies, as well as the difference between a patent, copyright, and trademark, and (2) for government officials to better understand why the registration of P-O-P-advertising intellectual property is important.

POPAI's Role in Protecting Intellectual Property

In 1997, POPAI produced the first edition of the "Point-of-Purchase Advertising Industry Standards of Practice Manual," which was updated in 2001. The manual was produced not only for association members but also for nonmembers, since many producers/suppliers, brand marketers, and retailers are unfamiliar with the laws that define intellectual property. Copies have also been shared with other advertising, marketing, and retail trade associations.

POPAI assists members in protecting their intellectual property in several additional ways. For example, POPAI has developed "spec label" language serving to educate business partners on both sides of the producer/client equation, about which a company asserts ownership over the particular design in question. Obtainable from the "Members Only" section of www.popai.com, this language can be downloaded and affixed to a proprietary design and serve to educate the reviewing party as to the participating company's assertion of ownership. See Figure 9-1.

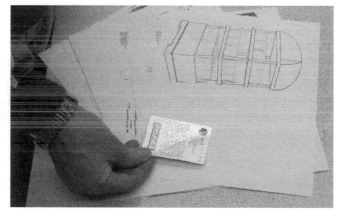

Figure 9-1

Producer applying spec label to
P-O-P designs

Another example of POPAI's work to assist members in protecting intellectual property is the establishment of POPAI's Intellectual Property (IP) Registry located on www.popai.com. The IP Registry serves as a repository for proprietary designs. Any company wishing to protect proprietary designs that they own can register a design in the IP Registry where the design's image will be both time- and date-stamped. In the event that there is a subsequent dispute over ownership of the design, the registering company can download the image from the IP Registry—complete with the date and time at which the design had been registered—thus being able to demonstrate the company's original assertion of ownership.

Federal Role in Protecting Intellectual Property

Although violations of an industry association's trade practices are certainly serious in their own right, of even greater consequence are violations of federal and state laws. The agencies of the federal government that monitor trade practices of businesses are the Federal Trade Commission (FTC) and the U.S. Department of Justice.

INTELLECTUAL PROPERTY

The term "intellectual property" is not a term familiar to most Americans, although the interest in and awareness of intellectual property has increased dramatically in recent years, thanks in part, to the growth of the Internet, which has spawned several intellectual property issues. Simply stated, individuals have not always recognized the significant—and often substantial—value of intellectual property, even though this value was clearly intended in the United States Constitution. Although ideas may be intangible, they are property.

It is worth noting that in Europe there exists a far greater sensitivity to intellectual property rights, specifically as they apply to the role of design, including the design itself. This may be explained by Europeans' longer-lasting and deeper appreciation of created works of art, ranging from literary works, paintings, and sculptures, to architecture.

Stephen R. Bergerson, a nationally known attorney specializing in intellectual property issues, prepared a special white paper for POPAI on these issues—it can be found in the POPAI handbook, "Point-of-Purchase Advertising Industry Standards of Practice Manual."[2] A member of the law firm Fredrikson & Byron, P.A., based in Minneapolis, Minnesota, Bergerson has practiced advertising and promotion law. Well-known in the advertising industry for his leadership on important legal, ethical, and governmental issues, he is a member of the National Advertising Review Board and chairman of the American Advertising Federation's Standards Committee.

In his white paper for POPAI, Bergerson lists four separate areas of intellectual property: *copyright, patents, trade secrets,* and *trademarks*.[3] Each provides different kinds of protection for different kinds of intellectual property. And each has proved confusing to the public at large, including members of the advertising industry.

Copyright

Copyright law protects the creative expression of ideas. Copyright is a form of protection provided by the laws of the United States (title 17, U.S. Code) to the authors of "original works of authorship," including pictorial, graphic, and sculptural works.[4] This protection is available to both published and unpublished works. Section 106 of the Copyright Act of 1976 generally gives the owner of copyright the *exclusive right* to do, and authorize others to do, the following:

1. To reproduce the copyrighted work in copies or phonorecords;
2. To prepare derivative works based upon the copyrighted work;
3. To distribute copies or phonorecords of the copyrighted work to the public by sale or other transfer of ownership, or by rental, lease, or lending;
4. In the case of literary, musical, dramatic, and choreographed works, pantomimes, and motion pictures and other audiovisual works, to perform the copyrighted work publicly;
5. In the case of literary, musical, dramatic, and choreographic works, pantomimes, and pictorial, graphic, or sculptural works, including the individual images of a motion picture or other audiovisual work, to display the work publicly; and
6. In the case of sound recordings, to perform the copyrighted work publicly by means of a digital audio transmission.[5]

What works are protected? Copyrightable works include the following categories:

1. Literary works;
2. Musical works, including any accompanying words;
3. Dramatic works, including any accompanying music;
4. Pantomimes and choreographic works;
5. Pictorial, graphic, and sculptural works;
6. Motion pictures and other audiovisual works;
7. Sound recordings; and
8. Architectural works.[6]

These categories should be viewed broadly. For example, computer programs and most "compilations" may be registered as "literary works"; maps and architectural plans may be registered as "pictorial, graphic, and sculptural works." Copyright does not, however, protect the ideas themselves; that is achieved with a patent. P-O-P advertising is obviously covered in the above descriptions and includes not only sketches and designs of point-of-purchase materials but models and prototypes as well.

Nearly all P-O-P advertising moves through these two important steps—design and prototyping. Whether done at the request of a client or on speculation, designs and prototypes *remain the property of the design firm* (the P-O-P designer and producer) unless it has been clearly agreed that the work is "for hire." Most P-O-P companies regularly affix a sticker or stamp to their work clearly stating this important point.

Copyright is secured automatically when the work is created. If a work of art (design) is created over a period of time, the part of the work that is fixed on a particular date constitutes the created work as of that date.

Registration of a work is not necessary but does provide a greater degree of protection and ensures quicker resolution of any potential dispute. Registration should be done within 90 days of creation or publication or before the infringement, whichever occurs first.

Although copyright law gives the copyright owner the exclusive right to the work and subsequent reproductions, including derivations, of that work, the immediate question is: *"Who owns the copyright in a point-of-purchase sketch, design, prototype, or model?"*

Most often it is the *creator* of the work—unless it is a *work for hire.*

Work for Hire

What defines a work for hire? *A work for hire* is described in section 101 of the Copyright Act of 1976, title 17 of the United States Code as (1) "a work prepared by an employee within the scope of his or her employment" and (2) "a work specially ordered or commissioned for use as a contribution to a collective work, as a part of a motion picture or other audiovisual work, as a sound recording, as a translation, as a supplementary work, as a compilation, as an instructional text, as a test, as answer material for a test, or as an atlas, *if the parties expressly agree in a written instrument* signed by them that the work shall be considered a work made for hire" (emphasis added).

As noted earlier, P-O-P producer companies create and manufacture P-O-P advertising materials in a variety of ways. While most companies have their own in-house design staffs, others use outside, independent contract designers to varying degrees.

Many brand marketers mistakenly believe that when they engage a producer to design point-of-purchase materials the ownership of that design automatically belongs to the brand marketer. *This is incorrect.* Unless the producer has signed a contract with the brand marketer assigning ownership to *the brand marketer, the producer retains the right to the design.*

If a brand marketer has another P-O-P producer manufacture P-O-P materials that are a derivative of the original design, *the brand marketer has infringed on the producer's copyright and is in violation of copyright law.*

Whether or not a work is made for hire is determined by the relationship between the parties. In 1989, the Supreme Court held that to determine whether a work is made for hire one must first ascertain whether the work was prepared by (1) an employee or (2) an independent contractor.

It is important to note that when a work is made for hire, the person for whom the work was prepared is the initial owner of the copyright unless both parties have signed a written agreement to the contrary.

The term of copyright protection for a work made for hire is 75 years from the date of publication or 100 years from the date of creation, whichever expires first. A work not made for hire is normally protected by copyright for the life of the author plus 50 years.

For further information
on copyright, contact:

Library of Congress
Copyright Office
101 Independence
Avenue, S.E.
Washington, D.C.
20559-6000

202.707.3000
www.loc.gov/copyright

Patents

Patents protect *inventions*. Under section 171 of title 35 of the United States Code, the patent laws provide for the granting of design patents to any person who invents a new, original, and ornamental design for an article of manufacture. Depending on the type of patent issued, the owner of a patent has exclusive right to his or her patent for 14 or 17 years.

The objective of a design patent protection is to give encouragement to the decorative arts by giving certain new, original, and ornamental appearances to an article of manufacture to enhance its commercial value and increase demand for it.

According to the U.S. Patent and Trademark Office, an agency of the U.S. Department of Commerce, "a design consists of the visual ornamental characteristics embodied in, or applied to, an article of manufacture. Since a design is manifested in appearance, the subject matter of a design patent application may relate to the configuration or shape of an article, to the surface ornamentation of an article, or both."[7] See Figure 9-2 for an example of a patented P-O-P display.

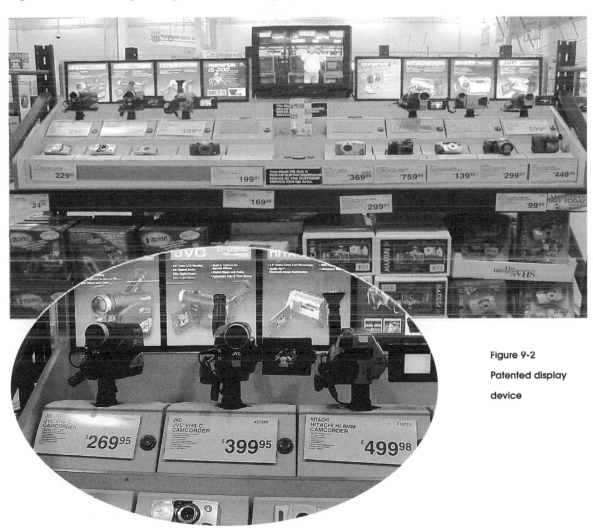

Figure 9-2

Patented display

device

For further information
on patents and patent
law, contact:

**U.S. Patent and
Trademark Office
USPTO Contact Center
(UCC)
PO Box 1450
Alexandria, VA 20231**

**Patent Assistance
Center: 800.786.9199
www.uspto.gov**

Patent law and copyright law differ significantly regarding the issue of ownership between the employer and employee. In most instances, the employee owns the invention unless (1) a carefully worded contract exists, (2) the employee was specifically hired or directed to develop the invention, or (3) when the employee "through words, silence, actions or inactions, has caused the employer to rely on the use of the employee's invention."[8]

The law prohibits employees from being forced by employers to sign agreements assigning inventions as a condition of employment. In addition, most states prohibit employers from including patent ownership language in employment agreements.

Trade Secrets

According to Bergerson, "a trade secret is (1) secret information which (2) is not generally known or readily ascertainable, (3) gained at its owner's expense and which (4) provides a competitive advantage of any kind."[9] A trade secret may be a process, technique, program, device, pattern, formula, or compilation. Generally known information, when uniquely combined, can qualify as a trade secret.

As long as a trade secret truly remains a secret, the owner has the exclusive right to use or sell it. If the trade secret is discovered through "proper means," including reverse engineering, the trade secret loses its protection.

Owners of trade secrets are permitted by law to take reasonable precautions to protect their trade secrets, including limiting access to such information and marking trade secrets as "confidential" or "secret." Confidentiality agreements can also be used to ensure that these secrets are not lost.

Trademarks

A trademark is a word, phrase, symbol, or design, or combination of words, phrases, symbols, or designs, that identifies and distinguishes the source of the goods and services from one party to those of others, according to the U.S. Patent and Trademark Office. Examples include the distinctive trademarks from (1) Wrigley Spearmint, (2) Frito-Lay, and (3) Miller Brewing, shown in Figure 9-3.

Figure 9-3
**Several well-known
trademarks**

A trademark is not a copyright or a patent. A copyright helps protect an original artistic or literary work; a patent helps protect an invention.

As noted previously, an independent contractor commissioned to design a trademark by a brand marketer, producer, or retailer should make certain that ownership of the design has been clearly established before undertaking the project. The company or individual commissioning this work for hire must obtain a written copyright transfer from the designer.

The Role of the Producer and/or Designer

The producer and/or designer of point-of-purchase materials has the responsibility for clearly understanding and communicating the parameters by which he or she is working-so that there are no misunderstandings.

Just as the producer and/or designer cannot proceed with designing a display for a customer without having all available information related to the function of the display, it is incumbent on that same producer and/or designer to make certain that all loose ends pertaining to intellectual property issues are raised and addressed. Producer sales personnel are too often reluctant to raise this sensitive issue for fear of upsetting the client too early in the process. The client will be far more upset when faced with a lawsuit for violation of intellectual property. It is far better to address this issue early on, rather than later.

The Role of the Brand Marketer

The brand marketer's role is quite similar to that of the producer and/or designer since the brand marketer is usually spearheading the project. Because the brand marketer usually is paying the producer, it is equally important that the brand marketer have a clear understanding of the process.

Because the brand marketer wants to please the customer—the retailer—the producer and/or designer has to please the brand marketer and the retailer. There is an additional challenge faced by the brand marketer: What happens when the retailer approves the brand marketer's product and P-O-P materials but suggests to the brand marketer than another producer be used to manufacture the approved P-O-P materials? This is a clear violation of intellectual property rights—but it takes a courageous brand marketer to point this out to a retailer who has been highly courted.

The Role of the Retailer

With the roles of the producer and/or designer and the brand marketer both defined, the role of the retailer is almost obvious. The retailer, as noted, is the brand marketer's customer. The larger the retailer, the more clout the retailer has to "call most of the shots" when it comes to the design and manufacture of the display. This is why clear, straightforward communication between the three parties—producer/supplier, brand marketer, and retailer—is crucial.

For further information on trademark protection, contact:

U.S. Patent and Trademark Office USPTO Contact Center (UCC) PO Box 1450 Alexandria, VA 20231

Trademark Assistance Center: 800.786.9199 www.uspto.gov

INTELLECTUAL PROPERTY CASE STUDIES

Following are four intellectual property case studies and three questions developed in attorney Steve Bergerson's white paper (included in POPAI's handbook on trade practices).[10] These case studies are conceptual only and should not be used to resolve specific issues, since each circumstance is unique and must be considered on its own merits.

EXAMPLE A

P-O-P Supplier A sees a display that has been produced by P-O-P Supplier B. Believing that he can produce a better display, Supplier A approaches the brand marketer whose display Supplier A saw and makes a proposal. The brand marketer is interested and asks for quotes on producing the display "as is" and with the changes proposed by Supplier A.

What are the legal implications of each of these scenarios?

Assuming that Supplier B, who manufactured the display, also designed it, both Supplier A and the brand marketer are headed for trouble. If Supplier A manufactures the display "as is," he will be copying Supplier B's design and, as a result, is infringing on the copyright which protects it. Even if Supplier A makes changes in the design, he will still infringe on the original design if the new version is "substantially similar" to the original, since the Copyright Act gives a copyright owner the exclusive right to create "derivative" (substantially similar) works. The brand marketer, at whose request the new display was made, will also be infringing on Supplier B's copyright.

If Supplier B did not register the copyright within three months following the first public use of the display or before the infringement, Supplier B will be entitled to recover whatever actual damages, as well as any profits on the infringements, Supplier B can prove are attributable to the infringement. If Supplier B did register within that time period, Supplier B would also be entitled to whatever statutory damages (up to $20,000) and attorneys' fees a judge believes are reasonable under the circumstances. If the infringement was willful, the judge may award additional punitive damages of up to $100,000, and a federal prosecutor might be persuaded to bring criminal charges.

EXAMPLE B

P-O-P Supplier A creates a "substantially similar" version of someone else's P-O-P display with similar graphics and the ability to hold the same amount of product, and which is manufactured from the same materials, and takes the display prototype to a brand marketer along with a competitive quote to produce the display.

What should the brand marketer do?

Since the Copyright Act prohibits the unauthorized creation of substantially similar ("derivative") works, Supplier A has infringed on the original creator's copyright rights. And, since the brand marketer would also be liable should such a project proceed, the brand marketer should obtain from Supplier A written assurance that the design belongs to Supplier A and that Supplier A will hold the brand marketer harmless from any liability for copyright infringement. If the brand marketer knows that Supplier A's concept was not original, it should decline the proposal.

EXAMPLE C

A retailer reviews a proposal from a brand marketer, which includes the means to merchandise its products in the retailer's stores, paid for by the brand marketer's co-op funds and based on the retailer's volume. P-O-P Supplier A has developed merchandising equipment working in concert with the brand marketer. The retailer informs the brand marketer that it wants the co-op funds but will have Supplier B produce equipment proposed by the brand marketer or the retailer will not accept the proposal.

What are the possible implications?

Assuming that Supplier A created the concept for the merchandising equipment and did not transfer the patent or copyrights to the concept, the brand marketer should advise the retailer that allowing Supplier B to produce the equipment could expose both the retailer and Supplier B to Supplier A's infringement claims. Should the brand marketer proceed on the basis demanded by the retailer, the brand marketer would likely be sued for having facilitated and participated in the infringing activities.

EXAMPLE D

A brand marketer commissions a design from Supplier A, obtains a bid from Supplier A, then checks bids with three other suppliers and returns to Supplier A stating that Supplier A must do the job for the lowest-price bid.

Must Supplier A comply?

While Supplier A may decide for business reasons to produce the display at the lowest-price bid, it is under no legal obligation to do so if it has retained copyright ownership of the design. And, if the brand marketer gives the assignment to a supplier who made the lowest bid, both could be liable for damages.

Question 1

Is a P-O-P invention that is patented in the United States protected elsewhere, such as Canada and Mexico? What about patents and trademarks?

Each country has its own intellectual property laws. Patent, copyright, and trademark protection must usually be obtained from each country. There are often advantages to seeking trademark protection in other countries promptly (usually within six months) after obtaining such protection in the United States. Most industrialized countries are members of a treaty that automatically grants copyright protection in all member countries

Individuals wishing to obtain a copy of manuals developed by other POPAI chapters can do so by contacting:

Point-Of-Purchase Advertising International
1660 L Street, N.W., 10th Floor
Washington, D.C. 20036

202.530.3000
www.popai.com

once it is protected under the laws of any one. Since copyright in the United States automatically springs into existence when a work is created, the work is protected in all member countries as of the same point of time. The extent of protection, however, varies from country to country.

Other POPAI global structures, including those in Canada, Australia and New Zealand, Brazil, Mexico, and Europe, have produced their own Standards of Practice manuals. These serve as guidelines to P-O-P designers and producers as well as brand marketers and retailers in those countries.

Question 2

Copyright law protects the expression of ideas, but not the ideas themselves. What protects ideas?

Ideas themselves are protected if they are patentable, qualify and are treated as trade secrets, and/or are disclosed within the context of a confidential relationship.

Question 3

Can a design be patented one time to cover all of Europe, or does it need to be patented in each individual country? What about copyright and trademarks?

Each European country has its own intellectual property laws. Patent, trademark, and copyright protection can only be obtained by complying with each country's laws.

How to Avoid Infringing on Intellectual Property Rights

How do companies avoid the embarrassing problem of infringing on intellectual property rights? Each of the principals in this arrangement-producer/supplier, brand marketer, and retailer-has a particular role.

Anyone who hires someone to develop a work for hire has the responsibility to make certain that everything is "buttoned down," since all forms of intellectual property are protected-copyright, patent, trademark, or trade secret.

A carefully written document will always be the best defense against possible future misunderstandings. That document should contain all understandings to which the parties have agreed regarding the use of a design, including assignment of its ownership.

The "Point of Purchase Advertising Standards of Practice Manual" can answer many of the questions and concerns that may be raised. A copy of the United States manual is included on the CD-ROM that accompanies this book.

POPAI's Ongoing Efforts To Promote Intellectual Property Protection

As the only global, nonprofit trade association of the marketing and advertising industry at retail, POPAI has taken the lead to help protect the intellectual property of all of its members. In recent years, large clients have sought to lower their costs by outsourcing the engineering and manufacture of P-O-P displays to offshore companies, particularly in China, or by conducting Internet-based bidding auctions for the manufacture of displays among a select number of American producers. Too often, the originators of the design or prototype being put up for bid were not fairly recompensed for their work—or paid at all. What's more, some large clients have demanded that producers of P-O-P displays relinquish all intellectual property rights before even submitting their designs and display prototypes for bid—a practice that denies producers fair recompense not only for their graphic designs but also for the engineering expertise that impacts prototypes of P-O-P displays—a three dimensional art form.

POPAI has held town meetings throughout the United States to bring together producers of P-O-P displays, brand marketers, and retailers to enable all facets of our industry to evolve a Best Practices Platform for protecting intellectual property and gaining it fair recompense. A copy of the Platform is available at www.popai.com. The problems POPAI seeks to address have been brought by the association to the attention of state and federal legislators involved with patent, copyright and trademark issues. POPAI remains committed to solving the challenges to intellectual property protection.

ENDNOTES

[1] Point-Of-Purchase Advertising International, "Point-of-Purchase Advertising Industry Standards of Practice Manual" (Washington, D.C.: Point-Of-Purchase Advertising International, 2001), 4. Also available online at http://www.popai.com.

[2] Ibid., 25–32.

[3] Ibid., 25–29.

[4] U.S. Library of Congress, Copyright Office, *Copyright Registration for Works of the Visual Arts*, circular 40 (Washington, D.C.: Government Printing Office, 1995), 2.

[5] U.S. Code, vol. 17, sec. 106.

[6] U.S. Code, vol. 17, sec. 102.

[7] U.S. Department of Commerce, Patent and Trademark Office, *A Guide to Filing a Design Patent Application* (Washington, D.C.: Government Printing Office), 2.

[8] Point-Of-Purchase Advertising International, "Standards of Practice Manual," 28.

[9] Ibid., 28.

[10] Ibid., 30–32.

10

"Marketing at retail has become the battleground to win the hearts and wallets of consumers. The P-O-P advertising industry is a $30 billion worldwide business, growing at the rate of seven percent annually."

Global Trends in Point-of-Purchase Advertising

ROBERT LILJENWALL, MANAGING DIRECTOR
PROCREATIVE SERVICES

INTRODUCTION

In a rapidly changing global economy, the universal "moment of truth" comes when the consumer reaches for a product and drops it into the shopping cart. It is at this moment that all integrated marketing communications comes to its final test: The final choice by the consumer. On the surface it is not a complicated decision, but, in fact, the decision to purchase that product began long before the product fell into the cart.

Whether this event occurs in Prague, Paris, Los Angeles, or Mexico City, all three stakeholders in this moment of truth—the retailer, the brand marketer, and the point-of-purchase producer—play pivotal roles in who "wins" this contest. They all have a strategic economic interest in how consumers make their decisions at retail.

> The universal "moment of truth" comes when the consumer reaches for a product and drops it into the shopping cart. It is at this moment that all integrated marketing communications comes to its final test: The final choice by the consumer.

Marketing at retail has become the battleground to win the hearts and wallets of consumers. The P-O-P advertising industry is a $30 billion worldwide business, growing at the rate of seven percent annually.[1] New technologies, new alliances, and aggressive retailers and brand marketers are influencing a global change in how products and goods are sold at retail. Consumers have become more sophisticated, smarter. They make their brand choices based on a wide variety of influencers, whether it is price, value, quality, brand knowledge, convenience, or "just out of habit". And "habit" (i.e., brand loyalty) is what every retailer and brand marketer is counting on: Make the buying decision automatic.

The global economy has slowly recovered since 9/11, and while the Asian economy sees a robust growth rate of 6 percent plus over the next three years, there is less projected growth of 2.5 percent projected for richer nations versus poorer nations, whose growth rate is projected at just 1.5 percent rate.[2] The booming Asian economy is clearly a new factor in the retail equation of how the three stakeholders grow and prosper.

GLOBAL TRENDS—ACROSS ALL BORDERS

In a survey of P-O-P leaders around the globe, nine significant trends were prominent in the major industrial markets of North America, Europe, and Asia. These trends reflect the volatile nature of technology, industry consolidation, and global building by retailers and brand marketers. While varying in importance and prominence from market to market, these trends also reflect the fast-paced growth of all retail segments and categories. Retailers and brand marketers scramble to keep pace with competitors in the battle to win consumers who have become more sophisticated and demanding shoppers.

The nine major trends are:

- The technology explosion.
- Global expansion of retailers.
- Private-label growth.
- Growing power of the Internet.
- Explosion of brands.
- Increasing control of retail environment.
- Outsourcing in China and Asia.
- Improved research performance.
- Increased emphasis on "team building."

All three stakeholders are major players in each of these trends, and they are constantly sensitive to the trends that are shaping their ability to survive. Staying competitive means staying ahead of the curve, whether it is buying smart in China or managing your business better at home. The P-O-P producer, brand marketer, and retailer, as you will learn, are all under attack from competitors.

THE TECHNOLOGY EXPLOSION

The technology explosion is occurring in all market segments–from the convenience store to Wal-Mart. For the most part, it is retailers who are driving this explosion, because technology begins or ends on their turf. And the retailer, who is less likely to make the investment in a low-margin business, is turning to the point-of-purchase supplier or an entrepreneur for a better, faster, cheaper way to get valuable information to the right source, whether that source is the retailer, brand marketer, or consumer. It is happening on all fronts.

While the average consumer experiences some of this new technology, such as interactive kiosks and plasma screens, the technology utilized by retailers and brand marketers is fueling this explosion. Sophisticated data capture and data mining programs enable stakeholders to better analyze shopper behavior. "Knowing the customer" is what everyone wants and needs to be competitive. XML (extensible markup language) is the new *lingua franca* or global language in data mining. XML has become the mantra to researchers and data mining executives who seek better ways to win "the moment of truth".

Getting Closer to Customers

The goal of the retailer, brand marketer and P-O-P producer is to get closer to the customer, to "grandualized down" the selling proposition to the individual consumer so that the retailer can easily extract more money from the customer's wallet. This is accomplished by giving customers what they need and want, and that is accomplished by knowing them better.

The hottest trend in retail technology is the rapidly developing interactive shopper systems that enable stores to get closer to customers. Utilizing a combination of touch screen and signal transmission technologies, retailers are now able to connect with each individual customer via a "smart touch screen" located on the shopping cart. Two major tests are taking place in Europe (Metro AG stores) and in the United States (Stop & Shop). These new customer-focused systems bring together radio frequency identification (RFID), infrared (IR), WiFi, Bluetooth, and loyalty programs that utilize the data mined from the customer's previous purchases (via the loyalty club tracking programs).

Using a variety of devices either on the cart or carried by the shopper, the technologies allow the store to immediately connect with the shopper and offer discounts and promotions for the items "the customer historically purchases." Metro's system offers full scanning and weighing capabilities; the customer does his or her own check out. The Stop & Shop (developed by Massachusetts-based CueSol) system identifies all of the customer's preferred items that are on sale and also allows customers to actually order from the deli without having to stand in line. Even more impressively, the CueSol system alerts customers as they proceed down the aisle that one of their favorite items is on sale. All of these systems use a variety of RFID, WiFi, IR, and data mining technologies being tested.

Self-Checkout

The drive to reduce retailer costs, especially labor, has resulted in the development of self-checkout systems, which supermarkets and big box suppliers such as Home Depot are turning to. One of the systems, USCAN, is being distributed through Kroger and its U.S. subsidiaries Ralph's and Fred Meyer. The self-checkout stations are composed of scanners where customers can self-scan bar-coded products, weigh produce, and do their own bagging. For example, at a Fred Meyer store in Astoria, Oregon, one station processed 33 percent of the grocery customers, which represents 47 percent of the revenues.[3] As supermarkets strive to reduce overhead to better compete against mass merchandisers, self-checkout systems are expected to increase their penetration.

The self-checkout technology is just another example of how retailers are finding ways to get as close to the customer as possible to facilitate choice, service, and efficiency, thereby reducing the retailer's expense and improving the shopper's ability to buy cheaper and buy more.

Presentation Technology

During the past five years, there has been an influx of new presentation technologies—interactive kiosks, large-format printers, plasma and LCD screens and a variety of electronic paper formats from which retailers and brand marketers to select. Retailers have embraced the large-format printers because they can reproduce high-quality graphics for a fraction of the cost of screen printing from preset templates, making the medium easy to use at the regional or, even, store level. Carrefour (France) is the master at putting up large-format P-O-P signage throughout their stores to promote items that go on sale the very same day.

Digital signage made a big splash several years ago (E-Ink and Mag-Ink were two of the prominent players), but it has been difficult for the technology to find a foothold because of cost and limited presentation quality.

The large plasma screen has been one of the more innovative and exciting retail presentations. Several companies have tested them in both vertical and horizontal formats and showed dramatic sales lift for advertisers. They are impressive in any retail environment, but retailers and P-O-P producers are at odds as to who pays for these systems.

Interactive kiosks work well in certain business models. The business model of selling tickets or products through kiosks or depending on advertising revenues have not been historically successful. However, interactive kiosks that provide information to customers work extremely well, especially ATMs and airport-based kiosks utilized by airlines to dispense boarding passes and tickets. And, of course, video gaming machines dominate the casino landscape.

Perhaps one of the most innovative kiosk concepts was introduced in 2004 by Eastman Kodak—a self-serve kiosk that will develop film in under five minutes, giving the customer the opportunity to select how many prints they want from the menu screen. Each roll of film is transferred to a CD (no negatives are provided).

The challenge with most presentation technologies is determining who will pay for the medium. Retailers are reluctant to share co-op dollars with outside vendors who want to install presentation technology and tout brand marketers to customers already in the store. But research has more than demonstrated that these presentation technologies, in fact, work and improve sales.

Global Expansion—The Wal-Mart Factor

From a pure economic point of view, Wal-Mart is the most dominating retail entity on the planet. Where Wal-Mart lacks in market penetration (currently in only nine countries), it makes up for in raw global power—ranking as the world's largest corporation. Wal-Mart's annual sales for 2003 were $244.9 billion, nearly three times its closest competitor's.[4] International sales reached $40.7 billion, a 15 percent increase over 2002, and Wal-Mart plans to open between 100 and 140 stores each year over the next three years.

The other major global retailers—Carrefour (France), IKEA (Sweden), and AHOLD (Netherlands)—are expanding and have a greater global penetration than does Wal-Mart in terms of number of stores and countries.

French-based Carrefour has a total of 5,532 stores in 29 countries. IKEA, a privately held Swedish furniture retailer is in 31 countries but has only 175 stores; and AHOLD has the largest global network of 9,000-plus stores in 27 countries.[5]

Since Wal-Mart entered Mexico in 1991, it has through acquisition and expansion become the country's largest retailer, with over $10 billion in sales and more than 93,000 associates.[6]

But what makes Wal-Mart such a force is its drive for dictating the rules by which vendors and P-O-P suppliers must play the game to get a share of its business. For example, Wal-Mart has indicated that by 2005 its top 100 vendors must have RFID identity chips on all shipments to its network—and recently suggested that by 2006 this may be required of all vendors.

If Wal-Mart mandates that its premier suppliers adopt an identity system, there will surely be a trickle-down effect for the rest of the retail industry, thereby spurring the integration of this identity technology.

Private-Label Growth

Retailers have discovered the power of private labels and the added profits they bring to the bottom line. Private labels have always lured retailers because of the edge they bring in generating higher margins than national or regional brands.

Notable private-label brands such as Marks & Spencer (U.K.), Sam's Choice (Wal-Mart), President's Choice (Loblaw, Canada), and Kirkland (Costco) reflect the fast-expanding role private brands have in today's retail market. In the United States alone, private labels accounted for more than $47 billion in sales among supermarkets, mass merchandisers, and drug outlets in 2003. Private-label sales have been growing at a four percent annual rate according to the Private Label Manufacturers Association in just the United States.

The statistics in Figure 10-1 indicate the power of private labels.

Figure 10-1
Percent of Private-
Label Market Share

United Kingdom	46%	Netherlands	19%
Belgium	26	Canada	19
Germany	23	Spain	17
United States	20.8	Italy	12
France	19	Japan	1

SOURCE: A.C. NIELSEN 2001; PMLA 2001

Retailers are devoting more space and resources to their private label programs by taking advantage of existing vendors and their learning curve. Private-label design has improved, and retailers are beginning to think like brand marketers using loyalty programs and their power of merchandising to drive customers to their in-house brands. Because retailers control the selling environment, they can effectively place their own brands in advantageous shelf positions.

Are private labels a threat to national brands? According to William Smith, Procter & Gamble's In-store Presence Manager and past chairman of Point-Of-Purchase Advertising International, "If you're in the top three brands, private labels will not be the threat that they are to brands in fourth or fifth position."

GROWING POWER OF THE INTERNET

When the dot-com became the dot-bomb in 2000, many retailers were relieved to believe that the Internet threat had gone away. The opposite has occurred. The Internet has been growing at a rate of more than 6 percent annually since 2001, according to the U.S. Census Bureau,[7] which tracks official e-commerce sales. Savvy retailers, who have adopted and adapted the Internet's best practices, have seen a dramatic increase in online sales.

E-tailing has seen as much as 25 percent market share[8] in the United States in total sales versus traditional retail in such 'Net-friendly categories as computers, software, books, toys, flowers, and travel. This means that a healthy percentage of retail sales has shifted from the traditional retail channel to the online channel.

Merchants are learning how to cross-promote and cross-sell between the two channels in a variety of creative ways. For example, Sharper Image (U.S.) attributes more than 10 percent of its total sales to its online channel but knows that in-store sales are greatly influenced by its robust Web site. Sierra Trading Post, a Cheyenne, Wyoming, retailer, now does nearly 50 percent of its business online.[9]

One of the Web's most successful retailers—Amazon.com—posted its first-ever profit for a full year of operation, $35 million for 2003, with net sales totaling $5.264 billion. Amazon sells everything from books to toys (for Toys R Us) to software, and, now, cheese.[10]

But the Internet also plays another important role in the point-of-purchase industry. The power of broadband enables all of the technologies we have discussed to exist and function in real time. Beyond the presentation technologies of retail television networks (e.g., plasma screens, interactive kiosks), the Internet is the data conduit that feeds the retailer's and brand marketer's thirst for instant knowledge. The Internet provides the engine to communicate with far-distance retail locations and servers that drive the information where it is needed.

THE BRAND EXPLOSION

Not only has technology exploded in recent years, so have brands. Combined with the proliferation of private labels and brand marketers' accelerating market segmentation, there are new brands hitting the shelves everyday—each targeted at new or growing niche markets.

Brand marketers, armed with research generated by mining consumer buying behavior data, are creating new products to not only reach better defined niche markets but also to respond to changes in lifestyle, such as the diminished demand for high-carb foods and increased emphasis on "heart-healthy" diets. Frito-Lay in 2004 will introduce a whole new line of low-carb snack foods to appeal to the low-carb market.[11] New sugar-free additives, such as Splenda, are enjoying increased sales in new products as consumers look for better ways to reduce refined sugar in their diets.

The brand explosion, however, is not confined to foods. It is happening across a broad spectrum of categories—consumer electronics, entertainment, media, automobiles, travel, and household products.

Figure 10-2 illustrates the explosion of choice that occurred in the United States between 1970 and 2000.

Figure 10-2
Explosion of Brands
in U.S. consumer
Market, 1970–2000

	1970	2000
Vehicle styles	654	1,212
Frito-Lay chips	10	78
Breakfast cereals	160	340
Radio stations	7038	12,358
Amusement parks	362	1,174

SOURCE: JACK TROUT, 2001

While the brand explosion has created more opportunities for the point-of-purchase industry, it has also created more communications clutter and intensifies an already-competitive environment for valuable retail space. Retailers are retaliating by seeking more control over their selling place.

The shifting roles of retailers and brand marketers

One of the more notable global trends is that retailers are becoming brand marketers (creating and promoting their own brands) and brand marketers are becoming retailers. Retail has become the battleground for retailers seeking to increase profit margins by increasing private-label programs (as discussed above), and brand marketers, feeling squeezed at retail, are flexing their brand muscles by creating their own stores within earshot of existing channel supporters.

Major consumer brands such as Apple and Sony have established their own signature stores, usually in upscale regional centers where they do not compete with established channels. Apple, which had traditionally used consumer electronic channels such as Best Buy, introduced its own retail stores in 2001—crisply designed, airy retail environments that attracted loyal Apple customers. They feature all of Apple's products, and shoppers can "test drive" each one. Apple users can get free advice from an expert at the "Genius Bar," and daily seminars are conducted on a variety of Apple-related topics.

Sony launched Style in 2003, a new retail concept that features only Sony products—televisions, computers, and other consumer electronics. Like the Apple stores, Style is interactive, allowing customers to sample all products.

These brand stores, of course, feature permanent and temporary P-O-P displays, each one fit to the overall store design. Environments are tightly controlled at corporate, and there is little or no clutter.

The World's Top Brands

In the world of brands, there is constant movement of global brands that cross all borders. Interbrand, one of the world's foremost brand consultancies, tracks consumer brand preferences, and historically, major brands such as Disney, Marlboro, McDonald's and Mercedes have enjoyed premier recognition in their global brand survey. However, Figure 10-3, taken from the last Interbrand survey released in early 2004, shows that Google.com is the world's number one brand and many of the previous top brands have slipped in the consumer poll.

1. Google.com	6. Ikea
2. Apple	7. Nokia
3. Mini (Cooper)	8. Nike
4. Coca-Cola	9. Sony
5. Samsung	10. Starbucks

SOURCE: INTERBRAND, 2004

Figure 10-3
Top Ten Global
Brands

The surprise entry is a relatively new-old brand – the Mini Cooper, a car that languished for years as an obscure British-manufactured small car, only to be resurrected by its new owner, BMW.

CONTROLLING THE RETAIL ENVIRONMENT

Retailers are no longer satisfied to give their stores over to brand marketers who want to buy their way in. Retailers across the board are installing more permanent point-of-purchase displays, while reducing the number and size of these displays to meet new design standards.

For example, Wal-Mart decided in 2002 to reduce the average number of P-O-P displays in its stores, which numbered approximately 700 per store on any given day. Citing the glut of displays and amount of management time to supervise this activity, Wal-Mart reduced the average number of displays to 300.

When Blockbuster Video redesigned its stores in 2000, it converted all in-store signage to a new Blockbuster-branded identity system and eliminated all movie displays. But when it discovered it needed studio-provided displays to hype the latest DVD promotion, it allowed a limited number of displays back in.

Movie chains, the historic centerpiece for movie P-O-P business, saw a major drop in business when some theater executives decided to "clean up" their lobbies. But the perceived benefit of cleaner lobbies did not make up for the pre-release promotion provided by the often-dramatic P-O-P movie displays, and movie displays are now prominent in theatres once again.

Retailers have sought to upgrade their store designs by reducing clutter, creating more permanent fixtures and providing a branded experience. For example, Costco and Sam's Club spice up their warehouse look with demonstration "food queens" who provide free samples of everything from cherry pie to the latest coffee.

Starbucks, with nearly 6,000 outlets worldwide, maintains a rigidly controlled selling environment that features attractive, permanent P-O-P displays, "living rooms" that feature large couches and chairs and the latest hot technology—WiFi capabilities that allow customers to access the Internet.

While some retailers have made efforts to reduce clutter and gain better control of their selling environments, supermarkets, super drugstores, mass merchandisers, and "big box" retailers continue to be the primary venue for P-O-P displays. Retailers with aggressive private label and loyalty programs are purchasing more P-O-P at the expense of brand marketers' desire to increase their retail presence.

Outsourcing

Perhaps the most notable global trend in the past 10 years has been the transfer of P-O-P manufacturing to China and other Asian countries. "Made in China" symbolizes the acceptance and awareness that all P-O-P manufacturers must reduce costs. Of course, this is not news to anyone in the display manufacturing business, or to anyone striving to reduce costs. The landscape, however, is littered with companies who naively moved manufacturing projects to China only to discover they made a costly mistake.

Gerard Grand, president of Design Solution Center in Canada, has done business in China for the past 25 years. His China-based subsidiary company, Dragon Fire Group, helps foreign companies set up manufacturing in China. Grand notes that many companies, lured to Asia with the promise of greatly reduced manufacturing costs, fail to do their homework and discover that the Chinese, while very savvy at manufacturing, are less proficient at data management, logistics, and product or industrial design. They also lack skills in packaging and P-O-P design, which have traditionally been Western strengths. Grand recommends firms do extensive research before committing to Asian suppliers unless they work with a recognized source.

China is not the only country firms are seeking out for outsourcing and lowering manufacturing costs. Ed White, chairman of E and E Display, has developed manufacturing and support alliances in Canada, Mexico, United Kingdom, Germany, France, and Spain. After 9/11, like many in the P-O-P industry in the United States and Europe, E and E experienced sales declines. Although sales have climbed back to its pre-9/11 level, E and E has shifted some of its manufacturing offshore to stay competitive.[12]

Mexico and Central and South American nations, which recently saw an influx of manufacturing from the United States, Canada, and Europe, have seen jobs disappear and shipped to China and other Asian nations. Mexico has launched marketing programs to keep manufacturing in the country by offering incentives and seminars on how to compete with China.[13]

Not all P-O-P companies are shipping their manufacturing overseas. Rapid Displays has an aggressive program to compete for business and keep it here, according to

Alan Forshay, category manager for Rapid Displays, who points out that "the production capabilities available in Asia are expanding and improving every day. The greatest challenge is delivering the benefit of reduced cost within the realities of limited lead time and transportation logistics."[14]

IMPROVED RESEARCH PERFORMANCE

One of POPAI's major initiatives has been its drive toward getting point-of-purchase advertising accepted as a measured medium along with radio, television, print, the Internet, and outdoor advertising. This challenge was answered when POPAI announced the results of its measured research study completed in mid-2003.

POPAI-sponsored research undertaken by the Advertising Research Foundation had the following goals:

- Increase awareness of the medium and its value.
- Include in-store advertising in media planning, forecasting, and tracking.
- Make informed decisions about media alternatives.
- Increase focus on executional excellence.

The results of the research as described by Doug Adams in the Special Report in this book clearly shows that P-O-P advertising achieves a measurable impact on retail sales. Retailers gain the benefit of these sales lifts in more ways than just increased sales— they do not pay for the displays and in fact often receive added promotional fees and discounts for letting the brand marketer install the display.

It is a win-win situation for both parties. Beyond these measured media studies, brand marketers and retailers have known through independent studies that well-designed point-of-purchase advertising is effective. Research in all countries will continue to demonstrate that point-of-purchase advertising is the one medium that works in the selling environment. Brand marketers and retailers alike rely more heavily today on pre- and post-promotion research than ever before.

INCREASED EMPHASIS ON TEAM BUILDING

The authors have emphasized the theme throughout this book — teamwork between stakeholders (P-O-P producer, brand marketer, and retailer) has become a necessity for all to succeed. Each stakeholder must become intimately involved in the planning, execution, and implementation process of achieving the maximum potential for every marketing-at-retail opportunity. With the globalization of retailers and brand marketers, the P-O-P industry faces worldwide challenges in serving its clients. As a result, P-O-P producers and advertising agencies continue to consolidate to serve this global economy.

Momentum, a division of Omnicron, provides a prominent example of how P-O-P producers have united to serve a global network of retailers and brand marketers.

Momentum is an amalgamation of many different support services—P-O-P design and ful-fillment, promotions, special events, and public relations—that was cobbled together through acquisitions over the past 10 years. It has 1,500 employees in 62 offices in 35 countries. Its global management practices feature face-to-face meetings between corpo-rate and local managers. E-mails exchange facts only, and everyone has accountability to an account.[15]

"We're flat. No CFO, no regional managers, and everyone is empowered to act local-ly," says Bill Kolb, Momentum president and COO. "We focus on research for every account, every day of the week. We want to know how our clients connect with the customers."

Perhaps most important was his advice to "become a part of your client's busi-ness model. If you don't do that, you become a commodity—just another vendor." He said that if you prove that you belong and that you provide substantial added value, "they will take you wherever they go." The goal is to create a permanent client bond.

THE GLOBAL SHOPPER

The most important member of the global P-O-P perspective is not the retailer, the brand marketer, or the P-O-P provider. It is the customer.

Between 1995 and 1998, POPAI chapters in North America, Europe, Brazil, and Australia sponsored research to determine the effectiveness of retail-level P-O-P adver-tising by analyzing customer behavior. The POPAI studies reveal one universal fact: More than 70 percent of purchase decisions made by shoppers in these studies were made *after* they entered the store. Results reflect statistics from each country. An Australian study conducted in only two stores is not necessarily representative of all consumers in that country.

Purchases Made

As indicated in Figure 10-4, the average shopper in Holland spends far less during each store visit than those in other countries surveyed. Shopping more frequently and closer to home, the Dutch tend to purchase fewer items and spend less money each trip, largely because Holland is a relatively small country in which shopping districts are within tight-ly inhabited areas. Brazilian shoppers, on the other hand, spend substantially more than shoppers in the United States, Belgium, and Holland.

Shopper Alone Or Accompanied?

As shown in Figure 10-5, the study found that more Brazilians (59 percent) are accompa-nied on their shopping trips than are shoppers in the other countries surveyed; in mass mer-chandise stores, even more Brazilians (71 percent) shop with others. Six out of 10 Brazilian shoppers are accompanied by either their spouse or children.

In Holland, shoppers tend to shop alone because they know what they want and make specific trips to purchase these items, therefore spending less time shopping. And

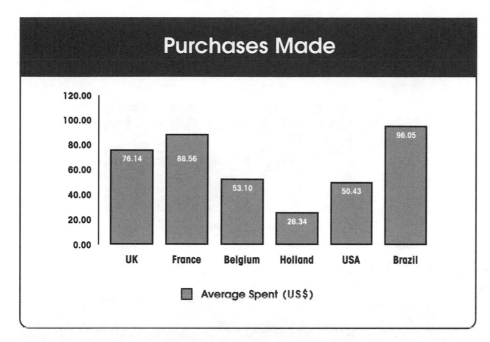

Figure 10-4

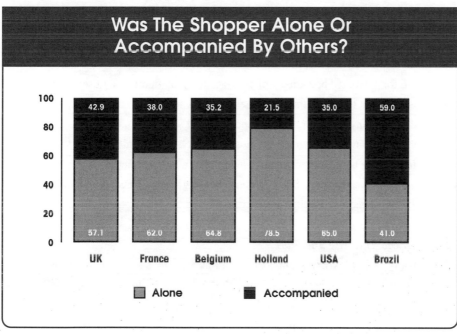

Figure 10-5

because of these "goal-directed" buying trips, they tend not to view P-O-P displays that exist in other parts of their shopping experience.

It is important to understand the makeup of the purchasing party. Because an adult who is accompanied by children may not make the buying decision, P-O-P messages may be aimed at both the child and the adult. Images, key words and phrases, recognizable icons, and spokespersons tend to trigger or activate the buying-decision process.

Figure 10-6

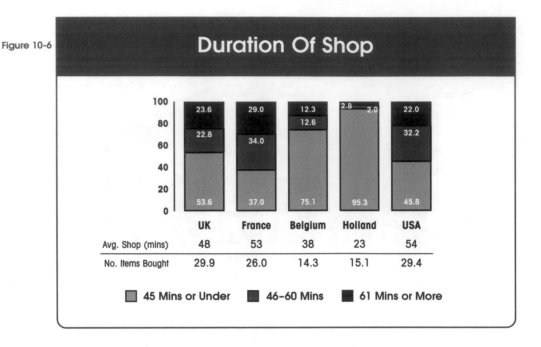

Duration Of Shopping Excursion

Average European shoppers spend 40 minutes per major shopping trip, make 1.2 major trips per week, and spend approximately five hours a month in a supermarket. See Figure 10-6 for a detailed breakdown of average shopping durations, in several countries. The research found that consumers were exposed to many other advertising media, and that there were many opportunities to expose P-O-P advertising to shoppers.

In markets where shoppers spend less time (such as convenience stores), the opportunity actually may be greater to make a sale than in a larger supermarket where the customer never visits a sales arena. Smaller stores ensure greater chance of visibility, but gaining space is much more difficult.

How Often Did They Use The Store?

Brand loyalty is just as important to retailers as it is to traditional brand marketers. POPAI surveys show that customers across the globe can be loyal shoppers and tend to revisit stores where they have pleasant and rewarding experiences. Brand loyalty is built by delivering on promises and performing in a consistent, quality manner over a long period of time.

Shoppers show consistency in choosing where they shop. One reason that shoppers frequented their supermarket or mass merchandiser was because they enjoyed the experience. Supermarket shoppers cited "clean environment" and "good customer service" as the top qualities comprising the shopping experience. In all markets, a majority of shoppers said they visited a particular store "all/most of the time." Figure 10-7 details how often shoppers in several countries shopped at a particular store.

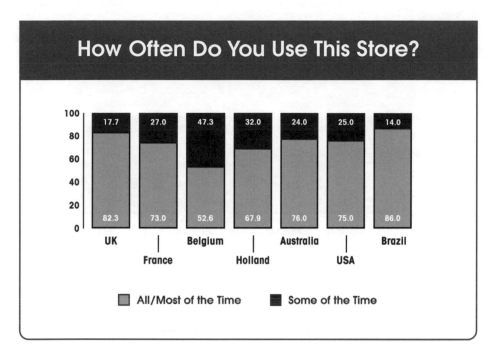

Figure 10-7

How Often Do You Use This Store?

One of the leading factors in building supermarket loyalty was the proliferation of "bonus" clubs. Fifty-nine percent of surveyed European shoppers were members of these clubs. In the U.S. market, the bonus club factor is a major marketing strategy for two of the three major supermarket chains.

The studies also noted that in Europe shoppers did not rate "Shopping an Exciting Experience" as highly as they did in other countries. This revealed the opportunity for retailers to enhance their in-store environment and activity.

In Brazil, location near the shopper's home is a key factor. Sixty-two percent of shoppers favored their supermarket or mass merchandise store because it was "near"—not "very near"—meaning they were willing to drive an extra distance to have the shopping experience they wanted.

With the exception of Belgian and Dutch shoppers, there is a high degree of loyalty. Eight out of 10 Brazilian shoppers consider themselves "loyal" to their stores, while 82 percent of U.K. shoppers feel that way.

Do You Use A Written Shopping List?

Understanding the value of P-O-P starts with the shopping list. The first objective of brand marketers is to get on the consumer's shopping list. The studies demonstrated that women are more likely than men to make shopping lists prior to store visits. Eighty-three percent of European shoppers are female; three-quarters of all shoppers are under 54 and married. As indicated in Figure 10-8, U.S. shoppers are, among those surveyed, the most likely to use a list.

Out-of-store marketing is obviously important in building top-of-mind brand awareness, and when a customer comes face-to-face with actual choices on the shelf

Figure 10-8

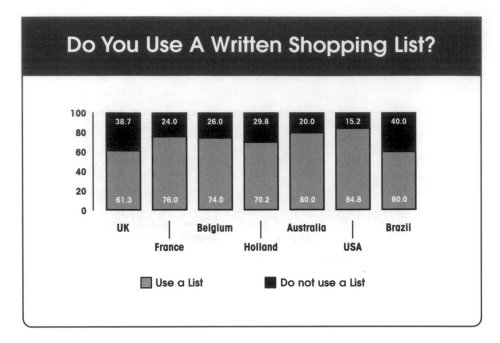

where no P-O-P inducement exists, customers tend to pick the brand leader. Because nearly 70 percent of all brand purchase decisions are made in the store, brand building prior to the store visit becomes critical where P-O-P is not present, which is most of the time for brand marketers.

Percentage Spent Over Budget

How much a customer spends in a store depends on how well he or she has planned the shopping experience (e.g., whether a list was made) combined with in-store decisions, which may be prompted by effective P-O-P advertising.

As indicated in Figure 10-9, the Dutch and Belgians have the lowest percentage spent over budget, while shoppers in the United States, France, and the United Kingdom have the highest. For all countries surveyed, there was a rather conservative over-budget percentage, considering that a majority of purchases are not planned but made in-store.

The conclusions of the research underscored the fact that most shoppers do have a general sense of how much they are going to spend in the store. But the data also recognize that after the basic needs that prompted the trip are purchased, shoppers use a secondary list to purchase additional, discretionary products

How Shoppers Went Through The Store

As shown in Figure 10-10, the studies found that, by at least 10 percent, Brazilians were more likely than shoppers in all other countries to visit all aisles. More than three-quarters of Brazilians visited either all or most aisles or sections, while only 57.4 percent of surveyed Europeans visited all or most sections.

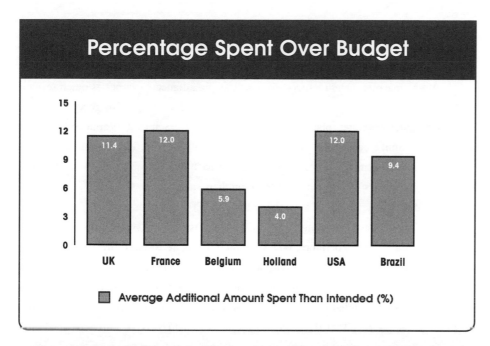

Figure 10-9

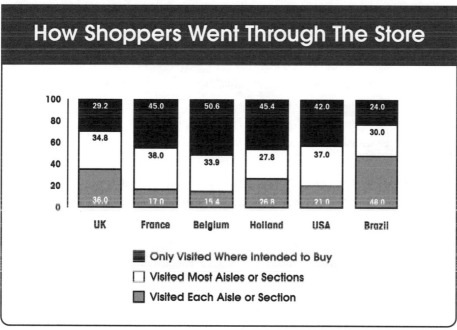

Figure 10-10

Why do supermarkets put milk and other daily staples in the back of the store? Consumers know the answer: This is the consumer's admission price for getting into the store free. Consumers know why storeowners want them to walk past thousands of other items for sale: Retailers and brand marketers want to entice them to buy on impulse.

Since a vast majority of shoppers surveyed said they "enjoy their supermarket experience" because it is in a clean and friendly environment, stores establish their traffic and merchandising plans to enhance the shoppers' experience and thereby maximize revenue streams from customers. Remember that customers control the revenue stream, not the retailer or brand marketer.

Brand marketers and retailers are in a strategic alliance to garner as much revenue from each customer as is possible. Placement of P-O-P advertising helps generate in-store sales. Computer-generated plan-o-grams, which are the essential footprint that retailers devise to maximize customer merchandising opportunities, are now so sophisticated that retailers can predetermine the best selling place for each product. They can even determine what colors work best and in what sequence on their shelves.[16]

And with generic brands accounting for some 20 percent of the sales (vs. traditional brands), retailers are balancing customer demands for brands versus their own higher-margin generic brands. Therefore, how customers navigate through the store influences where products are placed, which P-O-P advertising is accepted or rejected, and where it is placed. Hanger P-O-P displays are increasingly being used to attract customers in other aisles, which is why global retailers such as Wal-Mart extensively use wide-print-format technologies to produce P-O-P hangers.

In-Store Decision Making

Figure 10-11 clearly shows how powerful P-O-P advertising is to the entire revenue stream in any store. The in-store decision rate is the best barometer for measuring to what degree shoppers make their purchasing decision after they enter the store. In Europe, 75 percent of the purchase decisions are made after shoppers enter the store. In Brazil, the figure is 88 percent, and in the United States it is 70 percent. Dutch shoppers make more than 80 percent of their decisions after they enter the store. Each brand purchase is classified into one of four types:

- *Specifically planned*—Planned a particular item and brand.
- *Generally planned*—Planned a particular item but did not have a brand in mind.
- *Substitute product*—Planned to buy type of item or brand and bought another type of item or brand instead.
- *Unplanned*—Bought an item that was not planned prior to entering the store.

The "in-store decision rate" is made up of the total of generally planned, unplanned, and substitute purchase decisions.

POPAI further evaluated which purchases ranked lowest in terms of "in-store decision." Staples such as baby products, butter/margarine, water, fruit, soft drinks, hot beverages, milk, and meat all ranked high on customers' preplanned lists. Brand selections for many of the staples were still left to the in-store consumer decision process. Price, coupons, and P-O-P displays therefore still play a role in the shopper's mind as to which brand they select.

These studies confirm that P-O-P advertising remains a powerful merchandising

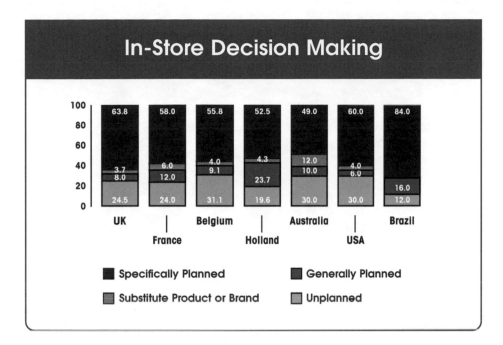

Figure 10-11

tool and influence regardless of where consumers shop. Retailers and brand marketers worldwide have this information plus their own private studies that clearly point to the significance of prompting the customer to make decisions once they are in the store.

ENDNOTES

[1] POPAI, 2003 marketing statistics

[2] World Bank Report, 2003

[3] Fred Meyer, interview by author, July 2002

[4] Wal-Mart.com, November, 2003

[5] Carrefour.com, November 2003

[6] Wal-Mart.com, International Markets, November 2003

[7] U.S. Census Bureau.com, 2003, 3rd quarter results

[8] e-Brand Letter, July 2002,

[9] e-Commerce Times, 2002

[10] amazon.com, financial results, 2004

[11] Barbara Dougherty, interview by author, 2003

[12] Ed White, interview by author, 2003

[13] McNeely Kroupensky, interview by author, Mexico City, Mexico, 2003

[14] Alan Forshay, interview by author, Rapid Displays, 2003

[15] William Kolb, interview by author, 2003

[16] Lynn B. Upshaw, *Building Brand Identity: A Strategy for Success in a Hostile Marketplace* (New York: J. Wiley, 1995), 126.

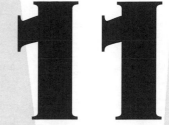

"A new, shelf merchandiser

providing better product availability,

visibility, and restocking . . .

. . . would represent a major

breakthrough for both the brand

and the entire warehouse

snacks category."

Global Reapplication
and Market Adaption:
A Case Study of Pringles
Shelf Merchandising

WILLIAM L. SMITH, JR., CPP, IN-STORE PRESENCE MANAGER
THE PROCTER & GAMBLE COMPANY

INTRODUCTION

Point-of-purchase advertising represents the brand marketer's final opportunity to influence consumers to buy a firm's product, as well as a chance to establish and reinforce long-term consumer equity behind the brand name of that product. Major packaged goods companies such as the Procter & Gamble Company have ever-increasing opportunities to sell brands across the globe as consumers become more connected to select products via advertising—advertising that appears not only on satellite television broadcasts and Internet sites that cross geographic lines and barriers but also through in-store advertising in both global and regional retailers.

Consistency of brand equity is vital as consumers shop worldwide in retail outlets they visit for the first time and in those they frequently shop. Consumers are absorbing more information and more choices as they attempt to select products that meet their needs. Brands with consistent visual cues and clear benefit messages make it easier for shoppers to select those products. This fact has important implications both for packaging design and for the use of similar in-store P-O-P displays and signage.

> Point-of-purchase advertising represents the brand marketer's final opportunity to influence consumers to buy a firm's product, as well as a chance to establish and reinforce long-term consumer equity behind the brand name of that product.

PRINGLES: THE IMPORTANCE OF SHELF MERCHANDISING

Pringles Potato Crisps is one of P&G's largest global brands. Shoppers can buy Pringles in more than 100 countries in a wide variety of retail outlets. Pringles offers several different package sizes to meet consumer needs for both immediate and future consumption, including on-the-go snacking, lunchbox packing, and social occasions. Although it shares similar consumption characteristics with other salty snacks, Pringles is unique compared to other potato chips, pretzels, and extruded snack products. Most salty snacks are distributed in defined regions, but Pringles is known across the globe. Much of the Pringles brand equity is tied to its innovative canister packaging, since most snack products are sold in bags. The distinctive packaging lends itself to a different retailer distribution system and in-store merchandising program not shared by other salty snack products.

Most salty snack distributors rely on direct store delivery (DSD) to ship their products to retail stores. DSD is designed to ensure that bagged products arrive safely on store shelves. This strategy also is consistent with the implementation of "push" marketing, which emphasizes strong in-store presence and promotion. Pringles, like most P&G brands, relies on warehouse delivery distribution. Thanks to its original concept of stacking potato crisps in a rigid cylindrical canister, Pringles can ship directly to retail store shelves via the retailer's distribution warehouse system with a high degree of whole chip product reliability. This factor, combined with P&G's traditional marketing acumen, results in "pull" marketing, as consumers shop at retail looking for a product with strong brand equity, distinctive product packaging, and strong media support.

Pull versus push in-store marketing requires a brand like Pringles to have a strong shelf presence at all times. Consumers must know where to look for Pringles in-store. In the United States, more than 60 percent of Pringles purchases occur from the snack aisle shelf at regular price; in contrast, less than 35 percent of all bag DSD chips are sold from the shelf in the snack aisle. The majority of snack purchases take place throughout the rest of the store, including the front-end cash registers, delicatessen, and the front and back end cap displays along the perimeter of the store. This generally requires the brand marketer to provide "arms and legs" in-store to supplement the placement and stocking of snack products both on-shelf and on-display. As do other P&G brands, Pringles depends on retail store personnel for regular shelf stocking and display merchandising.

Secondary-display locations and additional permanent placements in-store clearly help build Pringles' sales volumes and profit. Nonetheless, as a prominent, highly recognizable brand, Pringles must focus first on proper shelf space and position, which means two key fundamentals must be met:

- Product availability requires sufficient shelf space.
- Product visibility requires sufficient shelf position.

A broad distribution of Pringles package sizes and flavors requires sufficient shelf space to avoid out-of-stocks. While Pringles enjoys high brand equity, there are few, if any, deferred purchases in the snacks business. When the shopper is ready to buy, the impulse to buy, coupled with the absence of Pringles on shelf, equals "buy another brand." Product visibility is also essential for Pringles. Outstanding shelf position enhances its brand equity, reinforces desire, and increases sales. A mass presence of distinctive Pringles canister packages breaks through the profusion of bag snacks within the snacks department, making the purchase an easy one.

PRINGLES SHELF MANAGEMENT: GLOBAL SEARCH AND REAPPLICATION

Ever since Pringles' national U.S. launch in 1971, there has been a need to improve the brand's shelf space and position. The need became more acute by 1995 as volume doubled after a three-year period marked by improved product performance, insightful marketing, and lower list pricing. Over those three years, Pringles had moved from eight linear feet along the bottom shelves to 16 linear feet across four standard U.S. grocery shelves. Even with this additional shelf space, out-of-stocks and less-than-ideal visibility prevented Pringles from reaching its full shelf potential.

Figure 11-1

TTB Vertical-Block

Shelf

TTB Vertical-Block Shelving

In 1995 P&G's Food/Beverage Sales organization began selling the concept of a "top-to-bottom" (TTB) vertical-block shelf arrangement. Figure 11-1 shows the TTB vertical-

block shelving system, which resulted in an increase to 24 linear feet of shelf space, typically using six four-foot-wide shelves. Within two years, P&G was able to persuade more than 50 percent of its major supermarket and discount store customers to use a TTB vertical-block set for Pringles. The result was a significant sales increase for Pringles sales volume and profit growth.

The sale of the TTB vertical-block shelf concept was a first step toward improving both the product availability and visibility of Pringles. The additional shelf space for the Pringles brand added more shelf facings to best-selling products such as Pringles Original, Sour Cream & Onion, and Cheezums, which helped to reduce out-of-stocks. Also, incremental shelf space provided room to launch new flavors such as Pizza and Salt & Vinegar, as well as new package forms such as large-size twin pack, which was targeted for social occasions.

Red-Curved Shelving

Figure 11-2

Pringles Red Curved

Shelving

While the TTB vertical-block shelf concept was shared with other Pringles markets in both Europe and Asia, a new idea developing in the United Kingdom was quickly spreading to Western Europe. Pringles UK, in conjunction with a British P-O-P supplier, con-

ceived the use of distinctive and attention-grabbing red-curved shelving, in which red-curved material, manufactured from vacuum-formed plastic, is overlaid on top of standard gondola shelving. See Figure 11-2. The front lip of the formed curve provided sufficient space for retailer order tags, while the top of the shelves included formed dividers to keep the individual canisters in distinct rows. Additional in-store theater was later added, with branded logo and flavor stickers on the front lips and vertical aisle flags on each side of the red-curved shelves. When combined with the TTB vertical-block shelf set, red-curved shelving demonstrated significant volume increases for Pringles. Tests conducted in the United Kingdom, Italy, and Germany demonstrated 15 to 30 percent increases in sales of Pringles. Several skeptical European food retailers were impressed enough with the test data to implement the new Pringles shelving concept.

Canadian Black-Wire Shelving

Red-curved shelving provided a distinctive in-store presence for Pringles. The use of red-curved plastic shelving in the United Kingdom and Western Europe attracted the shopper's eye to the Pringles shelf section and helped to separate different package forms and flavors by using product dividers and color-coded flavor labels. However, there was a need to address two additional issues:

- Consumer shoppability—or the ease with which users can complete a purchase.
- Retail restocking.

In Canada, food retailers were looking for a more efficient way to address Pringles' out-of-stocks, both real and visual. The rapid growth in Pringles' sales in the mid-1990s made it difficult for grocers to stay in stock. The spreading use of top-to-bottom shelf sets for Pringles, coupled with the increasing use of deeper shelf fixtures, resulted in more visual out-of-stocks. Unless the product was checked regularly and "fronted" (pulled forward from the back of the shelf to the front edges), consumers could easily miss the last two or three cans of shelf inventory, causing a *visual out-of-stock*, particularly on the upper and lower shelves.

Working independently of Pringles in the United Kingdom and Europe, Pringles Canada worked with the P&G customer business teams to develop a shelving solution to reduce the impact of out-of-stocks. The principle of search and reapply revealed that several product categories, ranging from large two-liter soft drink bottles to small two-ounce seasoning jars, used gravity-feed shelving. Pringles canisters were ideally suited to this approach, particularly with their metal rims at the bottom of the package. Pringles Canada developed the black-wire shelving shown in Figure 11-3 to match the color of the standard shelving used by Safeway and other Canadian supermarket chains. The use of black contrasted with the assorted Pringles canister colors, particularly the best-selling red can Original and green can Sour Cream & Onion flavors. Product was always fronted and available for purchase, thus saving shelf-stocking labor time and eliminating visual out-of-stocks.

Figure 11-3

Canadian

Black-Wire Shelving

REAPPLICATION OF KEY GLOBAL PRINGLES SHELVING CONCEPTS FOR A NEW U.S. SHELVING SOLUTION

The U.S. Pringles business team wanted to take the brand's shelving program to the next level of excellence. Selling the need for additional Pringles shelf space, let alone holding on to existing space, was an ongoing challenge for the U.S. P&G customer business development teams. As the importance of selling more potato crisps to consumers while they shopped at retail continued to grow, Pringles recognized the benefit of improving its in-store presence. Creating relevant in-store theater that attracted the shopper's eye would not only increase sales but could also reinforce Pringles' brand equity at retail, much like television, print, and other media advertising.

Reapplying the use of red-curved plastic shelving from the United Kingdom and Western Europe could answer the need for Pringles' in-store retail theater in the United States. However, the customer business development organization realized that the use of red plastic shelves with curved fronts on top of existing shelf fixtures would not be enough to address the needs of U.S. retailers. Retailers quickly understood the benefit to P&G of the red-plastic shelving, but what would it do for them? There would undoubtedly be an increase in sales for Pringles, but that would be true for any brand using red-colored shelving to draw shopper attention to itself. Any successful merchandising solution had to offer more to the retailer than red-curved plastic shelf liners with Pringles signage.

Pringles U.S. next looked to the Canadian use of gravity-feed wire shelving. Like their Canadian counterparts, U.S. retailers grasped the benefits of gravity-feed shelving for eliminating the need for product fronting and the occurrence of visual out-of-stocks, and for easier recognition of real out-of-stocks before they occurred.

Many retailers recognized as an immediate advantage the labor hours saved at retail by use of self-fronting gravity-feed shelving. However, there were two limitations to the black-wire shelving solution used in Canada. First, the use of black was appealing to only a limited number of U.S. retailers and did little to build Pringles' brand equity or draw shopper attention to the Pringles section or the warehouse snacks department. Beige- or cream- colored shelf fixturing was more widely used by retailers in the United States, but the Pringles brand needed to sell retailers on using its equity red color at retail. Second, the use of wire shelving worked well in Canada, where distribution was primarily limited to one package size—the standard medium six-ounce canister. The wire dividers could be evenly spaced for common-width packaging, but the wire dividers did not provide effective flexibility to shelve multiple package forms. Individual by-item distribution and the number of facings per individual products varied by retailer; any shelf solution with product dividers had to provide flexibility. Although it offered durability, wire shelving lacked the flexibility to stock the small-size two-ounce cans, the standard medium six-ounce cans, and the large-size twin-pack canisters in the same package facing slot.

Since retailers are always receptive to any solutions that will help reduce the cost of restocking product on their store shelves, the goals that defined the design of a new shelving system were simple:

- Make Pringles easy to find.
- Make Pringles easy to shop.
- Make Pringles easy to stock.

Pringles also conducted consumer shopper interviews that revealed three key points of dissatisfaction with existing Pringles retail shelving systems:

- The shelf is very crowded and confusing.

- It takes too much time to figure out the product types
  and flavors, along with where to find them.
- Pringles is hard to find when placed on the bottom
  shelves of the snack aisle.

In addition, Pringles needed to create exciting in-store theater. It was time to raise the curtain.

The optimal shelving solution for Pringles would be discovered by combining the best elements of each idea from the United Kingdom, Western Europe, Canada, and the United States. A new, shelf merchandiser providing better product availability, product visibility, and product restocking that benefitted shoppers, retailers, and Pringles would represent a major breakthrough for both the brand and the entire warehouse snacks category.

PRINGLES SHELF MANAGEMENT: THE DEBUT AND LAUNCH OF "CENTER STAGE"

Development of Pringles Center Stage began in December 1998 with an objective of first placements at retail in July 1999 to coincide with the introduction of a large-size twin pack. Although seven months may have seemed sufficient time to launch a permanent shelving system including design, engineering, tooling and production, P&G Customer Business Development needed test data to answer the inevitable retailer questions regarding the volume lift for both Pringles and the warehouse snacks category by installing the Center Stage shelving system. Expensive hand-fabricated samples were required for controlled store testing by mid-February 1999 to conduct an eight-week market test that would provide documented results for presentations that May. With less than 10 weeks to complete the design and engineering required for the test samples and the start of injection-molded tooling, it was essential that Pringles clarify the in-store marketing objectives of this major shelf-fixture initiative.

PRINGLES CENTER STAGE: IN-STORE MARKETING DESIGN OBJECTIVES

1. Improved visibility of Pringles within the center store gondola shelving departments.
2. Quick identification of Pringles shelf set when shopping the aisle.
3. Better product presentation, easier shopping and improved shelf stocking within the aisle.
4. Flexibility to shelve a variety of packages and flavors.
5. Opportunity to customize Center Stage to meet retailers' merchandising requirements.

Each Center Stage design objective was tied back to the basic Pringles shelving goals for the shopper and the retailer as mentioned above: Make Pringles easy to find, easy to shop, and easy to stock.

How well did the Center Stage design meet the objectives?

1) Improved visibility of Pringles within the center store gondola shelving departments

A bright red header with large graphics, including the distinctive Mr. Pringles logo and familiar slogan, "Once you pop, the fun don't stop," was visible above the rest of the gondola shelving within the center store. The injection-molded sign had inserts that provided three different header sizes (8″, 12″, or 14″ high); retailers could select the right size for their stores, according to the different gondola and ceiling-height profiles within each retail interior. The header supports were also designed to accommodate two different product heights for the top shelf, depending on which Pringles packages were placed on the that shelf. Like many elements of Center Stage, the header supports were designed for easy retail installation.

Unlike many shelf headers that are designed to attach to the retailer's fixture supports, the Center Stage header supports were attached to the back of the top shelf. As the top shelf was placed into the back wall supports of the gondola fixture, the header also went into place. This eliminated the need for ladders during the installation process. Figure 11-4 illustrates the header's back-panel graphics that allowed shoppers to "join the Pringles Party" in the snacks department while shopping in the adjacent aisle. The front-side panel graphics could also be adjusted for quick changeover.

Figure 11-4

Pringles Center

Stage 8-inch header

Many retailers agreed that warehouse snacks was a underdeveloped category that deserved special in-store attention, and that Pringles was the right "signpost" brand to gain shopper awareness. Several grocery executives also noted that P-O-P signage is a critical element of retail merchandising for impulse products such as salty snacks, cookies, crackers, and soft drinks. Nonetheless, some retailers who desired a standard gondola height profile for their center store resisted the placement of the Center Stage header. Ultimately, the eight-inch was used by all retailers that installed the Center Stage header; injection-molded tool inserts to produce taller header sizes proved unnecessary.

2) Quick identification of Pringles shelf set when shopping the aisle

Once the shopper entered the aisle, the distinctive red-curved shelves and header quickly got the shopper's attention, immediately communicating Pringles' availability. The bright, red styrene plastic material was inherently attention-grabbing in a four-foot-wide by six-foot-tall vertical block. The red color was also synonymous with Pringles Original, the most popular flavor in the brand's product line. The center curve on both the shelves and the header helped communicate Pringles' unique canister packaging. The unique, curved shelves created a discontinuity among the rest of the shelving in the aisle, further attracting shopper attention to the Pringles vertical-block shelf set. The center part of the curved shelves stood out less than three inches from the standard shelf—not an excessive distance into the aisle. The bottom edges and corners had a smooth radius, eliminating any sharp edges. A metal frame to provide structural strength supported the injection-molded shelves underneath. The center curve, along with the radius-edged corners, provided safety benefits in the event of human contact with the shelves, added to the structural integrity, and was more resilient to cracks when the display was hit by consumer or warehouse carts.

Store operations managers expressed bipolar views on the red-curved shelving. Many grasped the Center Stage concept and understood the need to create a visual discontinuity in the aisle to grab the shopper's attention. Other managers disliked the discontinuity, preferring conventional straight-line shelving. Nevertheless, the design, engineering, and construction of the shelving made a very good impression.

Another key benefit for retailer operations was that the retailer could adjust the depth of the Center Stage shelf sizes. Because the shelves were inserted into the gondola shelf-fixture uprights, replacing the existing shelves, a store audit that measured the depth of the shelves within the warehouse snacks department was conducted before installation.

Using inserts in the injection-molded shelving tool, each Center Stage shelf was available in any one of six variable shelf depths, ranging in 2-inch increments from 18 to 28 inches. This ensured that the front corner edges would closely match the rest of the shelf depths along the entire length of the department, with only the two curved moldings protruding out into the aisle. This feature alleviated manager concerns as to how well Center Stage would fit in their center store aisles.

Figure 11-5

Clear styrene shelf fronts

3) Better product presentation, easier shopping and improved shelf stocking within the aisle

Perhaps the most popular feature of Pringles Center Stage was the gravity-feed shelves. Pringles product always remained front-faced, which eliminated visual out-of-stocks for consumers, particularly on shelves that were not at eye level. This feature also made work easier for retail store clerks, who no longer had to manually face all Pringles canisters to the front of the shelves. Molded-product dividers helped to keep each facing of canisters in its proper row. This improved product organization, helping shoppers find the desired package type, size, and flavor, and helping store clerks reorder and restock the correct Pringles products. When a product facing was down to one or two packages, the gravity-fed shelves revealed the need for product re-ordering; this was particularly beneficial for shelves not at eye level. The clear styrene-shelf fronts shown in Figure 11-5 were placed above the red-plastic shelving. This prevented the product from falling onto the retail floor and made it easy for both the shopper and store clerk to see which package was behind the shelf front. The fronts were fluted and sculpted for each row of canisters; all parts had radius edges to prevent cuts.

All product shelves contained an extrusion channel for retailer product order tags. This was easy to design, since most retailer product tags work within a standard one-inch-high extrusion channel. The extrusion channel could accommodate paper-back or sticker-back tags. While there was some initial interest in placing color-coded product labels on the plastic panel above the extrusion panel, it was determined that this would add to the shopper's visual confusion.

The Center Stage gravity-feed shelving system also had a pull-out drawer feature, which worked like a file drawer cabinet. See Figure 11-6. The pull-out drawer was designed to provide improved product rotation and restocking. The store clerk could depress by finger-touch two tabs located under the front left and right sides of each shelf. Once the tabs were pushed up, the molded shelves would slide down the supporting metal frame, thus making it easier to rotate and restock the product. The pull-out drawer was often not utilized at retail. The pull-out tabs were not visible, since retailers did not want consumers to pull out the shelves and leave them protruding into the aisle. Unfortunately, new retail clerks who could use the feature were not always told about it due to the lack of communication that follows the high labor turnover in entry-level stocking positions. Additionally, many clerks chose not to use the pull-out drawer.

Figure 11-6

Pringles Center Stage

pull-out drawer

4) Flexibility to shelve a variety of packages and flavors

Center Stage shelving was designed to manage three forms of Pringles packaging: The traditional, 6-ounce medium-size canisters, the 12-ounce large-size canister twin packs, and the 2-ounce small-size canisters. While the majority of product facings within the four-foot Center Stage shelving units would be used for the medium-can product, all shelves had to be designed to accommodate the placing of any of the product forms wherever the retailer desired. For example, Figure 11-7 is a four-foot shelving unit set up to accommodate all three forms of Pringles packaging. Depending on the retailer's shelving philosophy, they could approach merchandising Pringles in many ways to achieve the desired mix of sales volume and profit among the different product sizes.

The medium canisters were designed to glide on their metal rims at the bottom of the package between the standard molded dividers at a nine-degree shelf angle. Like the variable shelf depths, the product dividers also had specific lengths that provided the canisters with support and product orientation to the back of the gondola. Because the poly wrap around each of the twin-pack canisters prevented the packages from sliding down the gravity-feed shelves on their metal rims, Pringles large-size packages were supplemented with a coil-pusher system to maintain consistent product front facing. The pushers were also available in variable shelf depths to maximize product inventory on each Center Stage shelf. Two product pushers were used for each facing of the large-size twin pack, thus eliminating the middle canister product divider. The other two product dividers were left in place to keep the large-size packages better oriented within their product facing.

Figure 11-7

Four-foot Center Stage shelving unit set up to accommodate the three forms of Pringles packaging

The small-size canisters were designed with a unique two-tiered shelving system. The two-ounce canister "jump-shelves" helped to maximize inventory of these fast-selling items and eliminate excessive shelf air space when the small size was shelved next to the larger canisters. This feature was particularly appreciated by retail category managers, and store operations personnel who needed to maximize every inch of available shelf space.

The small-size jump shelves, like the product dividers and pushers, were available in variable shelf depths. One particular design challenge was to accommodate gravity-feeding of both the medium and the small canisters which have different package weights. The small-size jump-shelves had small "feet" or props molded at the bottom of their side supports, which changed the slope of the two-ounce product gravity-feeding to 12 degrees and enabled the medium and the small size to slide down the gravity-feed shelves at the same rate. This same "jump-shelf" design concept was applied when 23-gram, eight-pack Snacks Stacks product was added to the Pringles product lineup three years after Center Stage was first designed.

5) Opportunity to customize Center Stage to meet retailers' merchandising requirements

In addition to its strong Pringles branding, Center Stage was appreciated by many retailers because it could be customized to meet the merchandising requirements of each store within a retail chain. As noted above, Center Stage was not a free-standing fixture but was designed to work with the retailer's existing gondola fixturing.

Before a Center Stage unit was shipped to any store, an extensive shelf audit was conducted to determine the shelf gondola manufacturer and the specifications of the

Figure 11-8

Four-foot Center Stage shelving unit with six different shelf depths

Figure 11-9

Pringles Center Stage shelving unit with customized Albertson's "Snacks Central" graphics

shelf fixturing used in-store. Center Stage was originally designed to work with the primary form of four-foot-wide shelving used by the industry as manufactured by Lozier and Madix. Later Center Stage shelf adaptations were made to work with other manufacturers' shelving gondola systems including DixieCraft and Hussman. Because the overwhelming majority of interested retailers used four-foot-wide shelving, three-foot-wide gravity-feed Center Stage shelving was never designed or produced.

An essential element of Center Stage customization was the ability to custom pack each unit with shelving that matched the rest of the retailer's snack aisle shelf depth based on audit measurements taken in each store to assess the aisle's shelving depth. This ensured that the unique red-curved shelving Center Stage units did, in fact, properly fit each retail store and help to address many store operations managers' concerns.

Another important customization feature included the ability to custom pack a specified mix of different depth Center Stage shelving within each unit shipment. The shelf-depth profile frequently varied top-to-bottom. For example, the lower shelves were often deeper (22 to 24 inches) than the upper shelves (18 to 20 inches) in many older supermarkets. Whatever the variation in the audit, six Center Stage shelves could be packed, shipped, and installed with up to six different shelf depths, if required, as illustrated in Figure 11-8.

While most retailers maintain standard shelf plan-o-grams across their chain stores, many supermarket category managers supported Center Stage because they could select specific Pringles shelf hardware to support their own specific shelf-merchandising plans.

Customization of point-of-purchase advertising graphics was another option of Center Stage. The left and right front-header panels, along with the side-header panels, were designed to display "pop-in" graphic card sections that could be used for standard Pringles graphics or could be modified for retailer customization. Albertsons, the second-largest supermarket chain in the United States, took advantage of this option to customize by adding their signature "Snacks Central" department graphics to the front-end signage panels of the Center Stage unit shown in Figure 11-9. Surprisingly, only a handful of retailers took the opportunity to customize the panel signs with their own logos.

PRINGLES CENTER STAGE: SUMMARY AND KEY RESULTS

Since the 1999 inception of Pringles Center Stage shelving units, about 6,800 U.S. supermarket and mass merchandiser retail stores have installed more than 7,000 units. While most retailers agreed to placement of a four-foot unit, approximately 200 retail outlets installed two (8 linear feet) or three (12 linear feet) units in their stores. Figure 11-10 is an example of a 12-foot Center Stage unit.

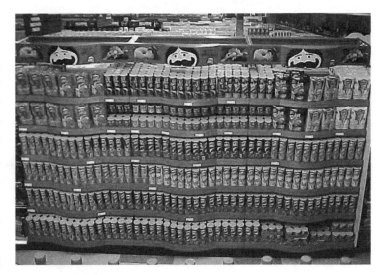

Figure 11-10

Pringles Center

Stage 12-foot

shelving unit

While not all of the brand's placement objectives were met, the list of participating retailers with 65 to 100 percent store placement within their chain was impressive. The largest U.S. grocery chain, Kroger, had participation by the majority of their Kroger Marketing Areas, including Fred Meyer, Fry's, and Smith's. Albertsons also installed Center Stage in most of its operating divisions, including Jewel and Acme. Two of the most influential U.S. regional food retailers that have supported Center Stage throughout the life of the program are Meijer and HEB.

Additional U.S. retailers that have placed Center Stage units include discounters (Kmart), upscale supermarket chains (Harris Teeter and Dierberg's), major regional supermarket chains (Giant Eagle, Hy Vee, and Brookshire Brothers), the U.S. Defense Commissary Agency stores, and many smaller chains and independents supplied by wholesalers such as Super Valu and Associated Wholesale Grocers (AWG).

In conclusion, Pringles Center Stage represents one of the largest placements of a brand marketer's in-line shelving unit that has ever been sold to the dry grocery merchandising segment of the U.S. supermarket industry. The success of Pringles Center Stage was acknowledged by Point-Of-Purchase Advertising International when POPAI honored it with the 2000 Gold Outstanding Merchandising Award (OMA) for Permanent Displays in the Snacks and Beverages category—a first for Pringles.

"The P-O-P advertising industry has begun the process of becoming a measured medium. The availability of in-store advertising measurement is expected to significantly increase the effectiveness of spending by brand marketers and retailers."

Special Report: Making In-Store Advertising A Measured Medium

Doug Adams, President
Prime Consulting Group, Inc.

Editor's Note: *The following special report is based on* P-O-P Measures Up: Learnings From The Supermarket Class Of Trade, In-Store Advertising Becomes A Measured Medium: The Convenience Channel Study, *and the paper*, In-Store Advertising Audience Measurement Principles. *The paper, authored by Doug Adams and Jim Spaeth, former president of the Advertising Research Foundation (ARF), was approved by the ARF Board of Directors in July 2003 and is part of the POPAI Measured Medium Initiative. All three reports are available at www.popai.com.*

INTRODUCTION

The time pressure felt by many consumers today has resulted in more buying decisions being made in-store. According to the *1995 Point-Of-Purchase Advertising International (POPAI) Consumer Buying Habits Study*, 70 percent of in-store decisions were made at the point of purchase in supermarkets. Clearly, a crucial location for advertising is at retail near the point of purchase. An integrated marketing communications (IMC) plan rewards the hard work of building brand awareness outside the store with the "recency" benefit of providing a related message at retail. With research having shown that advertising generally loses its potency rapidly after exposure, *recency theory*—or the belief that advertisements are more effective the closer the consumer is to a decision—places a premium on exposures timed for delivery the day before a purchase decision. Therefore, an at-retail exposure immediately preceding a purchase decision would be the most valuable of all.

Nevertheless, the essential metrics of media planning—*gross rating points (GRPs), cost per thousand impressions (CPMs), reach,* and *frequency*—have never been developed for in-store or at-retail media. Moreover, the most essential of all media metrics, *proof of performance* (i.e., whether the medium delivered the placements purchased) also has not been developed for in-store media. Finally, while there are well-accepted methods for determining the immediate sales lift from an in-store promotion action, a broad-scale knowledge base that could support using in-store media most effectively had yet to be developed.

These three unmet needs formed the basis of POPAI's Measured Medium Initiative, which had three goals:

- Goal Number 1   Measure Audience
- Goal Number 2   Prove Placement
- Goal Number 3   Quantify Sales Lift

Following a thorough study of key issues facing its community of producers, brand marketers, and retailers, POPAI adopted a major strategic initiative in 1998 to "establish in-store advertising as a measured medium, on par with print and broadcast." POPAI's long-term goal is to convert P-O-P advertising into a measured medium on par with print and broadcast. Such measurement of P-O-P advertising will allow producers, brand marketers, and retailers to:

- Increase awareness of the medium and its value.
- Include in-store advertising in media planning, forecasting, and tracking.
- Make informed decisions about media alternatives.
- Increase focus on executional excellence.

Measuring placement is invaluable to brand marketers and retailers if they believe, or can prove, that placement helps to enable their sales and profit objectives to be achieved. Therefore, to build interest for this new placement measurement, the value of placement must be demonstrated to the industry and to individual companies. Sales forces and retailers tend to focus on the immediate benefit—sales lift. Whereas all interested parties (producers, brand marketers, and retailers) express interest in measuring the sales and profit impact, brand marketers must also evaluate P-O-P advertising as a form of media capable of delivering impressions to an audience of current and potential consumers. This is referred to as *audience measurement*.

GOAL NUMBER 1: AUDIENCE MEASUREMENT

The point-of-purchase advertising industry has begun the process of becoming a measured medium. The independent availability of in-store advertising measurement is expected to significantly increase the productivity and effectiveness of spending by brand marketers and retailers. In addition, marketing at retail may now be on better footing to earn a larger share of the media budget if advertisers find the audience measurement results compelling.

The POPAI Measured Medium Initiative has broken a logjam that impeded in-store advertising progress for decades. It explains the measurement methodology for:

- Weekly reach (with an opportunity to see [OTS]).
- Frequency.
- Impressions/GRPs.
- CPMs.

In its early stages, the research faced the question of media vehicle. In traditional media, the vehicle might be a television program or a magazine, but not the ad itself. For in-store advertising, the store is the vehicle, which makes an OTS an exposure to the store, not necessarily the ad itself. This concept and the resulting measures for the supermarket and convenience store (C-store) channels are explored using chain-specific data and channel-wide estimates.

Approach

Although no current media measure was found to fit "as is," the principles that underlie the measures are readily adapted to a new in-store audience measurement system. At their core, the measures for in-store—like other media—must provide a measure of the consumer's opportunity to see the advertising. This concept is well ingrained in the media world as "OTS."

As "OTS" implies, audience measures do not guarantee an attentive consumer carefully absorbing the advertising message; rather it implies open eyes (or ears) in front of the media vehicle—an opportunity. In traditional media, the vehicle might be a television program or a magazine, but not the ad itself. For in-store advertising, the store is the vehicle, which makes an OTS an exposure to the store, not necessarily the ad itself.

It is anticipated that, as P-O-P ad exposure measurement evolves, vehicle exposure measurement may be refined to an area of the store in proximity to the display, through the use of shopper basket analyses or Personal People Meter (PPM) panels.

Starting with the basic exposure measure, we can build a small number of key media planning and buying measures such as exposure, audience, reach, and CPM. These measures are among those defined in the glossary of terms on the CD-ROM that accompanies this book.

To develop measures for in-store, media characteristics were examined to develop a comparable basis for in-store measurement. Television, print, and radio are targeted vehicles by which the brand marketer expects to reach a demographically specified audience that is segmented by age and gender. In most instances, age and gender are actually surrogates for the brand marketer's real target, which may be defined in terms of product purchase or usage behavior. Targeting media directly to shoppers [shoppers vs. users] is actually more effective because they are at the point of purchase, as opposed to potential buyers who are targeted by traditional media prior to actual purchase.

The recency theory adopted by the media industry over the past few years—that the closer the ad exposure is to the purchase occasion, the more effective it will be—lends support to in-store advertising.

Television, print, and radio attract their audiences based on content interest. Because of current data limits, brand marketers today generally accept the programming audience as the commercial audience. For other forms, such as outdoor advertising, there is no content draw. As a result, some brand marketers choose to discount the size of the traffic audience when estimating the number of persons actually exposed to the advertising. In-store advertising is more analogous to broadcast or radio in that consumers tune in for the content. In the case of the store, the content draw is to purchase products. In fact, in-store advertising, arguably, can be said to have a tighter connection between content and commercial because they relate to a specified product or service in the store.

Definitions and Data Sources

Development of the in-store advertising audience delivery measures relied upon data from Information Resources, Inc. (IRI) Shoppers Hotline for the supermarket channel and individual retailers for the convenience channel, along with various industry statistics as noted. The supermarket data are all household-based, whereas the convenience store data are transaction-based. Although neither is person-based, what they may lack in demographics they more than compensate for in propinquity.

Potential Weekly Reach

Potential weekly reach is the maximum reach achievable by an in-store message. The maximum assumes 100-percent store penetration. To develop the potential reach measure for in-store, two approaches were developed. The first approach assumes the availability of consumer-based information, whereas the second uses store measures and reasonable averages and approximations. The first approach (illustrated below) is more accurate, and therefore preferred, but the data are not always available.

To derive the number of households that shop in a store or chain in a week (or an average week), several sources can be used. These include:

- Retailer tracking.
- Household panel services.
- Diary panel services.
- Custom data collection.

In addition, depending upon the unit of measure in the available data, the following measures may be needed on a chain- or channel-specific basis:

- Average number of target persons shopping on a trip.
- Estimated number of trips per week per person.

The weekly people-with-an-OTS calculation is shown in Figure 12-1. The results show that in-store advertising in Chain A's 122 stores creates a potential reach of 552,782

		Chain A	Chain B
	Unique household trips (Avg./store/week) (1)	5,437	8,161
times	Avg. no. of adults per transaction (2)	1.25	1.25
divided by	Estimated number of trips per week (3)	1.5	1.5
equals	Weekly Potential Reach per store	4,531	6,801
times	Store count	122	160
equals	Weekly Potential Reach for chain	552,782	1,088,160
divided by	Population = Share of market	21.4%	42.3%

Figure 12-1

Opportunity-to-See Calculation for supermarkets in the Baltimore/Washington market shoppers in a week (21.4 percent of the market), compared to Chain B's 160 stores creating almost double that number—1,088,160 (42.3 percent). These two chains represent 63 percent of the weekly potential reach, yet only 53 percent of the grocery all-commodity volume (ACV), reinforcing their importance of chains in delivering in-store ad messages.

Actual Weekly Reach

Actual weekly reach is defined as potential weekly reach adjusted to reflect the actual store penetration level achieved. The adjustment reflects the fact that not every store will execute the campaign. The execution level, or proof of performance, is a critical element in this in-store audience measurement methodology.

Most in-store media planning and purchasing today involves an estimation of actual execution. Monitoring store-level execution ensures placement and helps adjust potential reach to actual reach by providing the following data:

- Actual store penetration (execution).
- Display condition (e.g., damaged, obscured, fully functional).
- Proximity of the P-O-P advertising to the product.

The actual store penetration is crucial to developing an accurate actual or realized reach. Today, store penetration levels can only be measured with sufficient accuracy through visual inspection of a store to confirm in-store ad placement. Such store audits, whether conducted routinely, randomly, or during key weeks (the sweeps concept), should be performed by a third-party service that is independent from those who will use the audit results.

Future Measurement of Execution (and Reach)

Whereas monitoring now requires store audits, various technologies that may provide passive yet accurate and independent verification of placement are under development. Such methods may require years of development and implementation. As a result, measurement approaches must be flexible to accommodate a variety of new data sources as they become available and accepted.

Frequency

A consumer can be exposed to an in-store ad message multiple times in the week measurement period. Weekly frequency measures, by chain by market, can be obtained from household panel services and from individual retailers (the latter primarily from frequent shopper data). Retailer-specific information, eventually at store level, is needed to avoid "averaging away" important distinctions and valuable information.

According to the Food Marketing Institute, the average shopper makes 1.5 trips to supermarkets each week. The comparable number for convenience stores is 1.7, according to the National Association of Convenience Stores. In the absence of market-store type and chain-specific data, these figures are reasonably accurate.

CPM

Understanding the cost of delivering impressions to the audience is just as important as the ability to measure the audience. CPM is the common denominator for comparing different media costs. It is used to allocate media budgets across different media, along with the tracking of actual performance.

A sampling of in-store advertising vehicle costs was gathered from sponsors of the 2001 supermarket channel study. These costs are not meant to be representative for the industry at large, but rather they were used to develop a formula to calculate and make comparisons to other media CPM.

$$\text{CPM} = \frac{\text{P-O-P advertising cost per event}}{\text{Audience}/1000}$$

The P-O-P cost per event includes the cost of P-O-P material, any specific ad placement fees, and the labor cost for setting up the material in-store for all the stores with placement. The audience, also known as reach, represents the actual number of people (in a week) who have the opportunity to see the material. Once CPM measures are calculated, in-store CPM can be compared to other media.

Application of Audience Delivery Measures

The application of audience delivery measures will be far reaching. In-store advertising can now be evaluated and planned with the same discipline afforded print and broadcast. The methodology outlined provides reasonable audience estimates, on a par with those used for traditional media. It can also be used in a variety of settings, including those that are data-rich and those less well measured.

Brand marketers will be able to include in-store advertising vehicles as part of the media planning process. Brand marketers and retailers will both be able to judge the reach of in-store activities along with the cost of delivering that reach. These measures may also extend into sales force and third-party support service applications focused on the importance of retail execution. After those uses will come scorecard development and negotiated levels of performance in both execution and audience delivery. In the future, we might expect a brand marketer to offer incentives to a retailer for providing a desired level of impressions for a target consumer segment.

When armed with independent, statistically valid evidence of the sales response from a particular combination of P-O-P materials, brand marketers, sales forces, and retailers will have compelling reasons to focus on execution and measurement—to achieve the maximum potential incremental sales from the promotional event or product placement. At the same time, some of the evidence may cause a redirecting of spending away from less effective materials toward those with a track record of delivering incremental sales profitably. This shifting, based on knowledge, is healthy for P-O-P advertising producers, as it will deliver greater value to brand marketers and retailers and will be rewarded by the consumer, who drives the entire process with the additional product purchases.

In-store advertising will now not only be measured but will also set the standard for planning and tracking the link between audience delivery and short-term sales response. As companies begin to experiment with audience delivery and sales effectiveness measures, new insights will be developed, which will likely refine this methodology and extend the various applications.

Defining the Next Goal

The POPAI Measured Medium Initiative studies have broken a logjam that impeded in-store advertising progress for decades. There is a good deal of work ahead to build the needed knowledge and fully implement its findings. Nevertheless, we can already begin to place the next set of goals into three broad categories: (1) tightening precision, (2) extending reach estimates, and (3) advertising exposure, that is, moving up the Advertising Research Foundation (ARF) Media Model hierarchy (of relevance) from vehicle exposures to advertising exposures. Let us briefly consider the three goals.

Tightening Precision

Many factors go into this methodology. Some rely upon generalized learning to provide a sound estimate but could be made more precise if more situation-specific data were available. These quantitative factors include cross-chain shopping, trip frequency, people involved in each transaction, and the level of at-retail execution. In addition to tightening quantitative precision, the following three areas of qualitative precision should be addressed as the measurements are refined:

- Quality of time exposure.
- Quality of P-O-P placement in-store.
- Quality of audience.

Extending Reach Estimates

The current methodology provides for weekly reach estimates. Media planners need to extend these estimates over longer time frames and combine them with other media to fully evaluate the contribution of various levels of in-store activity to the media plan. This will generally be handled as two related but separate projects.

The first project—extension of in-store reach estimates over time and multiple-week reach estimates—would be most useful, especially when tailored to the duration of the retail and media plans. The usual execution patterns of P-O-P advertising should inform this process and may make it fairly straightforward.

The second project requires some measurement of in-store exposure via the same method used to measure the other media to be considered. A number of such syndicated surveys exist, some on a national level and others on a more regional one. For example, circulation-per-copy is to print what the portion of traffic at a given store location is to in-store.

Advertising Exposure

The recently revised ARF media model[1] underscores the value of distinguishing between vehicle exposure and advertising exposure. There is general industry interest in moving the media currencies forward from vehicle exposure to advertising exposure. For example, in out-of-home advertising (e.g., billboards, bus benches), media practitioners use traffic counts as they relate to specific ad placement to translate vehicle exposure measures to ad exposure measures. In online media, too, practitioners are recognizing the distinction between vehicle and exposure. We can look forward to all media employing the same currency standard.

While not readily available today, chain-specific or market-level-by-store-type data could be collected on a periodic basis to map the traffic flow through a store and create exposure factors for various departments or sections of the store. With the first two phases of this multiphase initiative completed, we can already define the road map to standardized data methods and sources to enable the planning and management of in-store advertising as a measured medium comparable to traditional media. There will be refinements along the way, which tighten precision, extend reach, and evolve to measuring impressions. In the meantime, this progress allows brand marketers and P-O-P producers to include in-store in the planning and selection process with other "traditional" forms of media and to apply the same performance yardsticks.

GOAL NUMBER 2—PROOF OF PLACEMENT

The proof of placement is a commonly understood concept that has been sought on an individual company or agency basis for a number of years. However, no industry-wide standard of measurement or syndicated service has emerged to provide objective independent measurement. Tracking placement, also called "penetration" in media circles, is crucial in order for brand marketers, agencies, and P-O-P producers to link marketing stimulation with the resulting sales and profits.

The measurement of P-O-P placement has traditionally been accomplished through manual audits of a sample of stores. When developing the scope of proof of placement measurements, questions must be addressed concerning:

- Geographic scope.
- Range of retail stores.
- Timing of expected execution at retail.
- Specific P-O-P materials to be audited.
- Types of messages on the materials.
- Placement location within a store.

Many manufacturers have commissioned audits covering particular seasonal or holiday promotion drives that involve customized P-O-P executions. In several instances, the motivation is to validate placement, identify gaps in execution, or gather information to improve the execution process in the future.

Supermarket Study Audit Design

For the POPAI supermarket study, measurement scoping began with an evaluation of the goal: projectable results for the continental United States supermarket retail channel. POPAI and PCi engaged IRI to support the auditing needs. The store sample developed for the supermarket study was composed of 250 supermarkets from 22 major markets across the continental United States and drawn from the top 15 retailers plus strong regional retailers and independents. This sample was judged sufficient to provide a projectable estimate of the levels of execution.

The next decision involved the length of time needed for the audits. For store executions that involve only one placement (such as a semipermanent brand display fixture), one audit can provide the straightforward evaluation as to whether the material is present or not. Several audits may be required, spread out across a number of weeks or months, if an evaluation of the length of placement is desired. For several fast-moving consumer goods, execution in store changes weekly or biweekly, necessitating more frequent store audits to monitor the ever-changing levels of execution.

For the POPAI supermarket study, audits were conducted in three twenty-week waves, each focusing on different products. Twenty weeks was judged a sufficient period in which to see several complete retailer promotion cycles. The 250-store sample audited for twenty consecutive weeks translates into 5,000 store audits or potential observations of P-O-P advertising. Effort was made to audit products during their peak execution season of the year.

Once the geographic scope, type of retail stores, and timing of audits have been determined, three decisions remain as to what to audit for once in store: specific materials to be looked for, types of messages to be recorded, and locations within the store. This information can be of great value to the brand marketer and retailer. The POPAI studies have shown that the integration of the right material, right message, and right location in store are needed for successful P-O-P advertising that drives incremental sales.

Each store was broken into different areas for coding of the display or P-O-P ad placement, for example, main shelf, lobby, end cap, and open floor. Materials were coded based on their type: signage or collateral (e.g., inflatable, mobile, floor, coupon machine, and base wrap). Further information was captured about the signage content, including product photo, price, thematic message, brand message, and whether the sign was handwritten or preprinted.

Once the audits were completed, the data points were accumulated and analyzed according to like materials, placement levels, and various combinations of materials. These clusters of material combinations provided insight into merchandising execution and were instrumental in addressing the third goal—quantifying sales lift from P-O-P advertising materials.

Convenience Store Study Audit Design

When addressing the same study goals for the C-stores, projectability to the continental United States was still the goal, as was the key time of year for merchandising. The peak time of year for C-stores is summer. The range and type of stores were selected with the assistance of six leading retailers who provided access to a sample of 120 stores from 10 markets throughout the summer.

To accommodate the environmental considerations not applicable to supermarkets, such as outdoor merchandising, C-store auditing differed noticeably. Figure 12-2 illustrates the three sets of at-store audit parameters: locations at the store, materials, and messages on the materials. As in the supermarket study, once the auditing was completed various analysis steps were performed to develop lessons and insights about execution levels.

Figure 12-2

Three At-store Audit

Parameters

Where?

INSIDE
Checkout
Food Service Area
Front Window
On Cooler Door
Near Cooler
Gondola Endcap
On/Above Gondola
Open Floor Area

OUTSIDE
Perimeter
Gas Pump/Island Area
Gas Pump Nozzle Top
Sidewalk Area by Store
On Window
On Front Door

What materials at each location?

Branded Fixture
Generic Price Sign
Pre-Painted Sign/Banner
Branded Display Shipper
Branded Counter Display
Coupon Pad/Dispenser
Motion P-O-P
Inflatable/Mobile
Base Wrap
Prop/Standee
Wobbler/Dangler
Neck Hangers
Cooler Door Signs

What elements on each P-O-P?

Brand Message
Brand/MFG Logo
Chain Name/Logo
Theme
Coupons on P-O-P
Premium offer
P-O-P Shows Retail Price
P-O-P Shows Savings
(% or $)
Product Photo

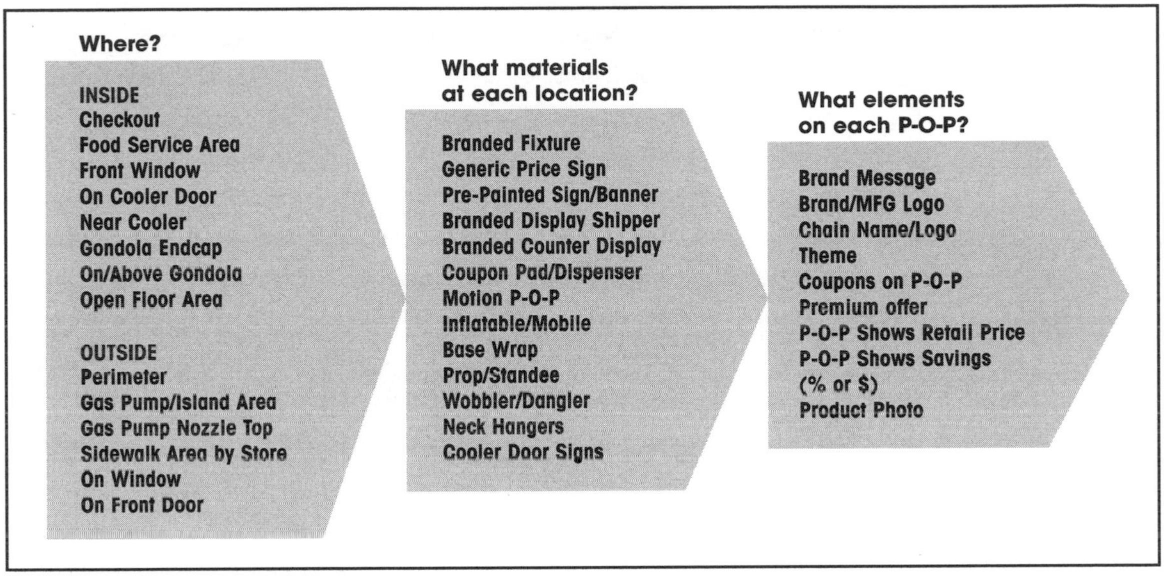

Future of Placement Monitoring

In the future, new approaches to monitoring placement will offer greater cost efficiency and more continuous access to placement information. The emergence of electronic chip and radio frequency identification (RFID) technology, allowing remote monitoring of P-O-P advertising presence, will provide new metrics and independent proof of placement verification. In the POPAI drug store study, one such new technology—from Goliath Solutions, Inc.—will be used to collect placement information for the study analysis. During the drug store channel research to begin in 2004, brand marketers and retailers will have access to placement information on a daily basis, opening up new areas of analytics and execution monitoring.

GOAL NUMBER 3—QUANTIFY SALES LIFT

Some brand marketers are satisfied with measuring the audience reach and the delivering of impressions that results from achieving Goals Number 1 and Number 2. Others are equally interested in both the brand-building impact and the immediate impact on sales. To address these interests, Goal Number 3 was established to isolate the immediate impact that P-O-P materials have on sales.

Clearly, there are numerous marketing stimuli at work simultaneously in the typical store today. Therefore, when developing the study methodology the study team evaluated two approaches: controlled-store testing and sales-response modeling. The team concluded that since P-O-P material is rarely the only form of marketing stimulation aimed at the consumer, sales-response modeling would more closely represent reproducible results. Therefore, sales-response modeling was used to quantify the sales lift. The same methodology was applied to both the supermarket and C-store studies, with just a few minor differences for environmental factors.

The models followed the pattern of standard statistical models used by many leading manufacturers and research firms. Data were gathered to develop historical patterns for the sample stores leading up to the audit time frame. The lift for each material was determined by statistically isolating the sales impact that resulted from placing that particular advertising material on the product display or at the main shelf. The effects of various other stimuli or causal factors such as a product display, location of the display (e.g., end cap, lobby, or floor), store differences, seasonality, price reduction, promotion, and other variables were factored out first to isolate the P-O-P lift effect. See Figure 12-3. Each brand was evaluated separately using its own response model. Statistical tests were performed to ensure that acceptable explanatory reliability was achieved for each brand.

Figure 12-3

Analysis

Methodology—

Sales Effectiveness

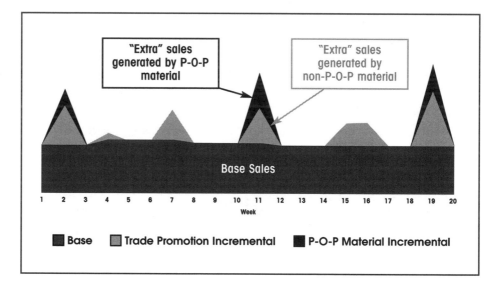

All "brand store week" observations for a particular material were used to obtain the sales lift. The models isolated the effects of each material by factoring out the mentioned variables, including other P-O-P materials. A sales lift was derived for an individual type of P-O-P material if that material was observed enough times by itself, meaning it was statistically valid to provide an *individual* lift for that material. The criteria to determine "releasability" (of single material lifts from model results) was a minimum of 25 observations (an observation is a store week) and an acceptable r-square for the model.

While brand material combination lifts were not modeled separately, the range between the additive and the multiplicative value of the individual material lifts was judged an acceptable estimate of the maximum lift attributable to that combination. An "average brand" lift was reported for each category by weighting the brand results according to volume for brands with sufficient observations.

Understanding the Value of and Applying Sales Lifts

The P-O-P effectiveness findings reported in this study represent the sales increase (or lift) for the P-O-P material *alone*. The lift is above and beyond the lift derived from the product display or price reduction. For example, if Material X delivers a 10 percent average brand sales increase, then adding Material X to that product's display would add 10 percent to weekly store sales above and beyond the product display lift or impact of a price reduction.

In general, small or infrequently promoted brands will experience greater percent lifts, because their base volume is smaller than that of a large brand. When combined with base volume, this smaller brand may not deliver as many incremental dollars in sales compared to a smaller sales lift for a larger brand. See Figure 12-4.

	Base Sales	Lift Percent	Incremental Sales
Brand A (frequently promoted)	$500,000	5.5%	$27,500
Brand B (less frequently promoted)	$150,000	12.9%	$18,000

Figure 12-4

Sales lifts for brands based on frequency of promotion

During the study, no attempt was made to determine a saturation level in either frequency of events or number of ad messages cumulatively present in a store. Both effects require separate study.

SUMMARY OF STORE STUDY KEY LESSONS

In-Store Advertising Works Half the Time—But Which Half?

The early twentieth century retailer John Wanamaker in often quoted to have said, "I know half the money I spend on advertising is wasted. . . . I just don't know which half." The advertising industry has not known in the past whether this holds true for P-O-P materials. The supermarket channel research revealed that Wanamaker's statement is equally applicable to P-O-P advertising. Based on the sales lifts found in the two studies, roughly half of P-O-P advertising was found to be effective. Forty-five percent of supermarket P-O-P materials and 57 percent of C-store P-O-P materials was found to deliver an immediate sales lift in the same week the material was seen by shoppers. Knowing which half of the in-store materials works is the first step to optimizing the P-O-P mix.

In the supermarket study, category results ranged from 23 percent to 70 percent of P-O-P advertising materials delivering sales lift at the main shelf and from seven percent to 67 percent at the product display. Hair care, beer, and laundry products had the most consistently effective P-O-P advertising at the main shelf. Beer and laundry, along with dog food and upper respiratory products, had the most consistently effective materials at product displays. For these categories, the results are not a reflection of how much advertising is used in-store but how effective the materials were in consistently increasing sales. Cereal was found to have the least effective P-O-P advertising among the eight categories studied. Not only was there little material to find, but the P-O-P material that was found did not achieve significant sales increases.

Not All P-O-P Is Created Equal

The supermarket and C-store studies both found wider variability than anticipated across the brands and product categories studied. In many cases, specific types of displays provided significant sales lifts for brands in one category but not in another. In addition, detailed analyses revealed that displays were rarely effective for all brands in that category, or the impact varied significantly between brands. For example, in upper respiratory products average brand sales increases in supermarkets for P-O-P displays ranged from 2 percent to 19 percent, depending on the material.

The average sales lift for P-O-P displays that were successful in driving incremental sales was 12 percent in supermarkets and just over 20 percent in C-stores. See Figure 12-5. With half of the displays scoring zero lift and the other half averaging 12 to 20 percent depending on the channel, brand marketers, producers, retailers, and agencies have plenty of motivation to know what works and what is not driving sales.

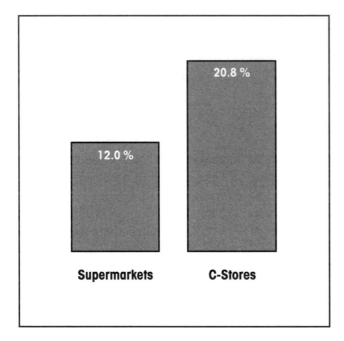

Figure 12-5
Sales Increase for
P-O-P Displays that
Worked

A few P-O-P materials delivered consistently across categories, either successfully or not. Consider P-O-P advertising use at the main shelf: not only was there consistent cross-category execution of two materials (shelf merchandising unit and retail price promotion sign), but both materials delivered modest brand sales increases for all categories. Combined, these two materials made up 80 percent of the main shelf P-O-P materials. Average brand sales increases were as high as 17 percent for a shelf merchandising unit, and up to 10 percent for a retail price promotion sign.

Store-provided price signs (item description and/or price only) also produced consistent results across studied categories. This material did not contribute any additional sales beyond the impact of the product display. Since this type of sign was found at two-thirds of all displays, consumers may have come to expect this primarily price message as part of the display and not as an additional advertising message.

The diverse results theme is amplified by looking at the best two material combinations. Although consistent sales effectiveness levels (14 to 27 percent sales lifts) were achieved across categories when combining the top two display P-O-P materials, the types of materials were different from category to category.

Placement Levels Are Low

Although more than 90 percent of product displays carried some signage in supermarkets, only one out of every four product displays (27 percent) had P-O-P advertising provided by the brand marketer (e.g., account specific, brand, or thematic). This means that three out of four product displays are found without brand-marketer-provided advertising support. At the main shelf, P-O-P advertising was found in only 12.7 percent of the store week observations.

Placement was better in C-stores, but still fewer than half (45.4 percent) of the product displays had advertising that was supplied by the brand marketer. High-volume beverage and snack categories received the strongest coverage yet rarely exceeded 50 percent, as shown in Figure 12-6.

Figure 12-6

Average Brand

Coverage by

Category in

Convenience Stores

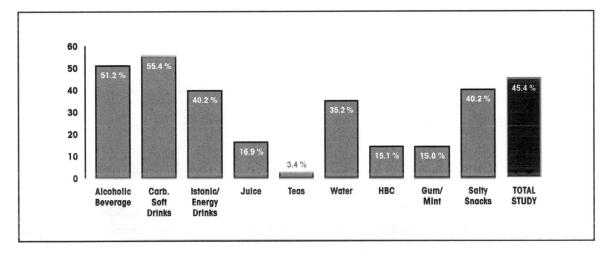

Execute at All Product Locations

The incremental sales-effectiveness measures for P-O-P materials contained in the report provide compelling evidence that tighter controls or more inclusive processes are needed to gauge execution compliance. Only one out of every four product displays in supermarkets and 45 percent in C-stores carried brand-marketer-provided P-O-P advertising. Additionally, the study found that every time that brand-marketer-provided P-O-P materials appeared on a product display, it was accompanied by a similar message at the product's main shelf location only 13 to 37 percent of the time. There is a huge opportunity to carry the marketing message from the product display to the main shelf location, to achieve higher levels of audience exposure and sales.

At the same time, with a decline in total store shopping, brand marketers and retailers may have only one location to provide consumers with an advertising message for a product. For some categories, such as health and beauty care products, the main stocking location is shopped by a majority of category shoppers. Yet for other categories, such as snacks, a large portion of consumers purchase from product displays found on several store floor locations from week-to-week. Therefore, the message needs to have *dual placement* (advertising placed simultaneously at the product display and the main shelf during the same week).

The strongest dual placement occurred in the beer category, with 37 percent of product display advertising tied to main shelf advertising. Upper respiratory brands had the least dual placement, with only 13 percent of product displays having simultaneous execution at the product display and main shelf. Across all studied categories, three-fourths of P-O-P display messages were not connected to the respective main shelf. Therefore, the customer who is shopping for the product at the main shelf—and does not walk past the display—has missed the advertiser's message.

While a retailer will not want to saturate the main aisle with P-O-P materials, appropriate main-aisle use requires knowing which brands are effective in their placement of advertising materials and knowing what types of material deliver incremental sales. Capturing this opportunity will require both education (retailer and manufacturer) and process change.

Location, Location, and Location

We have all heard the famous answer to the question, "What are the three most important things in real estate?" The same is true for real estate within a store for product displays and P-O-P advertising. During the supermarket and C-store studies, the quantification of sales lift added further evidence to this notion. For example, in C-stores P-O-P materials for products that are consumed on the go, such as single-serve beverages and snacks, performed well at the gas pump. Conversely, P-O-P advetising for take-home sizes of those products performed well on the front window or in open floor displays in the store.

Careful consideration in regard to the traffic flow of the target shopper for a product, not just the store's traffic flow, was found important. For example, single-serve beverages performed well in the food service area, where they complimented the mini-meals. Products that did not complement the food purchase did not achieve the same lift.

Consumers told POPAI that they remembered the first and last ad impressions a higher percentage of the time than they did impressions made in the middle of the shopping trip. And, as expected, consumers recalled familiar messaging more often, in part due to the repetition factor. As for messaging, consumers appear to recall and be interested in different messaging depending on the retail venue. For example, in supermarkets, thematic materials that engage shoppers performed better than brand messaging. Thematic messaging was less successful in C-stores, perhaps because of the fast nature of the trip allows less time to engage the shopper. Beer was the exception; thematic materials scored very strong sales lifts in both venues. In C-stores, telling the shopper of the savings, either in cents off, percent off, or multiples (such as 2 for 1) was just as important as showing the actual product price.

The study lessons point to the need to understand the location, retail channel, and in-store location when designing P-O-P materials and messages. Individual brand marketers, producers, and retailers will find their campaign results significantly enhanced if they have a thorough knowledge of what works and where it works.

APPLICATIONS

Operating in the Dark Is Hazardous to Your Brand

The supermarket and c-store channel findings clearly show inconsistent placement results and wide-ranging sales effectiveness levels. Without a formal and ongoing measurement system, all parties (brand marketer, retailer, and P-O-P producer) will continue to operate in the dark and forego the opportunity to work together to optimize this important portion of the marketing mix. Figure 12-7 illustrates how brand

Applications of Findings

Marketers to	Retailers to	Producers to	
			Proof of Placement measures will allow:
✓	✓	✓	• Evaluate/focus on improving execution levels.
✓	✓		• Measure compliance to intended execution levels.
✓	✓		• Establish performance standards and goals.
✓	✓		• Improve placement through acting on placement information.
		✓	• Offer value-added services to improve execution.
			Sales Effectiveness measures will allow:
✓	✓	✓	• Understand what works/what doesn't
✓		✓	• Bring better value to clients—insights on what works/what doesn't.
✓		✓	• Optimize the budget—get more sales from same spending.
✓		✓	• Move to value-added services—not just price negotiations.
✓	✓	✓	• Evaluate ROI or payback analysis.
			Audience Delivery measures will allow:
✓	✓		• Evaluate in-store with the same measures as print and broadcast.
✓	✓		• Plan in-store with the same discipline as print and broadcast.
✓			• Judge the reach and the cost to deliver that reach.
✓	✓	✓	• Value (currency) retail execution.
✓			• Negotiate for audience delivery levels.
✓			• Treat P-O-P as strategic part of your marketing mix.
✓	✓	✓	• Link execution with sales effectiveness measurements.
✓	✓	✓	• Redirect inefficient spending/execution.
✓	✓	✓	• Optimize P-O-P material selection.
		✓	• Suggest better performing material combinations.

Figure 12-7
Application of findings for brand marketers, retailers, and producers

marketers, retailers, and P-O-P producers can benefit from applying measures of proof of placement, sales effectiveness, and audience delivery.

Applying Proof-of-Placement Measures

Proof-of-placement measures allow brand marketers and retailers to measure compliance against intended execution levels. After compliance is determined, performance standards and goals can be established by using the placement information to address problem areas. Brand marketers, retailers, and producers can then work together to improve execution.

Applying Sales Effectiveness Measures

Once proof-of-placement verification measures are in place and communicated, brand marketers can work with producers to understand what works and what does not for their brands and category. Armed with specific sales lift figures by material, proof of placement findings, and material costs, they can measure return on investment (ROI) or develop a payback analysis to understand the profit generated by placement of P-O-P advertising. Brand marketers and producers can then further optimize P-O-P investments and educate retailers on the most effective use of these materials. Further, this analysis will allow brand marketers and producers to compare this P-O-P investment to other brand-building investments.

Applying Audience Delivery Measures

The new audience OTS measures have far-reaching implications for the industry. They provide the methodology for weekly reach estimates where none have previously existed. By combining audience delivery measures with the sales effectiveness information, brand marketers and producers will be able to use a more comprehensive scorecard to demonstrate the true profitability and ROI of their efforts.

Focusing on measurement statistics will afford brand marketers and retailers the ability to accomplish several strategic goals, including:

- Greater focus on execution of P-O-P at intended locations in the store.
- Quantification of potential incremental sales available from a specific campaign.
- An opportunity to fine tune the P-O-P mix and cost expenditures.
- Measurement of consumer exposure to in-store advertising messages.

Some of the above goals may cause a redirecting of spending from less efficient and less effective materials to those with a track record of delivering incremental profits. Collectively, these actions will be healthy for P-O-P producers, who will be able to deliver greater value to the consumer, and will be the basis for future and more innovative P-O-P material development.

EVALUATING P-O-P AS A TRADE PROMOTION

The evaluation of trade promotions for the more sophisticated retail trade classes (food, drug, and mass merchants) typically include:

- Sales increases, over base sales (lift) and over prior year.
- Penetration of the brand (percent of transactions with the brand purchased).
- Trade spending (off-invoice allowances, feature ad costs, etc.).
- Marketing agreement funds.
- Store execution levels.

The most common measures of trade promotion results are sales lift, cost-per-incremental dollar (CID), and spending as a percent of sales. By combining the sales effectiveness of P-O-P material with the material costs, these measures become available. This results in brand marketers being able to make comparisons to other forms of trade promotion such as:

- Thematic sign and inflatable/mobile on a product display compared to an extra 10-cent price reduction for the promotion.
- In-store advertising compared to coupons or retailer flyer advertising.
- Shelf-merchandising unit or shelf strip compared to price promotion.
- In-store signage compared to outdoor advertising.

The worksheet depicted in Figure 12-8 (shown on page 226) outlines how to calculate the appropriate promotion evaluation measures for P-O-P material.

The top half of the worksheet provides information on P-O-P materials used, the brand's base sales, lift factor (from the tables under each material's graph), and the resulting incremental and total sales. The bottom half details the various payback statistics. In the example, a Brand A promotion with a thematic brand sign and inflatable results in $663 of incremental sales from one store (in one week). Therefore, the $100 cost of P-O-P material delivered a 66 percent return. Evaluating cost per incremental dollar shows that every 15 cents of P-O-P material delivered $1 in incremental sales.

THE SALES OPPORTUNITY IS LARGE

The prize that may result from focusing on P-O-P optimization is large. The annual incremental sales opportunity is estimated at $2 to $6 billion in supermarkets and almost $1 billion in C-stores, depending upon the aggressiveness of the assumptions. These opportunity estimates assume

- No new product display placements.
- Dual placement focus: P-O-P at the shelf when on display.
- Executing brand-marketer-provided P-O-P ads on displays currently without displays.
- Optimizing the mix and performance of existing brand-marketer-provided P-O-P.

With the sales increases from P-O-P advertising averaging 12 percent in supermarkets and 20 percent in C-stores, there is no doubt that adding P-O-P ads to the existing shelf presentation or incremental display drives significant additional sales dollars. The challenge for brand marketers, retailers, and producers is to:

- Maximize the combination of location, material, and messaging that works.
- Take action to change the half of P-O-P advertising that was found ineffective.
- Secure P-O-P ad placement on displays that are not receiving coverage.

Taken together, these actions will deliver meaningful growth to brand marketers and retailers.

Figure 12-8

Sales and Payback

Projection Worksheet

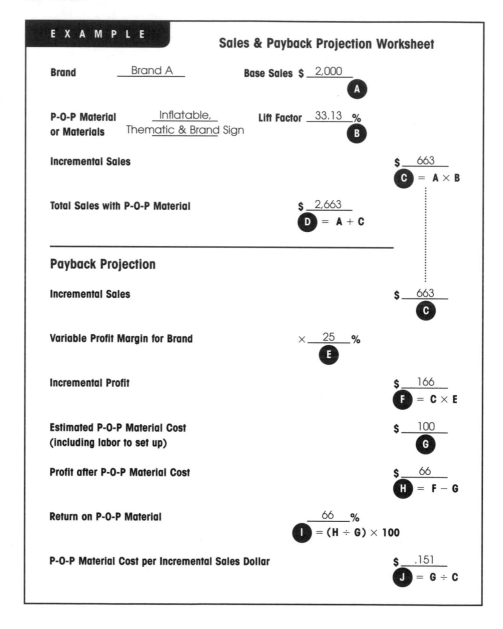

EXAMPLE

Sales & Payback Projection Worksheet

Brand   Brand A   **Base Sales** $ 2,000

Ⓐ

P-O-P Material   Inflatable,   **Lift Factor** 33.13 %
or Materials   Thematic & Brand Sign

Ⓑ

Incremental Sales $ 663

Ⓒ = A × B

Total Sales with P-O-P Material $ 2,663

Ⓓ = A + C

Payback Projection

Incremental Sales $ 663

Ⓒ

Variable Profit Margin for Brand   × 25 %

Ⓔ

Incremental Profit $ 166

Ⓕ = C × E

Estimated P-O-P Material Cost $ 100
(including labor to set up)

Ⓖ

Profit after P-O-P Material Cost $ 66

Ⓗ = F − G

Return on P-O-P Material   66 %

Ⓘ = (H ÷ G) × 100

P-O-P Material Cost per Incremental Sales Dollar $ .151

Ⓙ = G ÷ C

ENDNOTES

[1] "Making Better Media Decisions," (July 2002), The Advertising Research Foundation, 6.

13

Editorials

JOHN C. ANDERSON • **JIM EINSTEIN** • **MERRILL HOWARD** • **JOHN A. SAKALEY III, CPP**

Trends In P-O-P Advertising From The Perspective Of A Retailer

JOHN C. ANDERSON

U.S. MANAGER OF MARKETING/MERCHANDISING

BP OIL CORPORATION

In this busy world, retailers have less and less a share of the customer's attention as they try to entice the customer to purchase ever more goods and services. The question for the retailer becomes, "How can that be done?"

For many years, point-of-purchase materials have been increasingly used to better educate consumers. Retailers want consumers to better understand that the retailer has the product they want, that the price is "everyday" fair and low, and that the product is available for immediate purchase. Studies by BP have shown that in most cases our consumer is "on the run," coming into our convenience stores not always knowing what they want, but that they can and will make an impulse purchase decision if products are presented to them within the store.

We at BP also had to take into account the fact the average consumer is in our convenience stores for 90 seconds or less, so how do we draw attention to their needs and wants within that short a timeframe?

Three years ago, we decided to make our point-of-purchase materials colorful and direct and to use specific product imaging. We reviewed what "best-of-class" retailers were doing around the country. We reviewed what POPAI research was finding about the effectiveness of different types of point-of-purchase displays. And we conducted internal studies with our consumers, matching that information to what POPAI had learned in previous studies.

Once we figured out how we wanted to target our messaging specifically to consumers, we created a new look and feel for our P-O-P materials.

We discovered that our point-of-purchase materials should be strategically placed in the consumer's pathway and that the P-O-P messages should be reinforced throughout the consumer's journey. Doing so has helped us get and keep consumers focused on whatever kind of purchase we want them to make. Such strategic and repeated messaging has given BP an edge in daily communications with the consumer, thereby increasing our effectiveness and in-store revenues.

Our next challenge was deciding how to combine point-of-purchase advertising with our different site graphics packages. This was not an easy task. We had to review all the different color options, along with placement options for the P-O-P display. We wanted to ensure that the display would stand out and give the consumer a message that would be carried throughout the store. Once we agreed on a strategy, we placed the P-O-P display in a test store and evaluated how well the color and font choices stood out from environmental factors including store design and other point-of-purchase signage. Then we conducted customer intercepts to ensure that we had hit our targets with the consumer. We now use this process in testing all of our new point-of-purchase advertising in-store.

As you know, the point-of-purchase advertising industry has changed dramatically over the past five to 10 years. As it continues to change, it will be essential that marketers use the innovative ideas and suggestions developed by POPAI and others. People are always looking for ways to get things done faster, cheaper, and more effectively. That is why one must always look for new ways to improve business—for both for the customer and the shareholder.

Trends In Permanent Displays

JIM EINSTEIN

EXECUTIVE VICE PRESIDENT AND GENERAL MANAGER

ALLIANCE, A DIVISION OF ROCK-TENN COMPANY

Retailers generally don't care about growing individual brands. They care about growing categories to drive their bottom line. They also care about their own retail brand experience from the minute a consumer walks into the store to when they leave the parking lot, hopefully with bags brimming with purchases.

Within that concept lies the key to unlocking the future of permanent merchandising.

Today, retailers are focusing more and more on their stores as "brand" and spending millions to form the emotional bonds with consumers that were once the provenance of brands themselves.

Twenty years ago, think the Snuggle Bear and Jordache jeans. Today, think Niketown, Toys R Us, Pottery Barn, Starbucks, and Abercrombie & Fitch. Unless you have lived on an island for the past decade, the mention of those retail stores has struck an emotional chord. They are among the retailers who have used the store environment to successfully short-circuit the emotional bond that used to exist solely between consumer and brand to now exist between consumer and retailer. Welcome to the retail store as an overall brand experience.

Leading retailers are paying loads of attention to the most effective and consistent medium they have for communicating with their consumer audience—the retail stores themselves. Retailers understand the power of their own internal promotional networks reaching millions of consumers each day as other media struggle with a slippery grasp on audience.

Why are retailers now turning to marketing at retail? Consider that in 1995 it took three television spots to reach 80 percent of women. Five years later, it took 97 spots to reach them, according to a recent article in Fortune magazine.

As retailers build their own brand essence and attributes, permanent displays are vital elements in setting the stage for retail brand management and the ensuing brand partnerships that will proliferate from this point forward.

The following five trends are likely to shape permanent displays in the next five years:

Retailers supporting store-based selling events and strategic branding initiatives. Retailers, ever battling each other for shoppers, are looking at how to grow categories through a number of inventive ways that create incremental sales opportunities for brands. Look to permanent displays to be part of that strategically deployed effort in the form of category outposts, cross-merchandising, and special event promotions. Home Depot recently worked with Black and Decker to stage an out-of-category promotion of power tools to women, a nontraditional but expanding market. The result is a 38 percent increase in sales. New technologies and the use of mixed materials and modular formats mean that a six-month promotional window is now feasible with a permanent fixture.

Retailers providing a hands-on experience and theft deterrence. Each retail chain loses millions of dollars yearly due to shoplifting or "shrinkage". Still, today's consumer-sell is a very hands-on approach. This hands-on approach helps stores' brick and mortar locations differentiate themselves from their Internet portals and competitors. As retailers strive to balance an open-sell philosophy with reduced shrinkage, look for more innovative approaches to control theft that still permit consumer interaction-more products out of showcases, but controlled.

Retail partnerships that transcend class of trade boundaries. Retailers understand the value of category expertise and the importance of building their own brand essence. They are using permanent displays and merchandising to create hybrid stores-within-a-store and aisle environments in some nontraditional venues. Toys R Us is considering staking out sections of major supermarkets, and Office Depot will be selling products in special a section of the grocery chain Albertson's.

Retailers working with brands to grow category. Retailers have become proactive in working with the brands that are category leaders to grow their business within the retailer's strategic plan. Retailers solicit permanent merchandising concepts from their leading brands and award the project execution and prime space in the aisle to the brand that delivers the best understanding of growing the whole category, not just their own brand.

Permanent displays that are regionalized and event- and account-specific. As advances in materials and digital printing technology make low-quantity, high-quality permanent units cost effective, look for more regional and event- and account-specific promotions. Retailers are demanding more impact and more stability as traditional brands are synergistically incorporated into the retailer's overall brand positioning.

Retailers are working harder than ever to master and exploit every square foot of their most powerful promotional medium—the store environment itself. Permanent displays are an important tool for creating differentiation and an enhanced shopping experience.

Online shopping and the Internet as a research tool will grow simultaneously. As more consumers go online, retailers are controlling the role that their store plays in defining the consumer experience. They are expecting the brands that line their shelves to play along with them. Within that strategic alliance lies the future of permanent merchandising. For the brands that master this concept and strategically deploy permanent merchandising to secure their on-shelf real estate, this new era will yield phenomenal sales results for both the brand and the retailer.

Trends In Temporary Displays

MERRILL HOWARD
GENERAL MANAGER, DISPLAY DIVISION
ARTISAN COMPLETE

Temporary displays fill a large portion of the point-of-purchase market. They are often used to promote a newly introduced product or a product that the producer wants to have as a standalone to separate it from the competition. They can be shipped flat for assembly at destination or as prepacked displays, which many retailers prefer, to save stocking costs at the store level.

A major benefit of producing temporary displays versus permanent ones is cost. Many displays are needed at the retail level for only a short period of time, to increase sales during a high-volume period (e.g., candy at Halloween).

Because of the low cost, companies with many brands to promote can afford to produce temporary displays separately for individual products. A promotional impact can be created with a unique design and vibrant colors, without the high costs of a permanent fixture.

In the past, many temporary displays were produced as cheaply as possible—and looked it! As if the appearances weren't bad enough, there was poor construction that often did not support the product, creating havoc on the retailer's floor.

This still happens today. However, the trend—directed especially by the larger retailers who are now more specific in what they will allow in the retail environment—is to produce an attractive display that will enhance their store's image. Retailers want a temporary display that will not fall apart and, most importantly, will attract the consumer to it and increase product sales.

Today, budget concerns are increasingly driving the development of temporary displays Attractive displays, some including 3-D pop-offs, lights or motion, and stronger fillers to support the weight, will obviously cost more. Many brand marketers recognize the importance of point-of-purchase advertising and will opt for more durable, more attractive displays to increase product sales. Others do not see the value in the extra expenditures and need to be educated on how the improved display will improve the return on their investment

Using research information from POPAI, the P-O-P producer can demonstrate that investing a bit more in the point-of-purchase display will result in a more powerful, more effective display that will show immediate results.

Some of the standard temporary displays long used in retailing—such as sidewinders/sidekicks, pallet displays, and base/tray/header—can easily be designed to create an image that will attract the consumer. Don't forget, whether selling hardware or candy, it is the consumer who makes the decision as to which brand to buy, and it is the display's job to attract the consumer's attention.

How are these added features achieved on a display? One of the most effective techniques is to integrate new or different materials into the manufacturing process such as the use of transparent, colorful plastic inserts that catch overhead light. Another effective technique is to add motion, either battery-driven or from in-store air currents; LED lights; or dimensional add-ons for a 3-D effect. There are many additional things that producers are asking for, to draw attention to their products.

What trends are expected in the future? There will be a lot more store identification added to the displays along with the product branding, especially by the larger retailers. This added retailer customization means additional costs, specifically in the printing process. However, these additional costs ensure that the brand marketer is gaining access and getting the retailer's cooperation for the most advantageous placement.

We can also expect to see an increase in prepacked displays to save labor costs at the retail level, again increasing producer costs. Many of these displays are for one-time use and are disposed of when the contents are sold out.

Yet, contrary to this trend toward disposability, many producers are asking to make a display that can be refilled with product to amortize the display cost and be more environmentally friendly. This usually adds only a slight cost in order to increase the durability for longer usage in-store.

Another trend will be point-of-purchase advertising's increasingly larger portion of the advertising budget. Brand marketers and retailers, bolstered by research conducted by POPAI and others, are proving that marketing at retail is proving itself in return-on-investment analysis.

Where do we go from here? Although there will always be a need for the cheapest of displays to shelve product, display designers and manufacturers need to listen to producers, retailers, and consumers as to what is needed. More and more, we are being asked to stay away from the boring "square" display and create a display with innovative design and stunning color that will capture attention at the retail level.

Today, the display manufacturer is challenged with the opportunity to be uniquely creative and produce an attractive display by introducing new materials and complex shapes that will present the customer's product for a cost-effective, throwaway price.

Trends In P-O-P Advertising From The Perspective Of A Brand Marketer

JOHN A. SAKALEY III, CPP

VICE-PRESIDENT, MERCHANDISING

NINTENDO OF AMERICA INC.

How do brand marketers both grab the consumer's attention and interest and get the branding message across at retail? Only one medium does both—point-of-purchase advertising. Other media—such as advertising, in-store promotion, radio, print, out-of-home (theaters, outdoor signs, in-school, malls, bus shelters, and other place-based media), Internet, and tie-in promotions—are, of course, important to the overall marketing mix. But in the already-crowded retail environment, it is still that final three feet in-store that is vital and can spell the difference between success and failure.

Brand marketers must continue to tax their creativity, knowledge, and experience to identify the best and most cost-effective way to get their products from the shelves of retail stores into the shopping carts of consumers. To accomplish this, brand marketers need to find new ways to trigger the consumer's decision/purchase process of (1) being aware, (2) experiencing, (3) validating, (4) intention, (5) selecting what to acquire and where, and (6) making the final purchase. Brand marketers who realize the importance and value of P-O-P advertising will use the four following trends to win the battle at retail in the future.

Edu-tainment: To educate the consumer in-store, in a fun and entertaining way, will be paramount in the future. Brand marketers must bring their brands to life at the point-of-purchase by creating a vision experience through the use of audio/visual imagery, information gathering, price/value store escalation, and promotion.

The P-O-P display can no longer be just an extension of packaging—it must emotionally motivate the consumer. It also must educate in-store personnel by being unique and entertaining, thus validating in-store personnel's acceptance of a brand marketer's brand and products, while enhancing their ability to communicate their knowledge to consumers.

Data Mining: Brand marketers and retailers use *data mining*—defining the psychology and buying habits of the consumer—to find out as much information on perspective consumers as possible. The increased use of data mining has enabled the brand marketer and the retailer to gain critical, strategic knowledge about the consumer, using market segmentation to separate consumers into smaller "channels" (e.g., commonalities, lifestyle behaviors, media choices such as print vs. television vs. Internet, demographics, and psychographics).

Once their market segments are identified, brand marketers must synchronize their P-O-P advertising with their brand message and gear them to both old and new customers.

Technology: The use of digital compact flash media players, in combination with plasma or LCD screens (which can be continuously refreshed), allows displays to provide customized and time sensitive messages. It is important to avoid *white noise syndrome* (in which nothing is on the screen); rather, create an audio/visual "conflagration" that stops the consuming public in its tracks and causes increased sales and profits.

In the near future, OLED (organic light-emitting diodes) will be wafer-thin and have higher resolution and use little energy, changing P-O-P advertising forever as a result.

The Internet, already powerful, will become the ultimate transportation data device and will generate new deliverables (solutions and services) using a new form of P-O-P advertising—not just normal banner ads but, rather, "instant information" ads that are always up to the moment. Digital signal chips placed in packaging and P-O-P advertising will allow brand marketers to obtain daily inventories just by walking down the aisle.

Customization: Brand marketers must create and modify P-O-P advertising to better facilitate retailers. The day of "one for all" is gone. Creating customized, specific P-O-P advertising for each retailer's use is the way of the future. Moreover, P-O-P advertising that is able to provide customized content and messages based on the individual needs of the consumer will enable the brand marketer and the retailer to create a unique message tailored to each and every consumer.

Brand marketers need to take advantage of cross-channel marketing with special P-O-P advertising opportunities created for specific product categories. Store brands (private labels) are quickly developing their own unique brand identities that compete directly with major brands, creating tension between retailers and brand marketers. Brand marketers can sustain their power in niche marketing by using high-tech P-O-P advertising to aid their brand equity.

In conclusion, by using cutting-edge technology and futuristic entertainment environments geared to the whole family, brand marketers will be able to fulfill both short- and long-term branding strategies. P-O-P advertising, in conjunction with other marketing media, has to become both the beginning point and ending point. It is less about mass marketing and more about personalized marketing to the masses—not one message to all, but lots of messages to each individual.

Integrated marketing communications (IMC) throughout all of the brand marketer's merchandising and promotion efforts will be essential in maintaining a consistent brand identity in the marketplace. The brand marketer must create a vertically integrated yet consistent marketing approach, with seamless communication across the whole marketing mix.

How brand marketers disseminate information to the consumer will be even more critical in the future. P-O-P advertising can solve this challenge. Our call to action is "no need, no sale." Interactive information coupled with high technology is the solution.

14

Types of P-O-P Advertising Displays

TYPES OF P-O-P ADVERTISING DISPLAYS

This section provides short descriptions and some illustrations of types of displays available to the P-O-P marketer. Many of these, plus additional P-O-P advertising terms, are defined in the glossary of terms on the CD-ROM that accompanies this book.

- Case-stacker displays
- Combination counter/floor displays
- Counter displays
- Coupon dispensers
- Dealer-loader displays
- Dump-bins
- Duplex displays
- Easel cards
- Floor displays
- KD displays
- Mobiles
- One-way sell displays
- Pack-out displays
- Pallet displays
- Pole-topper displays
- Premium displays
- Pre-pak displays
- Revolving-floor displays
- Shelf talkers
- Sidekicks
- Table tents
- Three-way sell displays
- Walk-around displays
- Wall displays

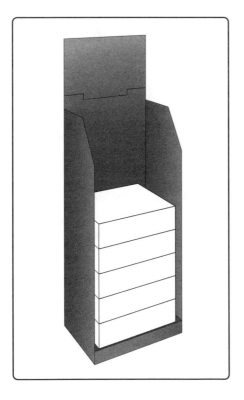

Case-stacker displays—These displays are created by simply cutting product cases open to expose the product and stacking the cases side by side and on top of each other to create a mass display. Case-stackers are usually used in conjunction with a pole display, an easel card, or a table tent. This is a very economical approach to getting a large quantity of product on display and is also a very easy and effective way of merchandising. These displays can be built from very small to very large, so they can be readily adapted to virtually any market size.

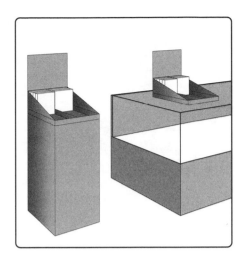

Combination counter/floor displays—The flexibility of this approach is ideal because it leaves the decision of where the display will be used to the retailer. If the retailer has more floor space than counter space, the floor base can be used with the product tray. If not, the tray of product can be placed on a counter and the base discarded. Its ideal feature is that the display will most likely be used since the retailer can make the decision best suited for his or her market.

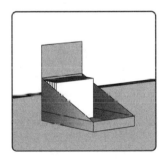

Counter displays—Counter displays are typically small and compact because counter space in most markets is at a premium. They can help to frame the product and set it off from the competing products. Like floorstands, they can also be designed as a one-sided sell, a three-sided sell, or as a revolving display.

Coupon dispensers—These dispensers are usually battery operated and offer instant coupons to the consumer. Placed next to the product, they attract attention through the use of graphics and color and often use blinking lights.

Dealer-loader displays—Also known as "dealer incentives." These displays have as an integral part some useful or desirable take-home unit for the dealer—tables, carts, grills, and so forth. For example, a display makes a premium offer to the consumer, and a sample of the premium is part of the display. When the promotion is over, the dealer is free to take the premium home as a "thank you" for the use of the retail space.

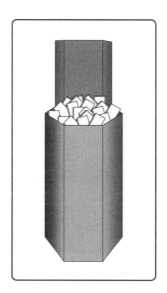

Dump-bins—These holders for bulk merchandise can be made of wire, corrugated, sheet metal, or other materials. They are used for a random order display of product, which is literally dumped or jumbled into dump-bins or dump displays. Obviously, this type of display is not suited for all products, but it does give the consumer the idea that this must be a special offer, often a sale item. Dump-bins are usually temporary in nature and quite simple to assemble. They are often used as "outpost" displays, offering a given product to the consumer in several different areas of a marketplace, for example, dump-bins of snack foods offered not only in the snack foods department but also in the soft drinks department, the produce department, and perhaps even at the checkout lanes.

Duplex displays—Duplex refers to a self-contained floor-stand shipper display that holds both a base and the product. It typically holds a plan-o-gram and has a header attached. The display is received at retail, the shipping tape is cut, and the unit is literally turned inside out, creating a display out of what had been a shipping carton. Duplex displays are very economical, and the assembly at retail is very simple.

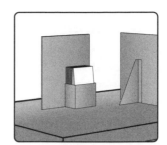

Easel cards—These displays are usually flat, two-dimensional displays that have a simple chipboard easel attached to the back. The retailer merely opens the easel and sets the display on a counter, a shelf, or a case stacker of product. Easel cards are often included in a complete P-O-P advertising kit, along with other items such as mobiles and table tents.

Floor displays—Floor displays, as the name indicates, stand on the floor at retail. Like all displays they are meant to feature the product or service, inform the consumer, and tell about the product's attributes, qualities, and, occasionally, price.

KD displays—These are "knocked-down" displays that are shipped partially assembled for reasons of economy in shipping, storage, or actual production. The degree of assembly required varies. The retailer must unpack the display components, carefully assemble the display as per the instructions, place the display in the desired location in the store, and fully load the display with product from cases.

Mobiles—Mobiles are displays consisting of several counterbalanced pieces suspended in such a way that each piece moves independently in a light current of air but can also be motorized so as to always be moving and attracting attention. They generally are used as image-building displays, not to merchandise product. Mobiles take up no floor space or counter space but hang above the retail spaces, can be seen from a distance, and are sometimes used to identify specific departments or centers. They are normally sturdy and lightweight and can be developed into more than just a flat, two-dimensional hanger.

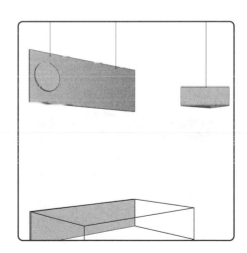

One-way sell displays—These are the most common type of floorstand. They can be backed up against a wall, placed on an end cap, or placed back-to-back. The product is only merchandised at the front.

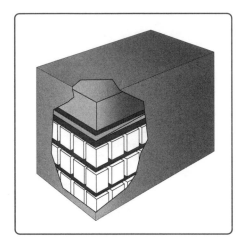

Pack-out displays—Also known as near-pack displays, these displays are received at retail either knocked down or assembled with the product included in the same carton but not in display position. The important concept is that both the display and the product are received at retail at the same time.

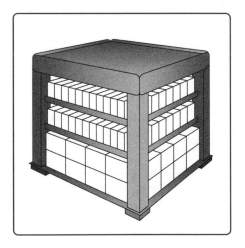

Pallet displays—Pallet displays are formed by a mass display of product built on a pallet and contained in corrugated or other structural components on the retail floor ready for display by just removing the protective shrouding and, in some cases, adding a riser.

Pole-topper displays—These displays carry the advertising message and are mounted on top of poles, usually paper tubes. Pole-toppers can be either two-dimensional or three-dimensional and oftentimes include motion and/or lights to attract attention. Pole-topper displays are usually supported at the floor by a simple corrugated pedestal or a set of wire feet. A quantity of the product is typically stacked around the pole at the floor level. A pole display can also be part of a floor display, functioning as the sign or header for the display.

Premium displays—Premium displays include some gimmick or item that is used to attract attention to the display or product in a secondary manner. The gimmick is intended to create interest initially in itself and then transfer the interest to the product. An example would be a display that offers a premium with the purchase of the actual product, such as a corrugated playhouse with the purchase of a package of Kimberly-Clark diapers. The customer buys the product, sends in a proof-of-purchase along with the price of the premium, and receives the playhouse in the mail a few weeks later. A premium of this type is normally meant to encourage the consumer to try a brand that he or she has not usually purchased in the past.

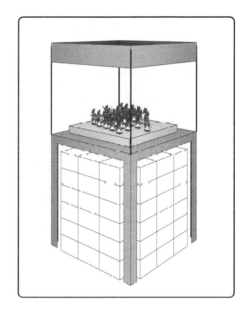

Pre-pack displays—These are designed to be packed with merchandise by the P-O-P producer and shipped to the retailer as a unit. Retail management often favors pre-pack displays because little time is required to assemble the display in the market and little or no handling of product is required.

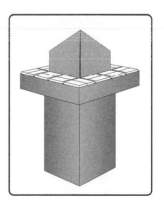

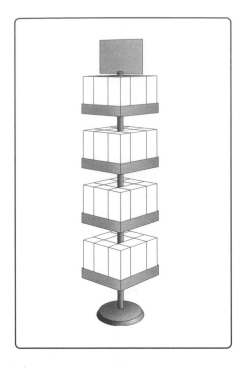

Revolving-floor displays—Since the consumer can manually spin these displays (sometimes called spinner displays), they can function as walk-around displays, against a wall or on an end cap. They are ideally suited for corners where the product on a regular walk-around would normally be hidden from view and would probably be inaccessible.

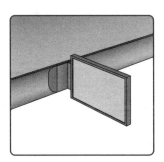

Shelf talkers—Shelf talkers are small signs affixed to the display shelf edge to call attention to the product.

Sidekicks—Sidekicks are used primarily in supermarkets, chain drug stores, hardware stores, and convenience stores. They are designed to be attached to the ends of end cap shelves and are meant to create display spaces to encourage incremental sales of products not normally sold in that area of the market. Sidekicks can be designed in temporary or permanent materials but, since they are normally considered to be promotional displays, they are usually designed in temporary materials and sent to the stores assembled and prepacked with product. Sidekicks used in multiples can create a larger floor display or even large, full-sized pallet displays. Sidekicks can be added to a base to create a floorstand or can be designed to function as counter displays, giving the option of store location to the retailer.

Table tents—Table tents are single-fold cards, set like a tent, for use on counters, bars, or tables, carrying an advertising message. They frequently have messages on both the front and back of the card.

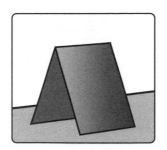

Three-way sell displays—This variation of the one-way sell display allows the product to be merchandised from the front, the left side, and the right side. This display is most ideally suited situated on an end cap or back-to-back with another three-way sell display.

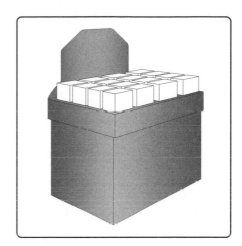

Walk-around displays—These displays offer product on all sides and allow the consumer to walk around the display, creating the feeling of a full-line merchandiser. The disadvantage of this design is that it is not readily accepted in some markets because of the amount of floor space required by the consumer to comfortably shop around the display.

Wall displays—As the name implies, these displays are designed to hang on the wall of a retail outlet or on the back wall of a store fixture. The display can be mounted flat against the wall or at a 90-degree angle to the wall, creating retail space on both sides for either copy or product.

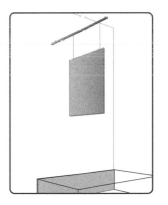

Illustrations provided by Rapid Displays.

NOTES